THE CAPETIAN KINGS
OF FRANCE

THE CAPETIAN
KINGS OF FRANCE

Monarchy & Nation
(987–1328)

BY

ROBERT FAWTIER

Membre de l'Institut, Professeur à la Sorbonne

TRANSLATED INTO ENGLISH BY

LIONEL BUTLER

Principal, Royal Holloway College,
University of London

AND

R. J. ADAM

Senior Lecturer in Mediaeval History in the University of St Andrews

ST. MARTIN'S PRESS NEW YORK

This work was originally published under the title of *Les Capétiens et la France* by
Presses Universitaires de France

Copyright © 1960 Robert Fawtier, Lionel Butler, R. J. Adam

Printed in Hong Kong
First published in the United States of America in 1960
Reprinted 1974, 1976, 1978, 1983

ISBN 0-312-11900-3

FOREWORD

TO THE ENGLISH TRANSLATION

THE preface to the original French edition has been here included, as it explains the circumstances in which the book was composed. It has been thought best that the text should stand as first published, and very few additions and corrections have been made. But it may be pointed out that very little historical work on the period has been published since *Les Capétiens et la France* first appeared, and certainly none which has rendered its general conclusions invalid.

I express my warmest thanks to my translators, Professor Lionel Butler and Mr. R. J. Adam, both of the University of St. Andrews. Their great merit appears to me to be the success with which they have avoided a purely literal translation. I venture to believe that their version of my text presents it to the English-speaking reader in the form best adapted to his own language.

ROBERT FAWTIER

PARIS
June 1958

PREFACE

THIS work has grown out of several years spent in studying the reign of Philip the Fair. The better to understand the events of the period and the documents through which they are known, I found myself compelled to turn back to the origins of the royal house of Capet and to assess the whole significance of its history. But the book itself would probably never have been written had not the Second World War broken out. For I was then required to replace at short notice a colleague called to the colours, and naturally enough I chose as the subject of my lectures the period best known to me.

I originally planned to give a course extending over two sessions. When the events of June 1940 overtook my country, I came to the conclusion that I should still complete this programme. I have always enjoyed the discipline of clarifying and setting forth my thoughts on history; and I was encouraged by the evident interest of some of those to whom I lectured. But there were also newer and stranger reasons behind my decision. In a time of national tragedy I found a source of strength, for myself and my audience, in the study of the beginnings of the French nation and of the actions of its first leaders. Such a study was, I found, not merely an escape from the horrors of contemporary reality. Like those monuments of antiquity which have provided the foundations for a whole series of later edifices, the original structure of France appeared to me so strongly built that it could not be completely destroyed. I hoped that something of this conviction might communicate itself to my readers, when my publisher was courageous enough to undertake publication. And even if his courage were to be ill rewarded, the book itself would always keep for me the character it acquired during the two years in which it was my companion in adversity, the good Samaritan giving me succour in a parched land.

The Capetian Kings of France is not a history of France from

987 to 1328, still less a history of Europe. It is intended only to be a study of the part played by the kings of the first Capetian dynasty in the creation of the French nation. Although my feelings have been deeply involved in its composition, two facts encourage me to believe that I have not distorted my themes: firstly, that I have had no need to deal with foreign affairs, so that questions of patriotism do not arise, and, secondly, that the remoteness in time of the entire subject has saved me from the unconscious prejudices which can influence the treatment of events closer to our own times.

I am very conscious of my debt to those historians, some of them my own teachers and friends, who have so skilfully and patiently reconstructed the history of Capetian France — all too often without general recognition of the importance of their work. This book is hardly more than a gathering together of their labours; such value as it has derives from them.

Notes and references have been kept to the minimum, for I have not tried to compose a treatise for specialists. My hope is that even those who know nothing of the subject will be able to read the book without too much difficulty. Nevertheless, I have been careful to justify any opinions which I have expressed by reference to the relevant sources. The first chapter contains, in addition, some basic bibliographical information, and those who wish to examine my views more closely will find the necessary material there.

I am well aware that a work of this kind cannot hope to be definitive. It can, at best, be only a general survey, based on the work of others as well as my own researches; and, like all surveys, it must be unequal in depth, precisely because previous work has not been equally distributed over the whole subject. But I hope that some younger historians may, as a result of reading this book, be inspired to take a closer interest in a period which still demands a great deal of study. And if my work induces the ordinary reader to ponder on the foundations of our native land, then my reward will be great indeed.

ROBERT FAWTIER

PARIS
July 1941

CONTENTS

List of Maps

ABBREVIATIONS

THE following abbreviations have been used in the footnotes:

B.E.H.E.   *Bibliothèque de l'École des Hautes-Études, Sciences Historiques et Philologiques.*

Lavisse   E. Lavisse (ed.), *Histoire de France*, 9 vols. in 18 parts (Paris, 1900–11).

L.T.C.   *Layettes du Trésor des Chartes*, 5 vols. (Paris, 1863–1909).

R.H.F.   *Recueil des historiens des Gaulles et de la France*, 24 vols. (Paris, 1737–1904).

2

The Evidence

Any study of the sources of Capetian history must start from the old but still valuable work of Auguste Molinier.[1] Rather than seeking to provide even a brief outline of these sources, this chapter aims only at emphasising the fragmentary — and often inadequate — nature of the historian's knowledge of the period, whilst at the same time giving some idea of what may be learned from the evidence which has survived.

History written in the vernacular was perhaps the last literary form to make its appearance in France. Throughout the whole Capetian period Latin was the historian's language, and churchmen, in consequence, were almost alone in writing for posterity. It is not surprising, therefore, that the history of the age has an ecclesiastical tinge, that kings appear as crowned monks, preoccupied with their good or bad relations with the Church, and that the events which are recorded by the writers primarily concern the Church. Thus Helgaud, a monk of the abbey of Fleury-sur-Loire, could write a life of King Robert the Pious (the *Epitome vitae regis Roberti*) which ignores his public life and recounts only his private virtues. Helgaud was possibly biased in writing of one who had (in his own words) treated him like a son, but more intelligent writers shared the same outlook. The life of King Louis VI written by Abbot Suger of Saint-Denis explains almost all that king's actions as arising from a desire to serve the house of Saint-Denis or some sister monastery.

In the thirteenth century a change can be detected; further, the growing number of records makes it less necessary for the student thereafter to rely so heavily upon chronicle evidence. For the

[1] *Les sources de l'histoire de France depuis les origines jusqu'en 1789: 1er Partie, Des origines aux guerres d'Italie (1494)*, fasc. 2 et 3 (Paris, 1902–3). A revised edition is being prepared by a 'groupe de travail' of the *Centre National de la Recherche Scientifique*.

first two centuries of the Capetian dynasty, however, these chronicles are almost the only source of information, and it is important to form some idea of the background and intellectual equipment of the men who wrote them. First and foremost, the writers were monks, men who rarely left their monasteries and who knew little of the world beyond their own estates. It would be too much to expect them to have written more than local annals, to have been as interested in the King of France as in the local counts or petty lords whose actions had a day-to-day significance for their houses. If a particular monastery happened to be in the tiny royal domain, or to have been a royal foundation, then the king took his place in its annals, but significant comment on the general history of the kingdom did not follow. We may suspect that the informed opinion of the age was more acute and had wider views, and that individual nobles and merchants were better able to interpret the course of events — but such men have left no writings behind them.

Early Capetian history, as a result, is a mosaic of incidental information drawn from the local chronicles of different monastic houses. The historian who arranges his own version of the mosaic has no means of testing the genuineness of the individual pieces, whilst if he rejects them entirely he has nothing to put in their place. To take an example: Suger supplies a list of battles between the kings of France and the Norman kings of England, each one ending in a French success. Norman chroniclers, describing the same events, give the victory on each occasion to their duke, the King of England. If we possessed additional evidence which would enable us to decide between these official communiqués their divergence would be unimportant. But when, as in this case, there is no other evidence at all, then it is impossible for us to do more than conclude that the two kings fought each other — and there are instances when we cannot even be certain of that.

In general, the chronicles of these early centuries record little but a long series of wars. The devout churchmen who wrote them were apparently almost exclusively interested in military operations. The paradox is hardly a justified one. The chroniclers might confine their interest to inconclusive battles and random sieges, but men lived, worked and thought throughout all these years, and we can do no more than regret that those who passed for historical writers could restrict their interests so narrowly.

A change comes at the beginning of the thirteenth century, when, for the first time, the rising authority of the crown is reflected in literature. The picture given by the chronicles of the abbey of Saint-Denis is that seen from the viewpoint of the monastery's protector, the King of France. Not all Frenchmen shared that viewpoint, but it commanded a new prospect which embraced the whole realm. The textual history of these so-called *Grandes Chroniques de Saint-Denis*[1] is obscure. A French version was presented to King Philip the Bold by the monk Primat in 1274, and is still preserved in the Bibliothèque Sainte-Geneviève in Paris. It is a translation, but not of a completely contemporary work. Latin chronicles had been written in the monastery since the beginning of the thirteenth century at the latest. The tradition that Abbot Suger, the contemporary of Louis VI, inaugurated this 'official history' of the dynasty has never been proved; it is more probable that it dates from the reign of Philip Augustus, though older writings may have been drawn upon by the earliest compilers. The great interest of the Saint-Denis chronicles for the historian lies in the emphasis laid in them upon the king and his actions, which are reported in considerable detail. But, although it is an advance to have for the first time a chronicle which takes the whole kingdom for its subject, it is still true that, like its predecessors, the Saint-Denis chronicle is the work of churchmen, as interested in hagiography as in the story of the dynasty.

Other contemporary works exist — sometimes ill-composed, but not without individuality. Such are the *Gesta Philippi Augusti* of Rigord, monk and doctor, and the *Philippide*, a long Latin poem composed by Guillaume le Breton, a canon of Senlis. Considered as a class, however, all these writings have a common defect. Not only were their writers all churchmen, but they all came from outside the charmed circle of the nobility, the only class which could look upon the king as an equal. As a result, almost all their compositions are eulogies, and the occasional

[1] Edited by J. Viard (Soc. de l'Hist. de France, 9 vols., 1920–37).

flashes of criticism are too tentative to throw any light on the personal characteristics of their heroes.

St. Louis was the first Capetian to attract a biographer close enough to have known him as a friend rather than a king. It is this that still gives the work of Jean de Joinville, seneschal of Champagne, a fascination shared by no other contemporary historical writing. There is, however, no evidence to suggest that Joinville set out from the start to write a life of St. Louis. He was himself a household officer and baron of the Count of Champagne, rather than a member of the royal court, and when he went on crusade in 1248 it was at his own expense. In Cyprus he entered the king's service, receiving a 'fief de bourse' (money-fief, or, in effect, pension) which made him a royal vassal. He continued to hold his fief in Champagne, and after his return to France in 1254 divided his time between his estates and the court of his royal friend. He was never, be it noted, employed on government business.

When Joinville, in 1272, wrote down the story of his six years' adventures in the East (1248–54), his intention was only to put on record his own personal crusade. Afterwards his suzerain, Joan of Navarre, Countess of Champagne (who had become Queen of France through her marriage to St. Louis' grandson, Philip the Fair), asked him to set down his reminiscences of his friend — reminiscences which the seneschal was clearly always ready to recount. Joinville did so, but it was not until 1309, four years after the queen's death, that the *Vie de saint Louis* was laid before her son, the future King Louis X 'the stubborn'.

In writing the *Vie*, Joinville drew on his own earlier memoirs. To these he added some anecdotes, and some extensive borrowings from Primat's French version of the Saint-Denis chronicles; he further supplied some details concerning the crusade of 1270, which he had refused to join, some information on the inquiry preceding the canonisation of St. Louis (in which he had been a witness), and finally a description of the actual ceremony of canonisation. The result was not a history of the reign of St. Louis, but instead a superb portrait, whose quality can best be seen by a comparison with the clerical biographies of the king by men such as Geoffroy de Beaulieu, Guillaume de Chartres, and Guillaume de Saint-Pathus. The contrast is striking. It is because of Joinville's precise and vivid word-pictures that St. Louis is the only Capetian whose character we know at all well.

But Joinville, for all his intimate knowledge of the king and his obvious admiration for him, was no mere hero-worshipper. He saw St. Louis' virtues, but knew better than to try to imitate them, for he saw too that they did not always have the best of consequences. Further, his portrait is of the man whom he knew, not of the king whom he served. There is no strong evidence that their friendship extended to discussions on matters of state. The historian is fortunate in the possession of Joinville's miraculous prose, but he must not believe that the man who wrote so well knew, at the same time, all the secrets of his master's kingship. Master Matthieu de Vendôme must have had a more interesting story to tell, but he, faithful to the oath of secrecy taken by all members of the King's Council, wrote no memoirs.

St. Louis' son, grandson, and three great-grandsons had no Joinville to record their lives. To some extent they therefore remain enigmas, although the chronicles of their times are not completely lifeless. This quality derives from the success of some writers, from the close of the twelfth century onwards, in breaking through the impersonality of their literary vehicles. The results are mixed. Much of the vernacular verse history written in the period is insipid. On the other hand, it is not obscured by the curtain of translation which lies over the earlier Latin chronicles. Three of the writers, indeed, were men of talent. The *Vie de Guillaume le Maréchal* was written to celebrate one of the great men of the Angevin court, but it contains much important detail concerning the struggle between the Capetians and their Anglo-Angevin vassals in the period 1186–1219. Some of the incidents are well told and gripping. Guillaume Guiart, a serjeant from Orleans, completed in 1307 the *Branche des royaux lignages*, which tells the story of France from the time of Philip Augustus to his own day in some 21,000 lines of verse. 8,000 of these relate to his own lifetime, and give, amongst other episodes, an eye-witness' account of the Flemish campaign of 1304. Lastly, the jingles written by Geoffroy des Nès, a clerk of the royal Chancery, echo the talk and thought of the Paris of Philip the Fair.

It should be remembered, too, that France was the political centre of thirteenth-century Europe. Every foreign chronicler worthy of the name thought it necessary to insert in his work notices of events in France. As a result, the politics of the Capetians can be seen reflected in the comments of English, Aragonese, Italian and Flemish writers.

But chronicles, however plentiful, can never be more than inadequate sources of historical information. In the Capetian period, they were written by men remote from the business of government, who most often had only the common talk of the day on which to rely for their knowledge of public affairs. Their position was not very different from that of the modern journalist, hearing only what those better informed wish him to know, and more often reporting inaccurate news than the reverse. The chroniclers were, in fact, even less well informed, for the Middle Ages always considered government to be a secret business. Something of this attitude still persists in the titles of those ministers designated 'Secretaries of State' — the titular descendants of those ' clerks of the Secret' who alone knew the real story of mediaeval government. The Capetians made those who thus shared in the 'royal secrets' protect their knowledge by an oath of secrecy — a precaution more effective then than now. So hampered were the chroniclers, therefore, that it would hardly be too much to compare the historian who relies on their writings alone to one who attempts to interpret contemporary history with no other sources than the columns of his local newspaper. It is fortunate that he has other resources to turn to, and that he can hope to find something of the secrets of the royal counsels in what are broadly called 'archives of government' — charters, administrative correspondence, inquests, financial accounts, and the like.

There is, however, one important condition which must be fulfilled: to be useful, archives must have survived the centuries. This is not always the case. The Capetians, to the inconvenience of historians, had at first no fixed archive depository, but followed the much less helpful practice of carrying their documents around with them. The habit was a dangerous one in an age in which kings rarely lingered long in any one place. The inevitable result was that they kept as few documents as possible, and that the routine of keeping copies and of making a register of the acts of the royal Chancery was slow to take root. The consequences for the historian are shown by Guillaume le Breton's account — confirmed by the English chronicler, Roger of Howden — of what happened at Fréteval in the Vendômois on 3 July 1194. On that day Philip Augustus, surprised by Richard I of England, lost not only a battle but also his treasure and his archives:

> 'Nec parcit raptor nummis, quibus arcta tumebant
>   dolia, nec saccis, quibus ornamenta latebant,
> *scripta tributorum, fiscique chirographa*, nec non
>   cum reliquis rapitur rebus regale sigillum.'[1]

Philip took steps to repair the damage, but naturally enough by reconstructing the 'modern' series of state documents, which had an immediate importance for the maintenance of royal rights. Older archives — if they had ever existed in any quantity — disappeared almost entirely.

On the other hand, it should be remembered that the royal archives did not at any time contain the originals of royal grants, but only minutes or copies written into registers. The charters themselves, carrying the king's great seal, passed into the custody of the subjects in whose favour they had been prepared. Where the muniments of these subjects have survived we may hope to find the originals preserved. Lay lords and town communities, however, were if anything less careful of their archives than were the kings; the towns, in any case, were comparatively late in the field. Only the clergy, in the earlier part of the Capetian period, grasped the value of royal charters and the importance of preserving them, and only monasteries, cathedrals, and other great churches retained their documents, either in their original form or as copies written into cartularies.

---

[1] v. *L.T.C.*, i, intro., p. xxv. For a sound estimate of the documentary losses at Fréteval, v. C. Petit-Dutaillis in *Recueil des actes de Philippe Auguste*, vol. ii (Académie des Inscriptions et Belles Lettres, Chartes et Diplômes, Paris, 1943), pp. vi–ix. For the history of the royal archives, v. H. F. Delaborde in *L.T.C.*, v.

Such wisdom has produced both good and bad results for the historian. Any surviving documents are of value to him, for their escape from the ravages of time and men is a happy accident. But a history of the eleventh- and twelfth-century Capetian kings, written from those archives that have survived, is liable to severe distortion. For extant royal charters record almost exclusively a long series of gifts to monasteries and churches, and reinforce the misleading impression suggested by a first reading of the chronicles.

In any case, the number of documents involved is not large. Distinguished scholars have assembled the evidence, edited and established the texts, and even, with marvellous patience, uncovered references to lost charters. The task has been accomplished for every reign before that of St. Louis, with the sole exception of Hugh Capet, who left very few records indeed.[1] The results may be set out thus:

Robert the Pious: reigned 34 years, 8 months and 25 days: 108 acts or mentions of acts.[2]

Henry I: reigned 29 years and 14 days: 125 acts or mentions of acts.[3]

Philip I: reigned 48 years less 3 days: 171 acts or mentions of acts.[4]

Louis VI: reigned 39 years less 2 days: 359 acts or mentions of acts.[5]

Louis VII: reigned 43 years, 1 month and 7 days: 798 acts or mentions of acts.[6]

Philip II: reigned 42 years, 8 months and 25 days: 2500 acts or mentions of acts.[7]

[1] Only a dozen authentic acts in ten years; v. F. Lot, *Études sur le règne de Hugues Capet*, (*B.E.H.E.*, Paris, 1903), p. 235.
[2] W. M. Newman, *Catalogue des actes de Robert II, roi de France* (Paris, 1937).
[3] F. Soehnée, *Catalogue des actes d'Henri Ier* (*B.E.H.E.*, Paris, 1907).
[4] M. Prou, *Recueil des actes de Philippe Ier* (Académie des Inscriptions et Belles-Lettres, Chartes et Diplômes relatifs à l'histoire de France, Paris, 1908).
[5] A. Luchaire, *Louis VI le Gros. Annales de sa vie et de son règne (1081–1137)* (Paris, 1890).
[6] A. Luchaire, *Études sur les actes de Louis VII* (Paris, 1885). This study is not exhaustive, and it has been suggested that a full quarter of the surviving documents escaped Luchaire's notice. This does not, however, invalidate the argument of the text.
[7] L. Delisle, *Catalogue des actes de Philippe Auguste* (Paris, 1856). A more complete catalogue was begun by E. Berger and H.-F. Delaborde (Acad. des Inscr. et Belles-Lettres, Chartes et Diplômes: vol. i, Paris, 1916; vol. ii, by C. Petit-Dutaillis, Paris, 1943).

Louis VIII: reigned 3 years, 3 months and 24 days: 463 acts or mentions of acts.[1]

Even allowing for the increase from the reign of Louis VI onwards, the clerks of the Chancery cannot have been overworked to produce such a number of charters; by comparison with their thirteenth-century successors they must in fact have had little to do. Mediaeval administrations were no different from their modern counterparts when it came to the proliferation of paper-work, and from the reign of St. Louis the Capetian government was no exception. Documents which in his reign are to be numbered in thousands come in tens of thousands in the time of his successors. The numbers are so great that the most devoted of scholars have been daunted by the immensity of the task involved in any attempt to catalogue them.[2]

Even so, the magnitude of these figures can be misleading, for far more documents have been lost or destroyed than have survived. Some early fourteenth-century government style-books[3] show an astonishing range of clerical activity. When we call to mind the physical conditions in which the writers worked, astonishment must give way to admiration. The mediaeval clerk sat on a narrow and uncomfortable stool; he wrote at a steeply sloping desk, using a goose-quill on parchment liable to turn greasy at the slightest touch; his office was most often a small room, usually badly ventilated and in winter still more badly

[1] C. Petit-Dutaillis, *Étude sur la vie et le règne de Louis VIII* (*B.E.H. E.*, Paris, 1894), pp. 449–510.

[2] I undertook in 1938, with the support of the *Centre National de la Recherche Scientifique*, to make a calendar of all documents issued by the royal authorities or received by them during the reign of Philip the Fair. The work is still in progress, but I have been able to publish three volumes of accounts (R. Fawtier, *Comptes Royaux, 1285–1314* (3 vols., Acad. des Inscr. et Belles Lettres, *Historiens de la France, Documents Financiers*, vol. iii, Paris, 1953–7)) and a calendar of the early registers of the royal Chancery (*Archives Nationales*, JJ 37–50), to be issued in 1958. The considerable materials collected are deposited in the *Archives Nationales* in Paris, where scholars interested in the period may consult them before publication. They include more than 15,000 royal letters and a far greater number of letters and papers from royal officials. The collection is known under the name of *Corpus Philippicum*.

[3] e.g. MS. Français 4763 of the Bibliothèque Nationale, probably compiled by a clerk from Amiens, and discussed by Ch.-V. Langlois ('Formulaires de lettres du XIIᵉ, XIIIᵉ et du XIVᵉ siècles', in *Notices et Extraits*, vol. xxxiv, part i (1891), pp. 9ff); Registers JJ 35 and 36 of the Trésor des Chartes (copies of a single original). A complete description and a calendar of the texts included in JJ 35 and 36 will be shortly published in the *Mémoires de l'Académie des Inscriptions et Belles Lettes*.

heated; even at midsummer the midday light was so inadequate that he had to use a smoky candle, to the detriment of both his eyes and his lungs — and yet with all these difficulties he and his fellows produced a mountain of documents.

For all their apparent profusion, his products have survived only haphazardly. Some remain only because a royal agent happened to remove his files to his own home, in order to work in greater comfort, and because after his death the returned papers appeared too daunting for examination, and were simply pushed into a corner and forgotten. Others exist only because some collector of the seventeenth or eighteenth centuries was unscrupulous enough to help himself to individual papers, or even whole files, which thus escaped those recurrent fires which have so simplified — from one point of view — the historian's work.

The problems of abundance, as opposed to dearth, appear at the same time in both the record and the chronicle evidence. They are accompanied by the growth, for the first time, of a significant number of 'private' documents, so valuable for the understanding of the social and intellectual background of history. Isolated examples can of course be found at an earlier date, such as the letters of Gerbert whilst he was still secretary to Adalbero of Rheims (the archbishop who helped Hugh Capet to the throne). Equally valuable are the letters of two Bishops of Chartres — Fulbert, a contemporary of Robert the Pious, and Ivo, a contemporary of Philip I and Louis VI — and those of Abbot Suger in the reigns of Louis VI and Louis VII. But this evidence, and the vastly greater weight of similar material from the thirteenth and fourteenth centuries, has its own complications. Much of it has survived, not because contemporaries thought it to be of historical importance, but because of a fashion in literary taste. The wish to preserve models of good style and composition led to the collection and copying of particular letters; others of equal or greater historical interest may well have disappeared. A similar hazard is evident in the transmission of more purely literary material. Ch.-V. Langlois has pointed out that many of the best of the thirteenth-century romances are known today from a single manuscript.[1] We can only guess at the number of works which have disappeared without trace, just as we must assume that many documents which would vitally affect our interpretation of the history of the age have suffered the same fate.

The documentation of Capetian history is thus very incomplete, and will remain so. Further, the relative abundance of sources for the later reigns of the dynasty does not automatically remove all the difficulties which confront the student. He must always suspect that a single lost document might invalidate conclusions perfectly legitimately drawn from the existing material. Chance, and the random activity of men, have provided the evidence, and we can never therefore be certain that our reproduction of a vanished age is an accurate one.

The incompleteness of the documentation, and its varying distribution, are reflected in the pattern of historical work upon the dynasty. The scanty material for the first two hundred years has been carefully and exhaustively collected. From it a series of competent studies have been written on the reigns of the eleventh- and twelfth-century kings;[2] some of these are in fact excellent. Only Henry I[3] and Louis VII[4] still await detailed examination. The later position is much less satisfactory. The three short reigns of Louis VIII (40 months),[5] Philip III (15 years),[6] and Philip V (6 years)[7] have alone been surveyed. There is no single adequate book on the reign of St. Louis,[8] and Philip the Fair has been the

[1] La vie en France au Moyen Âge . . . d'après des romans mondains du temps (Paris, 1924), pp. xxvii–xxviii.

[2] F. Lot, Les derniers Carolingiens (B.E.H.E., Paris, 1891); F. Lot, Études sur le règne de Hugues Capet et la fin du Xᵉ siècle (ibid., Paris, 1903); Ch. Pfister, Études sur le règne de Robert le Pieux (ibid., Paris, 1885); A. Fliche, Le règne de Philippe Iᵉʳ, roi de France (Paris, 1912); A. Luchaire, Louis VI le Gros (Paris, 1890); O. Cartellieri, Philipp II August, Koenig von Frankreich (5 vols., Leipzig, 1899–1922).

[3] The catalogue of royal acts (v. sup., p. 8, n. 3) is the only part of Fréderic Soehnée's École des Chartes thesis (Étude sur la vie et le règne de Henri Iᵉʳ, roi de France) to have been published. Professor J. Dhondt, of the University of Ghent, is working on the subject (v. inf., p. 16, n. 1), but his book has not yet (1958) been published.

[4] But v. the valuable, if incomplete, survey by A. Luchaire in Lavisse, vol. iii, part i, pp. 1–81; also M. Pacaut, Louis VII et les élections episcopales dans le royaume de France (1137–1180) (Paris, 1957).

[5] C. Petit-Dutaillis, Étude sur la vie et le règne de Louis VIII (B.E.H.E., Paris, 1894).

[6] Ch.-V. Langlois, Le règne de Philippe III le Hardi (Paris, 1887).

[7] P. Lehugeur, Histoire de Philippe V le Long (2 vols., Paris, 1897 and 1931).

[8] H. Wallon, Saint Louis et son temps (2 vols., Paris, 1875) is inadequate. There are a number of valuable studies of aspects of the reign by E. Berger: Histoire de Blanche de Castille, reine de France (Bibl. des Écoles françaises d'Athènes et de Rome, Paris, 1893); Saint Louis et Innocent IV (Paris, 1893; taken from the author's publication of the

subject of nothing more than sketches of varying merit,[1] whilst for Louis X and Charles IV we possess only the summaries of unpublished theses of the Ecole des Chartes.[2] Although there have been many detailed studies of particular aspects of these reigns,[3] it is difficult for the student to grasp the full significance of any one of them. That demands a historian of courage, who is prepared to spend his whole working lifetime on the task, and thereafter to distil the fruits of his knowledge into a work which can place the king, his court and courtiers, his kingdom and society in a clear relationship of action and interaction. Until every Capetian reign has been so treated, a study such as the present one cannot hope to be definitive; its value can lie only in demonstrating the immensity of the task yet to be accomplished.

Registers of Pope Innocent IV); *Les dernières années de saint Louis* (*L.T.C.*, iv, intro.). Despite their quality, these are not an adequate substitute for a history of the entire reign.
   [1] *v.* esp. Ch.-V. Langlois in *Lavisse*, vol. iii, part ii. E. Boutaric, *La France sous Philippe le Bel* (Paris, 1861) is now out-of-date.
   [2] By Renvoisé (1889) and Couderc (1885). A. Artonne, *Le Mouvement de 1314 et les chartes provinciales de 1315* (Bibl. de la Faculté des Lettres de Paris, Paris, 1912) examines one aspect of the reign of Louis X.
   [3] There is a bibliography for the period preceding 1270 in C. Petit-Dutaillis, *La Monarchie Féodale en France et en Angleterre, Xe-XIIIe siècles* (Paris, 1933; English translation, London, 1936). For the period 1270–1328, *v.* the references in J. Calmette, *Le monde féodal* (Paris, Collection 'Clio', 4th edition, 1946) and the bibliography in *Histoire générale: Histoire du Moyen Âge*, ed. G. Glotz, vol. vi, part i (Paris, 1940).

2

The Kings and their Counsellors

Between 987 and 1328 fourteen successive kings, all of the same family and descended in the direct line from the same ancestor, Hugh the Great, Duke of Francia, sat on the throne of France. During this epoch France was born. In all essentials the framework of the French nation was then assembled. Before we recount their actions and try to decide the part they played in the development of France, we must make a character-sketch of each of these kings, in the hope of illuminating his share in the dynasty's development. This task is hard — the harder for poor documentation; hardest of all when we turn from portraying kings to sketching their counsellors. Social and economic forces incontestably play a dynamic and often a preponderant part in history, but so do individual men and women, especially in periods like that under consideration, when a nation is neither territorially unified, nor conscious of its own existence.

Of the first Capet, King Hugh (987–96), the founder of the dynasty, next to nothing is known. Ferdinand Lot, who studied his reign in minute detail, came to the conclusion that it was impossible to reconstruct a portrait of Hugh Capet. 'We know nothing of his physical appearance, and little of his character. He was pious, and enjoyed the company of monks, disliked osten-tation and display, and was more the diplomat than the warrior. Hardly anything else can confidently be said of him. To supple-ment these meagre facts with fantasy and paint a "colourful' portrait would be easy and amusing, but frivolous.'[1] But Lot adds the important point that King Hugh set great store by the royal dignity.[2] To Achille Luchaire, another leading historian of the Capetian era, Hugh was no mediocrity. 'He was able to take the

[1] F. Lot, *Études sur le règne de Hugues Capet*, p. 185.   [2] *Ibid.*, p. 3.

13

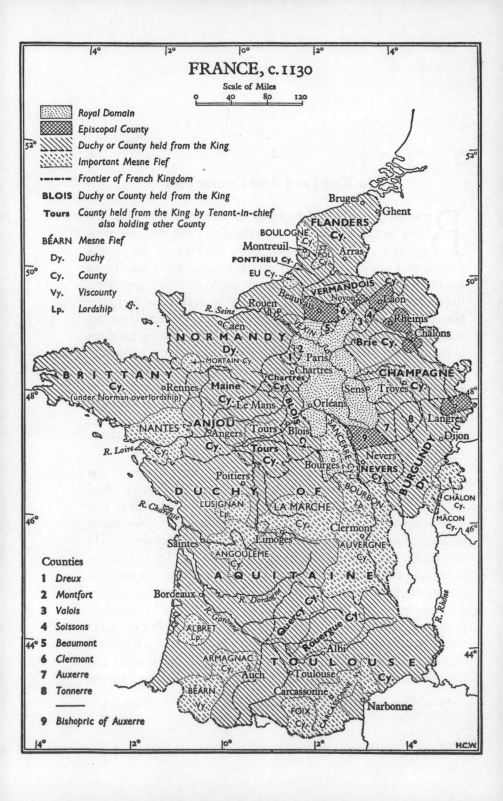

FRANCE, c. 1130

Scale of Miles

0   40   80   120

Royal Domain

Episcopal County

Duchy or County held from the King

Important Mesne Fief

-·-·-·- Frontier of French Kingdom

BLOIS Duchy or County held from the King

Tours County held from the King by Tenant-in-chief
also holding other County

BÉARN Mesne Fief

Dy. Duchy

Cy. County

Vy. Viscounty

Lp. Lordship

Bruges
Ghent
FLANDERS Cy.
BOULOGNE Cy.
Montreuil
ST. POL Cy.
Arras
PONTHIEU Cy.
EU Cy.
VERMANDOIS Cy.
Noyon
Laon
Rheims
Beauvais
Rouen
VEXIN
6
3 4
Chalons
Caen
5
2 Paris
Brie Cy.
N O R M A N D Y Dy.
MORTAIN Cy.
1
Chartres
CHAMPAGNE Cy.
B R I T T A N Y Cy.
(under Norman overlordship)
Rennes
Maine Cy.
Chartres Cy.
Sens
Troyes
Le Mans
7 8
Langres
ANJOU Cy.
Tours
BLOIS Cy.
Dijon
NANTES Cy.
Angers
Blois
9
NEVERS Cy.
Nevers
BURGUNDY Dy.
R. Loire
Tours Cy.
SANCERRE
Bourges
CHÂLON Cy.
Poitiers
BOURBON Lp.
MÂCON Cy.
LUSIGNAN Lp.
LA MARCHE
R. Charente
Clermont
Saintes
Limoges
LA MARCHE Cy.
AUVERGNE Cy.
ANGOULÊME Cy.
D U C H Y   O F
A Q U I T A I N E
Bordeaux
R. Dordogne
R. Garonne
Quercy Cy.
Rouergue Cy.
Albi
ALBRET Lp.
T O U L O U S E Cy.
ARMAGNAC Cy.
Auch
Toulouse
R. Rhône
BÉARN Vy.
Carcassonne
Narbonne
FOIX Cy.
CARCASSONNE Vy.

Counties

1 Dreux
2 Montfort
3 Valois
4 Soissons
5 Beaumont
6 Clermont
7 Auxerre
8 Tonnerre

9 Bishopric of Auxerre

H.C.W.

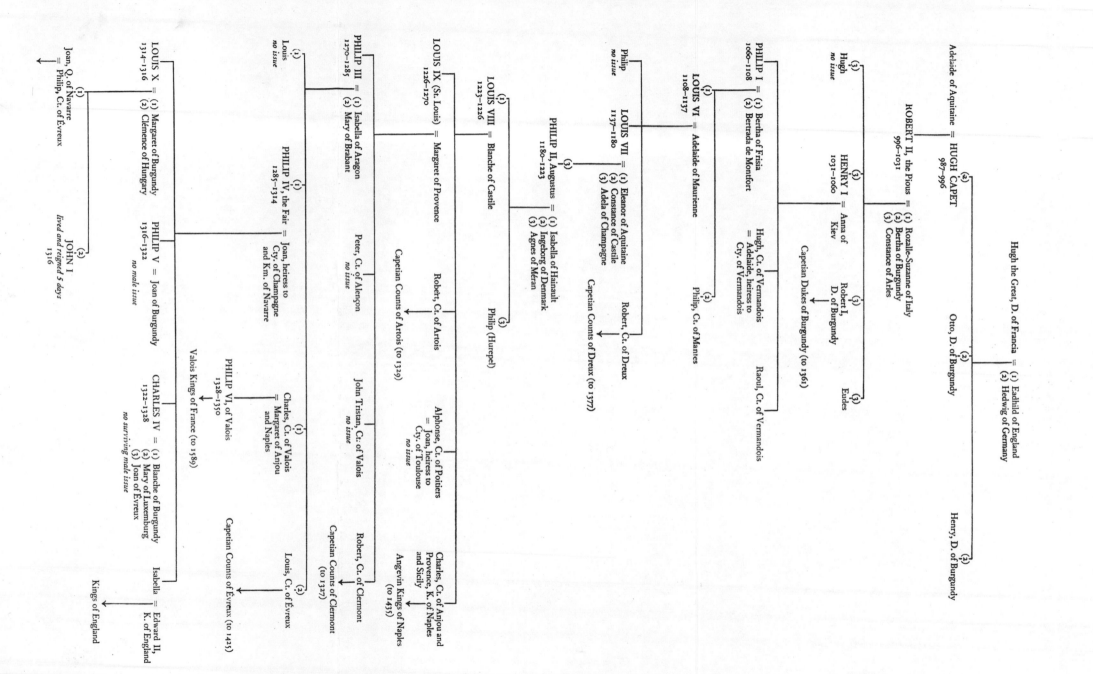

place of the Carolingian kings, keep what he had taken, maintain his own dignity in his relations with Pope and Emperor, and hand on his Crown, unopposed, to his son. Not all of this was mere luck.'[1]

Robert the Pious (996–1031) is a little better known to us through his biographer, Helgaud. We know that he was tall, slightly stooping, and rather fat, long-faced, mild-eyed, his nose big (or perhaps broad), his mouth 'benign, as if about to bestow the kiss of peace'. His beard was full. When he was on horseback, people noticed that he was afflicted by a grotesque deformity of all his toes. Helgaud relates that Robert was by nature gentle and humble, pious and virtuous, an affable man, a friend to the poor. As the pupil of Gerbert of Aurillac he was familiar with Latin and fond of books, and always carried a small library about with him. If we are to believe his biographer, Robert was a veritable monk on the throne. But Helgaud's is not a wholly reliable portrait, for he was drawing the king in his last years when, married to an unbearable wife, he sought consolation in his faith, and looked forward to a world in which Constance could no longer trouble him. A biographer has a natural tendency to forget that his hero passes by stages through youth, early manhood, and the prime of life to old age, if Fate allows him the Psalmist's allotted span. Robert, born in 970, lived to be sixty-one. The young prince associated with his father Hugh in the government of the country from 987 to 996, and the mature Robert who became sole king at twenty-seven were different men from the ageing ruler whom Helgaud describes.

Christian Pfister, in his classic study of Robert the Pious, describes the king as neither a great man nor an eminent ruler;[2] but a little later he gives Robert a very honourable position in the catalogue of the kings of France.[3] Achille Luchaire in one place says that Robert usually applied energy and method to the ruling of his lands; but in another that he was not a man to translate impulse into action.[4] For distinguished historians to contradict

---

[1] A. Luchaire, in *Lavisse*, vol. ii, part ii, p. 153.
[2] C. Pfister, *Études sur le règne de Robert le Pieux*, p. 386.
[3] *Ibid.*, p. 387.
[4] *Lavisse*, vol. ii, part ii, pp. 159, 161.

themselves like this illustrates how little is known of the history of this period and how hard it is by the feeble light of the surviving evidence to discern exactly the characters and policies of the kings of those days. But it is at least clear that Robert the Pious was able to keep himself on his throne for a long reign, and that when he died the Capetian monarchy found itself in a position slightly less unfavourable than at Hugh Capet's accession, and with another generation of existence behind it. In the circumstances Robert's achievement was by no means without value.

The poverty of the historical sources has made the first three Capetian kings shadowy figures in our eyes. (So obscure is Robert's successor Henry I (1031–60) that his courage is his one personal attribute of which we have knowledge.[1]) It is tempting but rash to conclude that they were men of no significance. For they accomplished a difficult task which was yet indispensable for the future of the monarchy. They lasted. They maintained the monarchical principle and the idea of the kingdom of France, and this at a time when it might have been expected that monarchy would perish in France and the country fall apart in a welter of separate and independent feudal principalities. Such principalities indeed arose, their lands far wider than the little royal domain, their lords much more powerful than the kings of France. But these overmighty subjects never swallowed up the royal domain. The king remained king. He did not dwindle into a mere Duke of Francia. To some extent fortune favoured the Capets. The great feudatories failed to see that the royal house might be a danger to them in the future. They never united against the king. Instead they frittered away in conflicts with each other the strength which they might have used against him. But the first three Capetians were able to turn this situation to their own profit, and they must take credit accordingly.

The king who came after them in 1060 is the Capet who has been most severely judged both by his contemporaries and by latter-day historians. Philip I (1060–1108) has had a bad press. In

[1] The Belgian scholar J. Dhondt, who devoted a good deal of work to the reign of Henry I, reached the conclusion that Henry considerably strengthened the royal power (*Revue belge de Philologie et d'Histoire*, xviii (1939), p. 948). More detailed study is required before Dhondt's views can be accepted.

his own day this fat monarch was reviled for his gormandising, his sensuality, his greed. Pope Gregory VII denounced him as a tyrant possessed by the Devil, as a perjurer and a robber. In our day Philip has been castigated for having failed to prevent the Norman conquest of England, and the virtual union of the kingdom of England with the duchy of Normandy; for having shown indifference and even hostility to the Gregorian movement for the reform of the Church; and for not having led the First Crusade. But a closer examination of the history of the reign suggests that Philip, despite his weaknesses and his mistakes, had a sure sense of the tasks his dynasty should concentrate upon. He realised that the king had first to make himself master in his own house, the royal domain, before he could master his kingdom at large. His reign saw the beginnings of the action which was to make the turbulent feudal nobles of the domain submit to the monarchy and eventually become its servants. There was a fortress called the Tower of Montlhéry which Philip adroitly got into his hands by arranging a marriage between the younger Philip, one of his sons by Bertrada de Montfort, and Elizabeth, daughter of Guy Troussel, lord of Montlhéry. Suger records that King Philip said to his heir, the future Louis VI, 'Look, son, make sure you never let the Tower of Montlhéry out of your keeping. It has caused me untold trouble. Frankly, that tower has made me old before my time.'[1] The lesson of this anecdote is that Philip I had a clear eye for the crude realities of his situation.

Likewise he saw how dangerous was his great vassal the Duke of Normandy. Philip, who was still a minor in 1066, could do nothing to forbid or stop William the Conqueror from aggrandising himself in England. But if he could not prevent the union of Normandy with England, he was at least the initiator of the policy which in the long run gave the victory to the Capets. For he made dexterous use of the family quarrels within the Anglo-Norman royal house. He egged on and supported Robert Curthose, first against his father William the Conqueror, then against his brother William Rufus. Louis VI in his day was to

[1] Suger, *Vie de Louis le Gros* (ed. H. Waquet, *Classiques de l'Hist. de France au Moyen Age*, Paris, 1929), p. 38.

make use of William Clito against Henry I of England; later still Philip II was to use Richard the Lion Heart against Henry II and John Lackland against Richard.

Philip I showed no favour to the Gregorian movement for church reform. The reformers attributed his opposition to greed, and in their justification it must be admitted that the king wanted to keep the regular income he got from the sale of bishoprics. Yet Philip seems also to have taken a broader view, and to have seen the general danger which the reforming movement presented, namely that a Church independent of lay control could be a menacing foe to royal power. Certainly he acted as if that was his belief, and from the monarchical standpoint it is hard to blame him.

Philip did not involve himself in crusading ventures. At the time when the First Crusade was being preached and organised he was disqualified from taking part in it, being under sentence of excommunication for his marriage with Bertrada de Montfort. There is no means of deciding whether he would have joined the crusaders if his circumstances had been different. What we know of Philip suggests that it was unlikely. He had no greatness of vision, only a clear eye for the tasks immediately ahead: to master his royal domain and to keep Anglo-Norman royal power in check. His resources did not allow him fully to achieve even these modest objects. It would have been a wild error to turn aside from them for an enterprise like the conquest of the Holy Land. Yet he made no move to oppose the First Crusade. Philip does not seem to have made the least trouble for those of his vassals — they included his brother, Hugh of Vermandois — who went to Palestine. Pope Urban II's decree of 1095, it is true, put the property of crusaders under the protection of the Church. Still, if Philip had been as unprincipled as his enemies alleged, papal prohibition would hardly have restrained him from molesting crusaders' lands had he wanted to do so. When Philip Augustus on a later occasion molested the Angevin lands few people blamed him.

Frequent as were Philip's brushes with the Church, he nevertheless kept his kingdom free of the troubles into which it would have been plunged by a conflict with the spiritual power over the burning question of Investiture. Co-operation and mutual aid between the Papacy and the French monarchy began with Philip's reign. It was a practice that became a policy and greatly benefited many of the French kings, not least Philip's grandson Louis VII. It is difficult — and in fact unimportant — to decide whether Philip I or Urban II should have the credit for inaugurating this policy. At least Philip took no steps to oppose it, and presumably he grasped its value to the crown. Unattractive, earthy, sordid, gross, he was also a practical man and a realist: the king for his time. When historians acclaim his son Louis VI as the sovereign whose reign saw 'the renaissance of kingship' in France, it must be remembered that Louis was following consistently the broad lines of Philip's policy.

Unlike his father, Louis VI (1108–37) is an historians' favourite. The secret of his high reputation is that not long after his death his friend Suger, Abbot of Saint-Denis, wrote his life, a glowing eulogy which is also the first biography of any length and discernment of a king of the House of Capet to have been composed, or at any rate to have survived. Yet in person Louis VI was as gross as his father. Henry of Huntingdon, an English chronicler of the time, takes both Philip and Louis to task for having deified the belly, 'the most baleful of all gods'.[1] By the time he had reached the age of forty-six Louis was too fat to be able to mount a horse. He was a sensualist—one bastard daughter of his can be traced, Isabella, whom he married in 1117 to a knight of the Vexin, William, son of Osmond de Chaumont. Not until he was thirty-five, and then only after much wavering, did Louis himself get married, to Adelaide of Maurienne. He was an avaricious man. He had a young Fleming flogged for refusing to reveal the hiding-place of the treasure of Charles the Good, Count of Flanders. In 1106, when he was still only king-designate, he let himself be bought — much against the advice of his more percipient father — by King Henry I of England. Like Philip I, Louis trafficked in justice. In the conflict between the bishop and the commune of Laon, the king sold his support to the side which bid the higher.

---

[1] Henry of Huntingdon, *De contemptu mundi* (ed. T. Arnold, Rolls Series, London, 1879), p. 312.

But Louis was Suger's friend and lived on good terms with the clergy. They for their part left on record their not implausible opinion that the king's good qualities made up for his faults. Suger makes Louis say: 'For the king to break the law is wicked and foolish, for the law and the king draw their authority from the same source.'[1] And, also according to Suger, when Louis knew that he was dying he gave this parting advice to his son: 'Protect the clergy and the poor and the fatherless. Do justice to every man. Arrest no man in your own court when summoned thither, unless he commits some offence there and then.'[2]

Like his father, Louis was active and courageous, a baron of his time, with the baronial virtues and the baronial shortcomings. Even more narrowly than Philip I he restricted his interests to the royal domain and the lands in its immediate vicinity. Whether he was pursuing a conscious policy of laying the foundations for a renaissance of royal power or merely striving to exploit undisturbed his inherited domainial revenues, is a question which the available evidence does not allow us to answer. But it is certain that all through his reign, undismayed by setbacks, he carried on an obstinate struggle with the feudal nobility of the domain. His attacks on this class were not the product of any overall military planning, but rather a series of vigorous reactions to the sporadic disturbances created by the barons of the Île-de-France and the Orléanais. Louis' conduct of these campaigns reveals no military originality and no grasp of strategy. He was waging feudal warfare in all its rough simplicity, and he was no better at it than his opponents.

But Louis VI built wisely and profitably on the foundations laid by his father. He relied on the Church, and defended it, and secured its support in return. And the current of history was running in his favour. Throughout France the greater nobles were tending to devote themselves more and more to improving the internal organisation of their fiefs. Thus preoccupied, they wanted to live at peace with each other and with the king. They saw that a victory of the Anglo-Norman royal house over the Capets would endanger their own interests. In his struggle with

[1] Suger, *Vie de Louis le Gros*, p. 106.   [2] *Ibid.*, p. 274.

Louis VI, Henry I of England got no help from the French magnates. Thibaud, Count of Blois and Champagne, Louis' only serious enemy among the great vassals, ended by siding with the king. Henry I died in 1135, two years before Louis, and the dispute over the succession to his throne plunged the Anglo-Norman monarchy into a time of troubles which greatly profited the Capets. To add to Louis' good luck, William X, Duke of Aquitaine, died in 1137, leaving as his heiress his daughter Eleanor. In law the wardship of the heiress and of her fief fell to the king. The text of William X's testament has not survived. Consequently it is not known whether it was his dying wish that Eleanor should marry Louis' son, or whether William merely gave the wardship of Eleanor to the king, who then exercised his right as suzerain and guardian to choose a husband for Eleanor. Whatever the truth, it was the future Louis VII whom Eleanor married, and this single event vastly enlarged the domains of the Capet family, so that their southern boundary was now the Pyrenees. Louis VI's relations with William X seem never to have been close, and with his son's marriage he was reaping the fruits not of long-term political scheming, but once more of good fortune.

Fortune was on his side in another field. His reign fell in the period when the townspeople of France were organising themselves in communes. Like all the feudal lords of his time, Louis had been induced to issue or confirm charters recognising the new communes and granting them privileges. This was enough to persuade the great romantic historians to represent him as a friend of the common people of France, an opinion which, though by now severely shaken and all but demolished, still faintly influences the views of modern scholars. The king whom Suger praised has always commanded the sympathy of historians; and he is one of those rare monarchs whose name lives on in popular memory.

The real Louis VI was an active king, and intelligent enough, it seems, to make use of the favourable circumstances in which he found himself. In the royal domain he did no more than pursue vigorously the traditional policy of Robert the Pious, Henry I and Philip I, whose activities there, as traced by the specialists who have studied their reigns, look like preliminary sketches for the work Louis was to accomplish. But if Louis fitted into an old tradition and reigned at the opportune time for reaping its benefits, he must take credit for not breaking it and for handing on to his successors a royal domain almost completely pacified. His reputation has been enhanced by his courage as well as his success. For biographer he had one of the most appealing — perhaps because one of the very few well-known — figures of his age. Everything needed to win him the esteem of his contemporaries and of posterity was his.

His son and successor, Louis VII (1137–80), though less well endowed by fortune, was more attractive in personality, as can be gathered from a couple of remarks of his which have come down to us through Walter Map. Thibaud, Count of Champagne, finding Louis asleep in a wood, guarded only by two knights, reproached him for his imprudence, and got the answer, 'I sleep alone, perfectly safe, because nobody bears me a grudge.'[1] On another occasion an Englishman was boasting about the vast possessions of his master King Henry II, and Louis contented himself with commenting, 'Now in France we have only bread and wine and our heart's desire.'[2] Louis was a gentle man, tender-hearted and courteous, pious and bookish. He lived simply; went unguarded amongst his burgesses of Paris; and showed tolerance to Jews, a rare quality in those days. He was scrupulously just. Walter Map relates that when Louis was building his country mansion at Fontainebleau he inadvertently seized a poor man's field. As soon as he found out what had happened, he made his workmen knock down the buildings which had been put up on that particular bit of ground, and handed the field back to the poor man.[3]

Historians have been surprisingly slow to appreciate Louis VII at his true worth; and yet his saintly character strongly reminds us of his great-grandson St. Louis. It is true that his reign was not marked by a series of military victories — rather the reverse; still, victory did not usually follow the royal banners before the

[1] Walter Map, *De Nugis Curialium* (ed. M. R. James, *Anecdota Oxoniensia*, mediaeval series, Oxford, 1914), p. 226.
[2] *Ibid.*, p. 225.
[3] *Ibid.*, p. 227.

time of King Philip Augustus (1180–1223). But, as historians have long acknowledged, in Louis VII's reign the prestige of the French monarchy was decisively established, and began to grow steadily. Louis was a realist. He grasped the need to assure the succession to the throne and to carry on the traditional policy of his dynasty in the royal domain. His expeditions against Gaucher de Montigny in 1137, Geoffroy de Donzy in 1153, Étienne de Sancerre in 1157, and Nevelon de Pierrefonds and Dreux de Mouchi in 1160 show him a worthy successor to Louis VI. The fruit of his policy was that from Louis VII's time onward the domain lands of the Île-de-France remained in submission to the monarchy. The descendants of the castellans with whom the Capetians had struggled for so long went over to the king's service, and were to become the trusted and indispensable agents of the royal will.

Louis was a loyal servant of the Church. When Pope Alexander III was driven from Italy by the Emperor Frederick Barbarossa, Louis gave him shelter and refuge, and treated him with extreme deference. But he displayed no weakness when the royal rights over the Church were called in question; and he was able to make use of the Papacy in his conflict with Henry II of England.

The difficulties which confronted Louis VII are easily under-rated. During his reign a feudal principality of unprecedented strength grew up within the borders of his kingdom. By his marriage in 1152 with Eleanor of Aquitaine, Louis' ex-wife, Henry II added the entire duchy of Aquitaine to his inherited fiefs of Normandy and Anjou. Shortly afterwards, in 1154, he became King of England. Louis VII strove to the best of his ability with this formidable new power. At times he blundered. But in his struggle to make use of the feuds within the Anglo-Norman royal family and to exploit his own position as feudal suzerain and his prestige as anointed king, he was at least working out a policy for dealing with his dangerous rival which in the hands of his son Philip Augustus was to win a great victory for the House of Capet. At the very time when Louis' situation was at its most critical, the bishops of the south of France turned to him and sought his protection. It may well have been that the

B

shrewdest way of dealing with the Angevin danger looming over his dynasty was to go on playing the part of the pious, gentle king, bearing malevolence to no man, and ruling in harmony with the intellectual currents of the age.

On the other hand, Louis has been severely criticised, especially by French historians, for himself creating the Angevin menace by repudiating Eleanor of Aquitaine as his wife. Yet it is by no means clear that to repudiate Eleanor was a mistake. In 1137 the French monarchy was hardly ready to assimilate the huge duchy of Aquitaine, whose feudatories were among the most turbulent in Europe. Draw as they might on their own portentous energies, and on the resources of England, Normandy, and Anjou, Henry II and Richard I could never subdue Aquitaine. The attempt to keep order there would have exhausted the Capetian monarchy, backed as it was by only its incompletely pacified little royal domain, and harassed as it would have been by great vassals seeking to profit from the monarchy's new preoccupation with expeditions to the south. The beautiful Eleanor's misconduct while on crusade at Antioch, if indeed it was Louis' true reason for divorcing her, was providential for the monarchy. Having lost his wife, Louis made a serious but short-lived effort to keep a hold on her lands and to stop her second marriage. He achieved neither purpose: perhaps because, in the long run, he lacked the will to do so, or descried too clearly the risks involved. Certainly the means at his disposal were inadequate. Despite appearances, the Capetian monarchy in 1152 was still a long way from being a great power, and was only to attain that status under Louis VII's successor.

Philip II (1180–1223) was the great king of the Capetian dynasty, and its exemplar long after his death. As a youth he seems to have taken after his grandfather Louis VI. There was the same corpulence, the vitality, the combativeness. Hard experience, early undergone — for he was king at fourteen, and at twenty-five, while on crusade in Palestine, he had a terrible illness, probably the sweating sickness[1] — turned him into a cautious, cynical, distrustful man, and left him with a sickly nervousness of disposition which he usually had the strength of will to master.

[1] A. Brachet, *Pathologie mentale des Rois de France* (Paris, 1903), pp. 253–82.

Philip's intellectual gifts were modest: he tried and failed to learn Latin; but he had a keen practical intelligence and was capable of making plans on a large scale and of executing them with a painstaking energy which ensured their success. His grandson, St. Louis, who was nine years old when Philip died, told his friend Joinville of a conversation he had had with the old king: 'He said to me that a king should reward his men strictly in proportion to the services they had done him, and that no man could become a good ruler who was incapable of being as firm in refusing as he was generous in giving.'[1] St. Louis' own dying words to his son — as Joinville reports them — were: 'Once upon a time one of the counsellors of my grandfather Philip insisted to him that the clergy were doing him grave wrongs, encroaching on his royal rights and obstructing his justices, and that it was astounding that he should put up with such treatment. The good old king answered that he believed this to be true, but that considering all the favours God had shown him, he would rather forfeit royal rights than quarrel with God's priests.'[2]

If there was no irony behind this second adage of Philip Augustus (and we have no evidence that there was) it lends admirable support to the first. Philip was a hard master, but he endeavoured to do justice to both God and man. His subjects were bound to do him good service, indeed this was in his eyes their sole function; and he readily acknowledged his duty to reward them for it — but the reward must be closely commensurate with the services rendered. And this was how a great king should think and behave. Yet he must set an example and himself be the foremost and most devoted servant of the crown. Especially in the latter part of his career did Philip Augustus act on these principles. He was tirelessly active, a brave and daring war leader, a prudent and skilful diplomat, reorganising his kingdom internally after a fashion that influenced the character of the French monarchy for centuries.

It must be admitted that good luck was on his side. A crossbowman's bolt rid him in the nick of time of his most dangerous

[1] Joinville, *Histoire de saint Louis* (ed. Natalis de Wailly, Paris, 1868), pp. 237–8.
[2] *Ibid.*, p. 265.

enemy, Richard the Lion Heart of England; and no one could accuse Philip of having had any hand in this fortunate accident. Thanks to the unbridled savagery of Richard's successor, John Lackland, the young Arthur of Brittany was removed from the scene, and with him the possibility of a strong opposition, supported by the nobility, to Philip's absorption of the Plantagenet inheritance on the continent. King John's blundering drove the English barons into revolt at the very time when a united England might have proved fatal to Philip. Innocent III's veto prevented Philip from embarking personally on the risky gamble of an attempted conquest of England. Innocent's policies also brought into the field against the Albigensian heretics the most adventurous spirits among the feudal nobility of France north of the Loire. From their conquest of the Midi the French monarchy was the ultimate gainer. Still, Philip was the man to turn Fortune's bounties, 'God's favours', to profit. On the field of Bouvines he was the heroic king in action, the courageous knightly leader. In the field of diplomacy he deployed a marvellous skill in his dealings with John Lackland and Arthur, with the English barons, with the Holy See. He was a master of legal argument, seizing on every advantage the feudal law offered a ruler in his position. All this had astonishing results. In forty-two years the King of France came to acquire and control effectively a vast royal domain. St. Louis' dictum 'There is only one king in France' was true from the reign of Philip Augustus onwards, as one of the best historians of the period has pointed out.[1] The speedy rise of the Capetian monarchy which Philip's exertions and his good luck had brought about would have been an ephemeral thing if his successors had been mediocre or incompetent; but few of them were mediocrities, and some were great kings. With Philip's example before it, the dynasty held fast to what he had accomplished.

King Louis VIII (1223–6) successfully carried on the work Philip had begun. But Louis lacked his father's physical stamina, and burnt himself out in a forty-months' reign of unresting activity. His premature death came at the high tide of success, when he had just victoriously established royal power in Poitou

[1] C. Petit-Dutaillis, *La monarchie féodale en France et en Angleterre*, p. 347.

and Languedoc. Languedoc had been all but independent, and but for Louis VIII the crusade against the Albigensian heretics might have put power there in the hands of a new feudal dynasty even harder to subdue than the old line of the counts of Toulouse.

The hour that struck the death of Louis VIII was arguably the most critical in the history of the Capetian family. The new king, one day to be St. Louis, was still a child. The trend of events in the previous two reigns had brought the higher nobility to realise that its independence would soon be seriously threatened. But a unique opportunity for a counter-blow had now arisen. And so opposition was raised to the regency of the queen-mother, Blanche of Castile, on the pretext that she was a woman and a foreigner. Yet this was not the first occasion on which the king's widow had acted as regent, nor the first on which a queen had played a part in politics. Philip Augustus had been the first Capetian not to involve his wife in the government of the realm. Before his time the queens of France had often intervened in affairs of state. Constance of Arles, not content with making married life difficult for Robert the Pious, had wanted to change the order of succession to the throne. She had led the opposition to Henry I, provoking and upholding his brothers against him, and she was perhaps responsible for the separation of Burgundy from the royal domain, to which Robert the Pious had joined it. Anna of Kiev, after the death of her husband, Henry I, had been one of the regents, and it was only her second marriage, to Raoul de Crépy, that took her out of politics. Bertrada de Montfort's influence over Philip I had been notorious, and so had her hostility to the heir to the throne, whom she had even been accused of trying to poison. Adelaide of Maurienne, despite a physical personality before which Count Baldwin III of Hainault is said to have recoiled, had held considerable sway over Louis VI, procuring the disgrace of the chancellor, Étienne de Garlande, and egging on Louis to the Flemish adventure from which her brother-in-law, William Clito, was to profit so much. Eleanor of Aquitaine — as St. Bernard had complained — had more power than anyone else over Louis VII as long as their marriage lasted. Louis VII's third wife, Adela of Champagne, had appealed to the King of England for help against her son Philip Augustus, when he had sought to free himself of the tutelage of her brothers of Champagne. Later, reconciled with Philip, Adela had been regent during his absence from France on crusade. From the beginnings of Capet rule, the queens of France had enjoyed substantial influence over their husbands and over royal policy.

But Blanche of Castile was to play a greater role than any of her predecessors. To all intents and purposes she may be counted among the kings of France. For from 1226 until her death in 1252 she governed the kingdom. Twice she was regent: from 1226 to 1234, while Louis IX was a minor, and from 1248 to 1252 during his first absence on crusade. Between 1234 and 1248 Blanche bore no official title, but her power was no less effective. Severe in personality, heroic in stature, this Spanish princess took control of the fortunes of the dynasty and the kingdom in out-standingly difficult circumstances. For in 1226 there arose the most redoubtable coalition of great barons which the House of Capet ever had to face. Loyalty to the crown, so constant a feature of the past, seemed to be in eclipse. This was at any rate true of the barons who revolted, for they appear to have tried to seize the person of the young king himself — an attempt without parallel in Capetian history.

Blanche of Castile threw herself energetically into the struggle over her son and his throne. Taking her father-in-law, Philip Augustus, as her model, she won over half her enemies by craft, vigorously gave battle to the rest, and enlisted the alliance of the Church, including the Pope himself, and of the burgess class, which in marked fashion took the side of the royal family. Blanche was able to fend off King Henry III of England, who tried to take the opportunity of recovering his ancestral lands, lost by John to Philip Augustus. She broke up the baronial coalition and reduced to submission the most dangerous of the rebels, Peter Mauclerc, Count of Brittany, and Raymond VII, Count of Toulouse. She adroitly took advantage of her victory to re-establish — this time definitively — the royal power in the south of France: her son Alphonse was married to the daughter and heiress of Raymond of

Toulouse. The way was now open for the union of all Raymond's rich patrimony with the royal domain.

The Capetian monarchy emerged all the stronger from a crisis which had threatened to overwhelm it. Blanche felt it her duty not to rest on her laurels. After her son came of age she continued to make herself responsible for good and stable government. By the force of her example she drove home the lessons which Philip Augustus seems to have wanted to press upon his grandson when they had talked together. To Blanche's initiative must be credited the measures taken to suppress the dangerous revolt of Trencavel in Languedoc, as also those taken to defeat the coalition broken up after the battle of Saintes. On these occasions Louis IX did no more than carry out his mother's policy. When he went off on crusade, Blanche once more officially shouldered the government of the kingdom. She maintained law and order, prevented the further outbreak of war with England, and successfully pressed on with the policy which was to lead to the annexation of Langue-doc. Likewise it was she who refurnished her son's crusade with men and money, and she took all the steps necessary for the safety of the kingdom when Louis was captured in Egypt.

But what posterity most remembers Blanche of Castile for is that she gave birth to and brought up Louis IX, the king who won and kept first place in French affections, who most strongly influenced the development of the French monarchy, and who obscured the glory of his forerunners and successors alike. After his time, men spoke not of the Capetians, of the royal house of France, of the throne of France: but of the line of St. Louis, the blood of St. Louis, and the throne of St. Louis.

In his youth Louis IX (1226–70) was a handsome knightly figure, slender and upstanding, with the face of an angel lit up by 'the eyes of a dove'. The man of mature years was an ascetic, his body wearied by the mortifying penances he inflicted upon it; yet all who came near him felt his unforgettable charm. Louis was simple in manner and dress, generally jovial, though capable of violent anger, and fundamentally good-natured, but with a zeal for justice which could, when the occasion demanded, arouse in him the energies called for in a great king. He was a dutiful son —

probably too much so for the taste of his ambitious wife, Margaret of Provence. He well understood the greatness of his mother's achievement, and sagaciously allowed her to govern the realm as long as she wished; but this is not to say that Louis was anxious to unload the burdens of kingship on to Blanche or that he had no will of his own. On the contrary, no King of France seems to have taken his high office more conscientiously. Kingship for him was not a mere opportunity of lording it over other men, or making his subjects happy, or conquering other kingdoms, or feathering his own nest. He approached it — as he approached everything else — with his Christian faith as his guide, a faith which was his lifelong inspiration, and was founded not on convictions reached through theological ponderings, but on the deep and sure belief that lies beyond all questionings and is marked by the tranquil joy which only those who experience religious certainty can know. Had Louis been born into a different social station, he would have taken vows and become a monk. He thought of so doing, indeed, but was restrained by his sense of the duties of kingship. God had put him on the throne, he believed, to serve the Christian faith and to lead his people not to worldly happiness but towards eternal salvation.

Such an idea, held by a king of different calibre, would have put the monarchy on the road to ruin. But it was not for nothing that St. Louis had listened to the counsel of his grandfather Philip Augustus — whom he freely quoted. Not for nothing had he come under the influence of the pious Blanche of Castile. Blanche is credited with the awe-inspiring remark that she would sooner see her son dead than cure him at the price of a mortal sin.[1] She taught Louis that a man may sin not only in his own person but also through another, that the sins of the subject become the sins of the king, and that no king can be without sin if his subjects live in iniquity. Now to lead the people out of their life of sin, a king must be strong and command obedience. With faith as his guide, he can and should take all decisions upon himself. And so an absolute monarch can, alone, lead his people to salvation. Reasoning thus, Louis IX sought to make the French monarchy absolute.

[1] Geoffroy de Beaulieu, in *R.H.F.*, xx, 4.

(He could hardly have foreseen the ultimately disastrous consequences of absolutism.) An absolute monarchy is perhaps what Philip Augustus had desired. Philip the Fair, Louis' grandson and faithful admirer, was to work towards the same goal, as were other French kings of the future, striving towards that ideal of monarchy by divine right which Louis XIV was most fully to represent. But the motives which worked upon these more or less conscious architects of absolutism were not those which fired St. Louis. The others thought of their kingdom or of themselves. St. Louis thought of the immortal souls of the men he ruled.

Louis IX surrounded himself with Franciscan and Dominican friars. His ideas on obedience and discipline were those which then prevailed in the two great Mendicant Orders, pervaded as they still were by the spirit of their founders. The influence of Francis and Dominic came all but directly to Louis. The disobedient, however mighty they were, felt the rough edge of his tongue. His brother, Charles of Anjou, had imprisoned a knight who with perfect legality had appealed from the court of Anjou to the royal court. 'There can be only one king in France', said Louis: 'and do not suppose that because you are my brother I shall shield you from the workings of justice.'[1] When Jean de Tourotte, irritated by the arrest of Enguerrand de Couci, who had illegally hanged three poachers, exclaimed that the king had nothing left to do now but hang all his barons, Louis retorted: 'What are you saying, Jean? That I am going to hang my barons? I certainly shall not hang them, but I shall punish them if they misbehave.'[2] Anyone — nobleman, clerk, burgess, countryman — who refused to do the royal will felt the hand of Louis IX heavy upon him. Nevertheless, the men he treated harshly, whose revolts he pitilessly suppressed, bore him no ill will for it in his lifetime. When he died he was mourned as no other king has ever been mourned. People did not wait for his canonisation by the Church before they began to adore his memory. His reign — the times of good King Louis — lived for centuries in the memory of Frenchmen as a sort of golden age which would never come back.

[1] Guillaume de Saint-Pathus, *Vie de saint Louis* (ed. H. F. Delaborde, Paris, 1899), p. 141.
[2] *Ibid.*, p. 139.

B2

It would clearly be inadequate to explain Louis' popularity by purely material arguments, even though it is true that the period from 1245 until his death in 1270 was a time of peace, which brought prosperity to France and a return to a sound currency and a gold coinage. French history has passed through other periods of peace and prosperity, inaugurated by kings or governments who got small credit therefrom. The Age of St. Louis has probably stood so high in the esteem of Frenchmen because of their realisation that, for a time, they were being ruled by a just man. In the *Instructions* which he drew up for his son, the future King Philip III, Louis expounded his conception of justice:

'Dear son, if you succeed to the throne, make sure that you have the qualities which befit a king. Be so just that you never deny justice to anyone on any account. If there is a dispute between a poor man and a rich man, uphold the poor as against the rich until such time as you know the truth of the matter — and then do justice. If you should be involved in a dispute with another man, uphold that man's cause even before your own Council. Give no appearance of favouring your own case until you know the whole truth of the affair, for otherwise your counsellors may hesitate to speak against you, a situation you should wish never to arise. If you should discover that you are in wrongful possession of any land or revenue, even if possession of it was acquired by your ancestors, surrender it forthwith, no matter how great its value. If the case is so involved and obscure that the truth of it cannot be disentangled, seek the advice of honest men, and then make such an agreement that your soul and the souls of your ancestors shall not go guilty in the matter. And even if men shall say to you that your predecessors made all the restitutions necessary, exert yourself to find out whether there is not yet some restitution to be made for the good of your soul and the souls of your ancestors.'[1]

Louis IX was not making an empty pronouncement. He was summing up for his son the rules he had imposed upon himself for the good of the kingdom. He had striven to be a just ruler, just to his neighbours, just to his subjects. The *enquêteurs* whom he had sent round the kingdom in January 1247 had been com-

[1] Ch.-V. Langlois, *La Vie en France au Moyen Âge*, vol. iv, *La Vie spirituelle* (Paris, 1928), pp. 37–8.

missioned 'to receive in writing and examine all pleas which any man may bring against us or our ancestors; and likewise all statements of injustices and exactions of which our *baillis*, *prévôts*, foresters and serjeants and their subordinates are alleged to be guilty since the beginning of our reign.'[1] The ordinances which the king laid down for his *baillis* and seneschals in 1254 and 1256, following upon these inquiries, are, in the apt phrase of Petit-Dutaillis, 'a moral code for the use of officials and subjects'.[2] Louis forbade prostitution and gambling; punished blasphemers under the ordinance of 1268–9; and banned the judicial duel and the carrying of arms in 1258. To ensure the reign of peace and justice, he extended the scope of his action beyond the royal domain, and legislated for the whole kingdom. Not content with striving to purify royal justice, he investigated seigneurial justice also. All his subjects, high and low, had access to his presence, and to all he did justice. He won the affections of men not only for himself but also for the kingship he personified: and he made the authority of that kingship reach out to all corners of his realm. In his day there was truly only one king in France.

Likewise there was only one King of France in Europe, a just king to whose arbitration many had recourse. All along the frontiers of the kingdom, in Dauphiné and in Savoy, at Lyons, in the Barrois, in Lorraine and in Flanders, disputants turned to him, besought him to decide between them, and accepted his decisions. At Amiens in 1264 he arbitrated in the dispute between Henry III of England and his rebellious barons. Louis did not intervene between Pope Innocent IV and the Emperor Frederick II, having a low opinion of those two rivals and taking faults to be equal on both sides. Neither Innocent nor Frederick, each doubt-less conscious of the weakness of his own case, dared appeal to Louis.

Practising what he had preached to his son ('I enjoin upon you, dear son, to refrain, as far as lies in your power, from making war upon other Christians')[3] Louis entered into treaties of peace with his neighbours — not without incurring the criticism of his

[1] *R.H.F.*, xxiv, p. *4.
[2] *Histoire générale: Histoire du Moyen Âge*, ed. G. Glotz, vol. iv, part 2, p. 272.
[3] Langlois, *La vie spirituelle*, p. 139.

subjects. By the Treaty of Paris (28 May 1258) with Henry III of England and the Treaty of Corbeil (11 May 1258) with James I of Aragon, he generously gave up various lands and rights claimed by the French crown, and expressed in these agreements the hope that he was 'fostering love' between his descendants and those of Henry and James. Capetian rights were not entirely sacrificed, for the two treaties secured for Louis the recognition of claims previously in dispute.

In the end, having established peace throughout France and on her frontiers, Louis turned back to the crusade, the grand enterprise he had never in his heart forsaken. He died under the walls of Tunis on 25 August 1270, thus adding the martyr's halo to the glory of the great lawgiver. By a bull of 11 August 1297 Pope Boniface VIII inscribed the name of Louis IX among those of the saints of the Church. But Frenchmen had not waited for the Church's decision before coming to believe in the king's sanctity. Guillaume de Saint-Pathus reports a miracle attributed to the relics of St. Louis even before they reached Saint-Denis. Near the elm-tree of Bonneuil-sur-Marne a mother prayed that her son should be cured by them, and their touch restored the child to health.[1] Guillaume also relates that in 1272 a hunch-backed old woman, hobbling along on crutches, went to tell her neighbours that 'she wanted to go to the tomb of St. Louis, where she hoped to be healed'.[2]

It was obviously not easy to succeed such a king as Louis IX, and the reputation of his son Philip III (1270–85) has been rather dimmed by proximity to so dazzling a predecessor. Philip III was a man of small intelligence who struggled along faithfully in St. Louis' footsteps. He is not undeserving of credit; at least he refrained from reacting violently against his father's policy and from putting in jeopardy the achievements of Louis IX, Blanche of Castile, and Philip Augustus. Instead he was content to retain in office the excellent servants his father had bequeathed to him, and to reap the benefits of the wisdom of his forebears, notably the vast heritage of Alphonse of Poitiers — Poitou and nearly all

[1] Les miracles de saint Louis, (ed. Percival B. Fay, Classiques français du Moyen Âge, Paris, 1939), pp. 173–4.
[2] Ibid., p. 134.

Languedoc — which was united with the royal domain in 1271. In Philip's reign there was also accomplished the marriage which was to add to the royal domain the counties of Champagne and Brie. Philip III has no great reputation, but it was under him that the royal domain was most widely expanded; and during the fifteen years of his rule peace was preserved. Still, his only positive achievement was to have left the old counsellors of Louis IX undisturbed for some years. He goes down to history as a king of largely negative personality.

This was just as well in view of what happened on the one occasion when Philip broke away from his father's policy. Urged on by his second wife, the young Mary of Brabant, and by his uncle, Charles of Anjou, he plunged recklessly into a war with Aragon. Once again, however, good luck was on the side of the Capets. The great expedition into Catalonia thrust a heavy financial burden on to the kingdom. Had it succeeded, it would have drawn away the attention of the French monarchy from much more urgent tasks. But it failed miserably. Philip III died in full retreat at Perpignan on 5 October 1285. He had not been at war long enough to have done any irreparable harm to his predecessors' achievements, though to have been the first King of France to embark on a war of foreign conquest was to have set a deplorable example.

Fortunately the lesson of 1285 was not wasted on Philip's son and heir. Opinions vary on Philip IV (1285–1314) but they all agree on the outstanding importance of his reign. Philip the Fair was tall and handsome, like his father and the sons who were to succeed him. Though quiet and cold in demeanour, he was a good-hearted, brave man of impeccable manners and considerable education. These qualities have led some historians to regard him as a great king. Others, going by the evidence of more or less well-informed chroniclers, see him as a weakling in the hands of unscrupulous counsellors. A prolonged study of the reign has led the present writer to conclude that Philip was a great king who gave his counsellors his full support and made no move to visit disgrace on any of them — even when such a gesture would have markedly lessened his difficulties. If they were the initiators of

Philip's policies, then they had his confidence. If the initiative came from the king himself, he was presumably happy that his counsellors were carrying out his instructions effectively.[1]

Like Philip Augustus, and even more like his grandfather St. Louis (whom he venerated and whose canonisation he procured from the Pope), Philip IV intended that there should be 'only one king in France'. But the France of which he wanted to be sole ruler was a different France from the kingdom of his predecessors. Philip III's acquisition of the heritage of Alphonse of Poitiers and Philip IV's marriage to Joan of Navarre, Countess palatine of Champagne and Brie, brought the French crown's possessions close to the Alps, the Meuse, and the Scheldt. To acquire the narrow fringe of territories separating him from these desirable frontiers Philip IV no more envisaged armed conquest than St. Louis would have done. Instead, like Philip Augustus, he exploited his feudal rights, sometimes very astutely, as opportunity arose. But the kingdom of France in Philip IV's day still included regions — the duchies of Brittany, Aquitaine, and Burgundy, and the county of Flanders — in which the royal power, though in theory supreme, was in practice overshadowed and at times eclipsed by that of the great vassals. It is true that Brittany and Burgundy made no move to resist Philip's appellate jurisdiction and the ordinances which he was now issuing for the entire kingdom. It is also true that by skilfully enlisting the support of his magnates he persuaded the whole realm to acquiesce in a series of new fiscal measures; for despite the huge increases in the royal domain in 1271 and 1285, its resources were still inadequate to meet Philip's commitments. But in Aquitaine the royal interests clashed with those of the duke, who was also King of England. In Flanders the crown fell foul of urban communities which were among the largest in Europe. Philip and his officers were accustomed to the relatively easy management of rural and

---

[1] It is possible (but not certain, because the evidence can be interpreted in different ways) that Philip IV on his deathbed took upon himself all the responsibility for his policies. Baudouin de Mony has published an interesting news-letter from Guillem Baldrich to his master the King of Aragon, dated 7 December 1314, and full of precise details about Philip's last days, including the following: '*Et inter cetera dixit et recognovit defectus et vitia sua et quod in multis erraverat et offenderat Deum, malo concilio ductus, et quod ipsemet erat causa mali consilii sui*' (*Bibliothèque de l'École des Chartes*, 1897, p. 12).

semi-rural populations. To control the turbulent industrial society of Bruges, Ghent, and Ypres was utterly beyond them.

Philip IV saw a religious quality in his kingly office. He was all the more exasperated by the resistance he met with in Aquitaine and Flanders, regarding it as inspired by heresy if not by the Devil, to judge from his correspondence on Flemish questions. To break with the traditional practices of Philip Augustus and St. Louis was as distasteful as it was difficult, but Philip felt that he had no choice, and man of peace though he was, he resorted to force. In Aquitaine he went to war with the duke, Edward I of England; and the last dozen years of his reign were marked by almost annual and sometimes disastrous campaigns into Flanders. The cost mounted high. Finance became the king's leading preoccupation. To meet his unquenchable need for money every royal right was exploited in ruthless and mercenary fashion. The *enquêteurs* who now ceaselessly scoured the country still employed his grandfather's methods, but despite all pretence to the contrary they no longer acted in the spirit of St. Louis. Their one object was to seek out new sources of royal income.

This endless quest for revenue brought the monarchy into conflict with the Church. The Popes were also acutely in need of money to finance their Italian policy. Boniface VIII (1294–1303) advanced in its extreme form the Gregorian theory of the superiority of the spiritual power over the temporal and asserted the right of the clergy not to be taxed by secular governments. When this great issue of principle arose the Papacy and the French monarchy collided for the first time over the dangerous question of the relations between the spiritual and temporal powers. Each side was firmly convinced of the justice of its claims and of the sacrilegious nature of its rival's position. Philip, strong in the knowledge of his own indisputable legitimacy as King of France, assailed his opponent on personal grounds, making skilful use of the circumstances which had surrounded Boniface's election as Pope. It was left to pamphleteers to criticise the Papacy on matters of principle: there is no evidence that they were working under Philip's orders. The king was attacking not the Holy See but the man who had ascended the throne of St. Peter after the resignation, considered by some to have been canonically impossible, of his predecessor Celestine V. Philip was borrowing from the Church itself a most useful weapon against Boniface when he claimed the right as a prince of Christendom to take his dispute with the Pope to the judgment of a General Council. The whole body of his subjects was called on to support his demand. It remains in doubt whether or not this step was originally thought of by the king himself.

Philip IV's victory was overwhelming. There was a brief episode when his agents actually held the Pope prisoner at Anagni. A month later, on 11 October 1303, Boniface died. But Philip resolved that his victory must be sealed with the approval of Holy Church herself. By threatening a post-mortem trial of Boniface, he succeeded in extracting from the next Pope but one, the Gascon Clement V, a bull, dated 27 April 1311, which quashed and deleted from the registers of the papal chancery all the acts of Boniface and his successor Benedict XI which had been directed against the French king. The bull further declared Philip to have been moved throughout solely by his zeal for justice. And so, by the unrelenting efforts of the royal government, the temporal power had won a notable contest with the spiritual power in France. In one instance, the suppression of the Knights Templars, the crown was even to supplant spiritual authority. It was Philip IV who took the initiative in the trial of the Templars, thus breaking the church's close monopoly in matters of faith.

The mainspring of Philip the Fair's actions in both the secular and the religious fields was probably his faith: faith in the Capetian dynasty, faith in his kingly office, and religious faith too, deeply rooted, and affronted by the lack of spirituality in the religious Order of the Temple and in the person of Boniface VIII. But this faith, unlike that of St. Louis, reveals a hard streak of pride, the pride of a king told by the Pope that he is guided by the Holy Spirit.[1] It is known that Philip was a great reader of Boethius' *Consolation of Philosophy*. At his request Jean de Meung, the

[1] In one of his letters Clement V solemnly recalled that he had said to Philip that his ambition to set up his brother Charles of Valois as emperor of Constantinople was inspired by the Holy Spirit (*Mantissa Codicis Juris Gentium diplomatici*, ed. Leibnitz, Guelferbyti, 1747, ii, 243).

second author of the *Roman de la Rose*, translated the *Consolation* for him into French. Philip made it clear that he wished the translation to follow the Latin text as faithfully as possible.[1] He seems to have had an unusual interest in Boethius, and the vein in which Boethius wrote is disillusionment allied with contempt for the material achievements of men; his saving grace is a certain stoicism. It is conceivable that in the mind of the Roman senator whom Theodoric put to death Philip the Fair found his own reflected. Like Boethius he had schooled himself to face manifold difficulties coldly and unflinchingly. Exasperation with Philip drove the Bishop of Pamiers to declare: 'The king stares at men fixedly, without uttering a word. . . . He is not a man, not a beast, he is a graven image.'[2] This frigid, silent man left a deep mark on the history of the French monarchy. In his reign the royal administration reached a new and mature stage of its development. It was a body filled with zeal for its task, insatiable in its demands, keen to swoop on the smallest detail, more devoted to the interests of the crown than was the king himself. Against the tendencies which would have subordinated the royal authority to feudal law and custom, the administration more or less consciously set Roman Law — long preserved in Languedoc, which had recently been annexed to the royal domain — with its theory of the will of the ruler as the sole source of law. Yet despite the reputation of Philip IV and his administrators for over-governing, the people's regard for the monarchy did not slacken. Contemporaries praised Philip for his benevolent qualities.[3] That the monarchy was

[1] 'A ta royal majesté, très noble prince, par la grace de Dieu roy des François, Phelippe le quart, je, Jehan de Meun . . . envoie ore Boece de Consolation que j'ay translaté de latin en françois, ja soit ce que tu entendes bien latin, mais toute voies est moult plus legiers a entendre le françois. . . . Et pour ce que tu me deïs, lequel dit je tieng pour commandement, que je preïsse plainement la sentence de l'aucteur sens trop ensuivre les paroles du latin, j'ay fait a mon petit pooir si comme ta debonnaireté le me commanda. Or pri tous ceulz qui cest livre verront, si leur semble en aucuns lieus que je me soie trop esloignés des paroles de l'aucteur, ou je aie mis aucunes fois mains, que il me pardoingnent, car, se je eüsse espons mot a mot le latin par le françois, li livres en fust trop occurs aus gens lais. . . .' (Langlois, *La vie spirituelle*, pp. 275–6).

[2] *Cf.* the evidence of Maître Guillaume Montaner at the trial of the Bishop of Pamiers (P. Dupuy, *Histoire du différend d'entre le pape Boniface VIII et Philippe le Bel*, Paris, 1655, p. 648; there are omissions in this text).

[3] A curious echo of this praise may be detected in a letter dated 4 January 1315, from Guillem de Canet, lieutenant of the King of Majorca, to James II of Aragon. The Majorquin agent at Perpignan adds the comment: *'Quod est valde mirabile'* (see M. R. Avezou in *Bulletin hispanique*, xxix (1927), p. 181).

popular in his lifetime may be judged from the absence of any stirrings of revolt as long as he remained on the throne. Trouble did not break out until after his death.

Philip IV's three sons succeeded him in turn. Each reigned for only a short time: Louis X (1314–16) for eighteen months; Philip V (1316–22) for five years; Charles IV (1322–8) for six years. They were all strikingly handsome kings, but their characters are obscure. They played, rather more intelligently, a part similar to that which Philip III had played as successor to St. Louis. They went on with the work of Philip IV, and no doubt regard for their father helped them to make their choice when circumstances called upon them to set definitively the future course of the French monarchy.

From 1314, the last year of Philip IV's reign, onwards, the French nobility — possibly under the influence of contemporary events in England — reacted vigorously against the absolutist tendencies of the monarchy. The crown was in acute need of money. It either could not or dared not as yet break with the feudal tradition that barons must be asked to consent to the levying of subsidies from their lands; and it was anxious to preserve harmony with the Holy See. For these reasons the royal government was led to hold assemblies of nobles, clergy, and burgesses, which had a somewhat different character from the assemblies of the *curia regis* in its widest sense, which the Capetians had always been in the habit of summoning from time to time. Confronted with the royal requests for money, the barons sought, for a time with success, to extract from the crown charters in which their liberties were solemnly recognised. Between 1314 and 1325 it looked as though a parliament on the English model would develop in France.

But the sons of Philip the Fair decided to continue with what had been the dynasty's traditional policy since the time of Philip Augustus. The kingdom was too big for the entire nobility ever to be able to assemble conveniently in one place. The monarchy took advantage of the situation to hold regional assemblies. The nobility, riven by particularism, contented itself with extorting purely local charters of liberties from the crown. It did not and would not exact a general charter for the whole kingdom. Its lack of political maturity played into the monarchy's hands, as did the loyalty which the townspeople and the peasantry felt towards the throne. The development of a French Estates-General still lay in the future.

The baronial movement caught a glimpse of victory during the reign of Louis X, but it soon petered out, leaving little trace behind. What Philip Augustus, Louis IX, and Philip IV had wanted still held good. The monarchy's course was firmly set in the direction of absolutism. But in the very hour of triumph for the traditional Capetian policy, the dynasty itself foundered. The three handsome sons of Philip the Fair left only daughters to succeed them.[1] The crown passed to a cadet line, the House of Valois, the head of which, Philip VI, became King of France in April 1328.

*   *   *   *

It has been possible to attempt character-sketches, however imperfect, of the Capetian kings. A similar treatment of their counsellors is impossible. The servants are still less well known than their masters. Except for Abbot Suger, the faithful adviser and minister of Louis VI and Louis VII, and for a few of the servants of Philip the Fair, the royal counsellors are little more than names. Poor documentation prevents the historian from putting together a detailed account of any of them. But a general impression may be offered, in the hope of discovering whether the evolution of the counsellor runs parallel to that of the king.

To begin with, the title 'counsellor' has modern associations which must be discarded. The men of the royal entourage were not functionaries, or at any rate they were more than merely functionaries, and the royal council only appears as a regularly constituted body in the last years of the Capetian dynasty. The king's counsellors were his friends, his *familiares*, and naturally in

[1] It is true that Louis X's queen had a son, John, born after his father's death, but this infant, born to Queen Clémence during the night of 13 November 1316, died five days later without having reigned. Nevertheless, he used to be counted among the kings of France, and for that reason King John (1350–64), the only French king of that name, is styled John II.

the days when a king like Philip I was little more than the lord of the Île-de-France, the royal friends were of a different type from the companions of St. Louis and Philip the Fair. The king's friends came of very varied origins. They included clerics, both secular and religious; great vassals and members of the minor baronage; princes of the blood royal; and, beginning with the reign of Philip Augustus, royal officials of every kind. A complete list of them cannot be drawn up; nor would such a list tell us much. When so many kings are shadowy figures, little can be said of the lesser mortals clustering around them. In some instances the careers of royal counsellors have been reconstructed,[1] but the resulting bald recitals of offices held and favours received shed no light on their characters or on the really important question of the influence they had over the king.

One of the best-known king's counsellors, Maître Guillaume de Nogaret, keeper of the royal seal from 1307 to 1313 and the kidnapper of Pope Boniface VIII in his palace at Anagni, has been the subject of a conscientious monograph by Holtzmann,[2] who has traced in careful detail the functions he carried out and the missions with which he was entrusted. Nogaret was a lawyer. From that, Holtzmann was irresistibly tempted to deduce that he was also a knave. When Philip IV was quarrelling with the Pope, Nogaret produced his view of the conflict in documents strongly favourable to his royal master's cause, asserting that the king and he were moved solely by their concern for the Christian faith. To Holtzmann this was proof of hypocrisy as well as knavery. The brilliant Renan had already leaped to the same conclusion. The impeccable scholarship of Langlois was later to be directed to its reinforcement; and it became the interpretation of Nogaret's character which all historians accepted. Nevertheless, the discovery

[1] e.g. Luchaire's notices of a few intimate counsellors of Philip I, Louis VI, and Louis VII in the appendix to his *Histoire des institutions monarchiques en France sous les premiers Capétiens*, vol. ii (Paris, 1891), pp. 319–26; and H. Stein, *Recherches sur quelques fonctionnaires royaux des XIII⁰ et XIV⁰ siècles originaires du Gâtinais* in *Annales de la Société historique et archéologique du Gâtinais*, vol. xx (1902), pp. 1–23, 192–7; xxi (1903), pp. 343–72; xxxii (1914), pp. 195–221; xxxiv (1919), pp. 1–103.

[2] R. Holtzmann, *Wilhelm von Nogaret* (Freiburg, 1898). Ernest Renan's article in *Histoire littéraire de la France*, xxvii, 233–371, remains of use; the substance of it was reproduced in his three articles in *La Revue des Deux Mondes*, 15 March, 1 August, and 15 August 1872.

of a particular letter from Nogaret's own hand to his friend Étienne de Suisy has revealed the supposed hypocrite to have been a man of such ardent faith that he prayed God to stay his hand, if need be to strike him dead, if the task he was about (Nogaret was writing on the way to Anagni) were contrary to the divine will.[1]

What has been said about Nogaret underlines the need for caution in forming judgments of the characters of royal counsellors. We should also consider the difficulties of estimating the influence the king's friends had over his decisions. Pierre de La Broce, for example, one of the few 'court favourites' known to Capetian history, and chamberlain to Louis IX and afterwards to Philip III, was feared by everyone during Philip's reign 'because he did as he pleased with the king'.[2] The chronicle ascribed to Baudouin d'Avesnes asserts that Pierre 'attended the royal Council at any hour he chose, and when the barons had given the king their wise counsel, it was rejected if Pierre disagreed with it'.[3] Langlois, who studied Pierre's career in minute detail, came to the conclusion that 'he left no constructive, political achievement behind him. ... We should think of him as a vulgar upstart struggling with the misfortunes his ambition had deservedly brought on him. ... There is hardly any lesson to be learned from Pierre's history except that the king was unbelievably deluded by him, and displayed singular weakness, first of all by making Pierre's fortune for him, and then by abandoning him against his own will.'[4]

Langlois' learned and masterly study of Philip III's entourage has a value far transcending the narrow limits of the period he worked on. Its close attention to detail makes it clear that the king's very numerous counsellors had to share with each other their influence over their master, and as a result the individual pull exerted by any one of them was never strong. Repeatedly it fell to them to suggest to the king what steps he should take, but the final decision was always his. They were the general staff, planning

---

[1] 'Domine mi, orate ad Dominum ut si via mea Deo placeat me in ea diriguat, alias me per mortem vel ut sibi placeat impediat' (*Journal des Savants*, nouvelle série, vol. xv (1917), p. 323). Ch.-V. Langlois himself discovered and published this letter.
[2] Guillaume de Nangis, in *R.H.F.*, xx, 494.
[3] *R.H.F.*, xxi, 180.
[4] Ch.-V. Langlois, *Le règne de Philippe III le Hardi* (Paris, 1885), p. 32

campaigns for the commander-in-chief, but they could do nothing unless he willed it.

It thus appears impossible to portray the royal counsellors convincingly, still less to single out with precision the contribution made by each of them or indeed by any one of them to the dynasty's general achievement; but there seems to have been one important respect in which their action probably helped to reinforce the dynastic views of the Capetian kings. The Capetians were remarkably loyal to their counsellors. In so far as the history of their council is known, disgrace appears rarely to have been visited on its members. Étienne de Garlande, archdeacon of Notre-Dame de Paris, and chancellor and seneschal to Louis VI, Pierre de La Broce, and Enguerrand de Marigny, the cynical Norman adviser of Philip the Fair, are the only royal counsellors known for certain to have been disgraced. For that matter, Marigny was deserted not by the king he had served, but by his son Louis X, who lived to experience remorse for it. Counsellors frequently survived the king who had first admitted them to his council, nor did the royal favour shown them die with him. Out of filial respect a new king, on succeeding to the throne, would usually retain his father's counsellors in his service. The association of the heir-presumptive with the throne during his father's lifetime helps to explain this policy during the reigns preceding that of Philip Augustus; so does the quasi-hereditary nature of the functions of some of the great offices of state. But in Philip Augustus' time these last two factors finally ceased to operate. All that now counted was the regard of a new king for his father's memory and his father's works. Louis VIII retained all the counsellors of his father, Philip Augustus. After him, his widow and son retained the services of the Hospitaller Guérin and of Renaud de Roye, who had been reared in the school of the victor of Bouvines. Until the closing years of his reign, Philip III allowed the old servants of St. Louis to carry on his father's policy. Many of Philip the Fair's officials began their careers under Philip III, and, after a temporary eclipse, Philip the Fair's counsellors very largely made up the council of his three sons.

The relative permanence of the royal counsellors helped to

create a kind of political continuity for the whole Capetian period. For two centuries, each Capet king in turn was associated with his father in governing before coming to rule on his own. Every king of the dynasty was surrounded by counsellors who had already worked with his predecessor and sometimes with the last king but one. And every king was persuaded to follow the same broad lines of policy, the more so as the very exigencies of his situation set him on the path he must tread. Hence Capetian policy was not cursed with the vagaries characteristic of so many dynasties and governments. A last contributing factor was the modest and reasonable character of everything they purposed and accomplished. Excess was foreign to their natures. The only wild-goose chases known to have been proposed to them were recommended by the lawyer Pierre Dubois in his *De Recuperatione Terrae Sanctae* and his *Summaria, brevis et compendiosa doctrina felicis expeditionis et abreviationis guerrarum ac litium regni Franciae.* Dubois was never employed by the dynasty, and it turned a deaf ear to his schemes.

The moderation of Capet policies derived in part from the fact that for a long period they commanded relatively meagre resources. It was also partly due to the diversity of the counsellors surrounding them. The great vassals belonged to their council as of right, but it also included a striking number of representatives of the lesser baronage of the royal domain and of the bourgeoisie — the latter being either clerks of urban middle-class origin or royal officials who were laymen. In particular, the dynasties which successively occupied the office of royal chamberlain throughout the Capetian period belonged to the minor nobility of the royal domain. They were king's men in the strictest sense of the expression, men entirely devoted to the royal service by family tradition and the traditions of office. The chamberlains were a link with the early days of the dynasty, when the monarchy was a mere lordship, its pretensions limited by its slender means. Loaded with gifts by the kings they served, the chamberlains were not the men to persuade the monarchy into wild adventures. It may be no exaggeration to suppose that the attitude of some of them towards the high spirits and adventurous outlook of the nobility was that of the most famous of all this class of the monarchy's counsellors, Enguerrand de Marigny, who in 1314 wrote in a celebrated letter to Simon of Pisa: 'This blazing ardour, Brother Simon, does not surprise me, remembering the hot weather we have just been experiencing, but I hope that after mid-August, when the temperature begins to drop, the Flemings will cool down, and will not be half so hot for war as they are at present. I am certain that you have found your people's blood so inflamed and their feelings so high that you have not dared to tell them what we said at Arras; and I assure you, Brother Simon, that I for my part have not been able to speak of it, for our lords here are in high dudgeon, and spoiling for a fight. I realise that, considering the emotional state both our barons and the barons of Flanders are in, it would be bad policy to speak of it. But if the situation does not get better soon, it will get far worse: one side or the other must be the first to calm down. What cooling waters, Brother Simon, must be poured on the flames by whoever would bring these troubles to a happy issue!'[1]

At the close of the thirteenth century and during the last decades of the dynasty, after the French Midi had been annexed to the royal domain, there appeared in the royal circle the group known as the 'Legists'. These counsellors, who often originated from the Midi, were well versed in Roman Law, which some of them had studied at Montpellier and others at Orléans.[2] Their careers often began in minor departments of the royal administration, where they were distinguished by their tireless application to business. When they were promoted to high office, the king conferred knighthood upon them, and with it nobility. The monarch had raised them up, and they served him with a fervent zeal which impelled them to transform the very nature of kingship. In their eyes he could no longer be the feudal king, the supreme suzerain, more suzerain indeed than sovereign, bound by custom

[1] F. Funck-Brentano, *Philippe le Bel en Flandre* (Paris, 1897), p. 657.

[2] They had had precursors in the royal administration who were not southerners. The *Conseil à un ami*, a juridical compilation strongly impregnated with Roman Law, was written between 1254 and 1258 by Pierre de Fontaine, Beaumanoir's predecessor as *bailli* of Vermandois. The *Livre de Jostice et Plet*, written about 1260 by Philippe de Rémy, father of Beaumanoir and *bailli* of the Gâtinais under Robert of Artois, is of similar character

and by his respect for illustrious ancestors whose example he was obliged to follow. They were bent on making of him a new kind of king, an absolute sovereign whose will should be law.

What they were doing was in harmony with the Capetian tradition, which had sought to make men recognise that there was 'only one king in France', but the sense in which the legists were using the term 'king' was that conveyed by the *princeps* of Roman Law. So omnipotent a prince could not possibly have abstained from the excesses, the *démesure*, which the dynasty of Hugh Capet had always been able to avoid. Could the Capetians have resisted the offer their legists were making them? Philip the Fair and his sons, steeped as they were in family tradition and feudal convention, did not, on the whole, succumb to the temptation. And fortune, always favourable to the Capetians, brought the dynasty to an end at the very time when it might have abandoned the line of conduct it had followed with so much success.

The Capetian kings and their counsellors had laboured together to construct the framework on which the French nation was to be created. We must now watch them at their work.

3
The Dynasty

Hugh Capet was crowned King of France at Noyon on 5 July 987. He was the son of Hugh the Great, Duke of Francia, the grand-nephew of Eudes, Count of Paris and King of France (888–98), the grandson of Robert I, King of France (922–3), and the nephew of Raoul, King of France (923–6). His accession was due as much to the intrigues of Archbishop Adalbero of Rheims as to his own personal actions. Contemporary opinion probably did not look upon the occasion as the inauguration of a new dynasty. We may even suspect that those who elected Hugh as king would not have done so, had they been able to read the future. The great feudal magnates of France north of the Loire who chose the Duke of Francia to be their ruler had no intention of committing themselves to his descendants. Indeed, everything suggested that they would react to his death as they had done to that of the last Carolingian, Louis V, and make a free choice of a successor.

Hugh Capet had rather different ideas, and these were shared by his descendants. A few months after his election — on 25 December 987 — the king's son Robert was crowned and associated with him on the throne. Robert, who reigned alone after his father's death in 996, in his turn associated his eldest son Hugh with himself in 1017; when Hugh died his younger brother Henry took his place, in 1026. On 28 May 1059 Henry, who had been sole king since 1031, had his own son Philip crowned at the age of seven. Philip succeeded in 1060. His son Louis was made co-ruler at some unknown date between 1098 and 1100, when he was chosen *rex designatus* by an assembly of nobles and bishops, though he does not seem actually to have been crowned during his father's lifetime. In the same manner, Louis VI had his son

Philip crowned on 14 April 1129. It was after Philip's death that his younger brother Louis was anointed by Pope Innocent II, on King Louis' request, in Rheims Cathedral, on 25 October 1131. Louis VII waited until 1 November 1179, when he was on his death-bed, before he had his only son, the future Philip Augustus, crowned; the latter was already fourteen years old. Philip himself was the first of the dynasty to feel secure enough to omit the formality of association, and to leave his heir to succeed without previous coronation.

The kings thus acted deliberately to secure hereditary succession. There does not seem to have been any very determined opposition. The only reported instance came at the association of King Robert with his father, but the poverty of the sources may conceal other cases. The opposition to Robert's successor Henry came mainly from the queen-mother Constance, and arose from family quarrels. It should be noted, however, that despite this lack of opposition the Capetians never made a specific claim to a hereditary right to the throne. Philip III, his son, and his grandsons made arrangements at various times for the succession, or for a possible regency, but they never laid down by ordinance any rules for the inheritance of the crown.

The idea of election, which had brought Hugh Capet to the throne, never gave way completely before this cautious introduction of the hereditary principle. It survived in the assemblies of prelates and barons which every ruler, until 1179, convoked to give formal designation of the heir-apparent as associate-king. It survived also in the homage which every new king received from all his vassals at his accession, and, in a symbolic form, in the *acclamatio* which accompanied the ceremony of anointing, and which had once been more than a mere symbol. The idea was still alive in the fourteenth century, as was shown in 1316, 1322, and 1328, when fortune at last deserted the royal house. Louis X, Philip V, and Charles IV all died in quick succession, leaving only daughters as heirs. On all three occasions females with undoubted hereditary rights were passed over — twice in favour of brothers of the dead rulers, and once in favour of a cousin-german, Philip of Valois. Further, these important decisions were in contradiction of the wishes of the dying kings. They were taken by assemblies of prelates, nobles and burgesses of Paris. These assemblies would have been of doubtful legality if the Capetians had ever dared to lay down that the succession to the crown went by primogeniture inside the house of Hugh Capet. The caution of their ancestors thus lost the crown to the granddaughters of Philip the Fair, and the dynasty ended through the very processes which had inaugurated it.

Given similar circumstances, it might have ended long before. But fortune long favoured the Capetians. Every king from 987 to 1314 left — and was careful to leave — a male heir to succeed him. There is considerable evidence to suggest that the continuity of the dynasty was never far from their minds.

In 988 Robert the Pious, when only sixteen, married Rozalle-Suzanna, daughter of King Berengar of Italy. The new queen was no longer young, and her husband hardly exaggerated in calling her 'an old Italian'. Her first husband was Arnoul II, by whom she had a son, Baldwin the Bearded, who became Count of Flanders on his father's death in 988. Her marriage to King Robert was politically advantageous to the Capetians. Nevertheless, he repudiated her in 992, to the great scandal of the virtuous, as for example the chronicler Richer. The reason given was the great disparity in age between husband and wife, but it may not have been irrelevant that after four years of marriage no heir had been born.

At some unknown date, the young king acted as godparent at the baptism of a son of Bertha, wife of Count Eudes of Blois and daughter of Conrad the Peaceable, King of Burgundy. We do not know whether it is from this event that we must date Robert's infatuation for her; it may have begun even earlier. In all events, Bertha, some years older than the king and the mother of five children, was left a widow at very much the same time as Robert became sole king through the death of his father, and they were married, most probably late in 996. The marriage was not a fortunate one for the king. It aroused the anger of the Church, for the two were related in the sixth degree, and in addition had acted together as parent and godparent. In 997 Robert was threatened with excommunication if he failed to separate from her.

In 998 a council held at Rome by Pope Gregory V anathematised him, should he not submit at once. Robert was recalcitrant, and did not give way until 1001. Then he separated from his wife. His precise reasons are unknown, but Bertha, after four years of married life, had not presented him with the desired heir, and reasons of state may well have prevailed. Two years later the king married Constance, daughter of Count William I of Arles; she led him no easy life, but gave him four sons and a daughter, so assuring the succession.

A century and more later King Louis VII was faced by a similar problem. Duke William of Aquitaine, when on his death-bed, had given his daughter and heiress, Eleanor, in marriage to the king, a year before he succeeded to the throne. The marriage was politically important, for it added to the small royal domain the enormous duchy of Aquitaine, which embraced the whole south-west of France, from Bourges to the Pyrenees, and from the mouth of the Loire to the Cévennes. Eleanor was beautiful, intelligent, and extremely attractive to the young king. His obvious devotion to her was disquieting to St. Bernard, who suspected her of hostility towards churchmen. After fifteen years of married life, during which only two daughters had been born, the royal couple went together on the Second Crusade in 1147. Trouble developed, in the shape of an obscure scandal at Antioch, and they returned to Europe on very bad terms with each other. In March 1152 they were formally separated, on the legal ground that they were cousins in the third or fourth degree. It is difficult to believe that they had not discovered this apparently awkward fact sooner. Both remarried very soon afterwards. Eleanor married Henry Plantagenet, Count of Anjou and Duke of Normandy, and bore him four sons in rapid succession. Louis married, in 1154, Constance, daughter of the King of Castile. When she died childless on 4 October 1160 he married yet again within five weeks; this time his bride was Adela of Champagne, who gave birth, on 21 August 1165, to the future Philip Augustus.

A third instance is the well-known episode of Ingeborg of Denmark, Philip Augustus' own queen. The only child of Philip's first marriage, with Isabella of Hainault, was a son, born on 5 September 1187, who later succeeded as Louis VIII. Isabella died in 1190, after giving birth to twins who did not survive her. Her only surviving son, Prince Louis, was not robust, and was critically ill with dysentery in 1191. The line of the dynasty was thus dangerously thin, and it was hardly surprising that the king should remarry in 1193. On the very morrow of the wedding, however, he had developed a compulsive horror of his new queen, the unfortunate Ingeborg. Whatever its cause, this repugnance made the birth of a further heir unlikely — and it is clear that Philip badly wanted a second possible heir. Only this will explain his anxiety to find a third wife and his marriage to Agnes of Méran, in 1196, in the teeth of the united opposition of the Church. Agnes did in fact produce a son — called Philip 'the shock-headed', as his father had been — in September 1200.[1] She died in August 1201, some three months before her son's legitimacy was recognised by Pope Innocent III on 2 November. Shortly there-after some sort of agreement was reached between Philip and Ingeborg, and though they were not fully reconciled the king made no move to take another wife. But the succession was now guaranteed by the existence of a second heir.

Episodes of this sort are rare in the story of the Capetians. Their marriages were generally fruitful, and, what was equally important, their sons were usually loyal, or at least obedient. There are remarkably few instances of rebellion against paternal authority. Robert the Pious did take arms against his father, probably in 996, and his own two sons Henry and Robert united against him in 1030; but these were isolated instances. The only other example that can be offered is the quarrel between Philip I and the future Louis VI, which may be attributed to the malicious intervention of the prince's step-mother, Queen Bertrada. If it demonstrates anything, it shows the patience and loyalty of Prince Louis under considerable provocation. No contemporary royal, or even noble, family can show anything approaching so favour-able a record in this respect.

The characters of the individual kings go some way towards explaining this absence of family strife. The Capetians were good

[1] O. Cartellieri, *Philipp II August, Koenig von Frankreich*, vol. iv, p. 83, n. 4.

husbands. Only two bastards are recorded for the fourteen kings of the dynasty: Isabella, daughter of Louis VI, who married Guillaume de Chaumont, and Pierre Charlot, the son of Philip Augustus and that 'damsel of Arras' whose name the chroniclers delicately omit. Only three scandals can be pointed to: the elopement of Philip I with Bertrada de Montfort, wife of Fulk of Anjou, on 15 May 1092; the estrangement of Philip Augustus and Ingeborg of Denmark in 1193; and the tragic episode of the daughters-in-law of Philip the Fair in 1314. The only excuse put forward for the first affair was the excessive obesity of the lawful queen ('*praepinguis corpulentiae*', according to William of Malmesbury);[1] it would not be unfair to point out that the king himself, at the age of forty, was already very fat also. Dr. Brachet has plausibly explained the behaviour of Philip Augustus as the consequence of the impact of a momentary anaphrodisia on a nervous system already strained by illness.[2] Certainly, the adventure of the damsel of Arras apart, he does not appear to have led an irregular life. But we must look more closely at the third episode, which throws a vivid light on the moral values of the royal family.

Early in 1314 Philip the Fair arrested his three daughters-in-law — Margaret of Burgundy, first wife of Prince Louis, King of Navarre (the future Louis X); Blanche of Burgundy, first wife of Charles, Count of La Marche (the future Charles IV); and Joan of Burgundy, wife of Philip, Count of Poitiers (the future Philip V). The first two were accused of an intrigue with two knights, the brothers Philippe and Gautier d'Aunay, and Joan of having been aware of the offences and of having failed to denounce them. The two knights were at once put to death, and the three princesses were imprisoned. Margaret died in prison; Blanche defended herself for seven years whilst detained in Château Gaillard, and finally died in a convent in 1326, having been repudiated by her husband in 1322. Joan soon dropped out of the case; it may be noticed in passing that the county of Burgundy had come to the royal family through her marriage. Her sisters' guilt must remain doubtful. The wicked Isabella, their sister-in-law, who later had

---

[1] *De Gestis regum Anglorum*, (ed. W. Stubbs, Rolls Series London, 1889), vol. ii, p. 315.
[2] *Pathologie mentale des rois de France*, pp. 307–30.

her own husband Edward II of England assassinated, has been suggested as their accuser; if this be true, then the charges must be considered very dubious indeed. But one aspect of the whole affair deserves notice: the king was prepared to expose the scandal of adultery within the royal family by a public punishment. Morality could hardly demand more.

The Capetian kings found their brothers no more difficult than their sons. The exceptions were the brothers of Henry I, Robert and Eudes, but thereafter the younger Capetians developed a tradition of loyalty to their elders. Robert of Dreux, the brother of Louis VII, who was the focus of a feudal revolt in 1149, was only a partial exception, for at that date the king was still in the East, and the real object of hostility was the regent Suger. By contrast, Hugh of Vermandois was described by contemporaries as the *coadjutor* of his brother, Philip I. St. Louis' brothers, Robert of Artois, Alphonse of Poitiers, and Charles of Anjou, never caused him any difficulties, and the same can be said of Peter of Alençon and Robert of Clermont in the reign of their brother Philip III. Even the disturbing Charles of Valois, with his designs on the crowns of Aragon and Constantinople, was always a faithful servant to his brother Philip the Fair, and to the latter's sons. The declaration which he made when on the point of invading Italy in the service of the Pope is revealing:

'As we propose to go to the aid of the Church of Rome and of our dear lord, the mighty prince Charles, by the grace of God King of Sicily, be it known to all men that, as soon as the necessities of the same Church and King shall be, with God's help, in such state that we may with safety leave them, we shall then return to our most dear lord and brother Philip, by the grace of God King of France, should he have need of us. And we promise loyally and in all good faith that we shall not undertake any expedition to Constantinople, unless it be at the desire and with the advice of our dear lord and brother. And should it happen that our dear lord and brother should go to war, or that he should have need of us for the service of his kingdom, we promise that we shall come to him, at his command, as speedily as may be possible, and in all fitting state, to do his will. In witness of which we have given these letters under our seal. Written at Saint-

Ouen-lès-Saint-Denis, in the year of Grace one thousand and three hundred, on the Wednesday after Candlemas.'[1]

This absence of such sombre family tragedies as Shakespeare immortalised had a real importance. In a society always prone to anarchy the monarchy stood for a principle of order, even whilst its material and moral resources were still only slowly developing. Respectability and order in the royal family were prerequisites, if the dynasty was to establish itself securely. Disorder would have embroiled it with the Church, provided leaders to the feudal opposition, and brought the royal house down to the level of the great noble families, when it was essential that it should acquire a status apart. But in itself a united and respectable royal family was not a complete answer to the problem. Possession of the throne had to be supported by stronger sanctions, if the Capetians were to rise from being simple feudal overlords into sovereigns. In particular, the dynasty had to be invested with a distinctive religious — and even priestly — aura.

As a start, the original usurpation which had brought it the crown had to be obliterated, for it involved the dispossession of the legitimate line of Charlemagne. The obvious course was to associate the new dynasty with the old — a fact which the friends of the Capetians early recognised. By 1045 a chronicler of Sens, the monk Odorand, was painting a vivid picture of Hugh Capet receiving the crown from the last Carolingian, Louis V — *donato regno Hugoni duci*[2] — and a more or less contemporary monk from northern France went so far as to state that Hugh was unwilling — *invitus* — to accept it.[3] In a short time a whole group of legends grew up, based on these misleading assertions. The last Carolingian is shown leaving not only his kingdom, but also his wife or sometimes his daughter, to the founder of the new dynasty. The marriage of Robert the Pious and Constance of Arles was also brought into service by the supporters of the Capetians. Constance's mother, Adelaide of Anjou, had married, as her second husband, King Louis V. But the assumption that Constance

---

[1] *i.e.* 8 February 1301. The text is published in Du Cange, *Histoire de l'Empire de Constantinople sous les Empereurs françois* (Paris, 1657), preuves, p. 40.

[2] *R.H.F.*, x, 165.

[3] *Liber de inventione corporis sancti Judoci*, in *ibid.*, x, 366.

was thus half a Carolingian was false, for Louis repudiated Adelaide, and it was her third husband, William of Arles, who was the father of Constance. In the same way, stress was laid on the Carolingian origin of Adela of Champagne, third wife of Louis VII and mother of Philip Augustus, and her son's entourage were careful to underline the point; Guillaume le Breton, in the dedication of the *Philippide*,[1] addressed his king as *Karolide*. Philip's son was in even better case, for his mother was another descendant of Charlemagne, Isabella of Hainault, whose ancestor was Ermengarde, the daughter of Charles of Lorraine; Louis VIII had thus Carolingian blood on both his paternal and his maternal sides. In him, as the Saint-Denis chronicler was at pains to point out,[2] 'the line of the great Charlemagne, who was Emperor and King of France, returned after seven generations'.

There were reasons why this union of the two dynasties should have been thus emphasised. At the beginning of the eleventh century the monks of Saint-Riquier, perhaps seeking to strengthen the position of the family of their benefactor Hugh Capet, had set down a pious tale. In it St. Valéry appeared to Hugh, and exhorted him to return his body, and that of St. Riquier, to their original resting-places; in return, he promised that one day Hugh would wear the crown, and that his descendants to the seventh generation should be kings.[3] An allusion to this story in the Saint-Denis chronicle shows that it was taken seriously, and it is by no means impossible that Louis VIII himself had some misgivings about the position of his dynasty. He was the seventh descendant of Hugh Capet to wear the crown. On his death-bed at Montpensier he was clearly in some anxiety about the succession. He demanded, on 3 November 1226, that his prelates and barons should take an oath to swear fealty and do homage to his eldest son Louis (or, should Louis die, to his younger brother Robert), and to have him crowned without delay after his own death.[4]

Though the surviving texts make no mention of it, there may have been some similar idea behind the opposition of the greater

1 *Philippide*, ed. H. F. Delaborde (Paris, 1885), prologue, l. 28.
2 *Les grandes chroniques de France*, ed. Viard, vol. vii, p. 3.
3 *R.H.F.*, x, 147–9.
4 *L.T.C.*, ii, p. 96, no. 1811.

nobility to the regency of Blanche of Castile. A half-formed conviction that the day of the Capetians was over, that the prediction of St. Valéry was about to be fulfilled by a change of dynasty, may well have played its part. Further — though no great weight should be placed on the fact — St. Louis married his daughter Margaret to John I, Duke of Brabant and Lower Lorraine, 'who is the heir to the kingdom of France by hereditary right, as the eldest of the race of Charlemagne' (according to the author of a contemporary genealogy of the dukes of Lorraine).[1]

One answer to dynastic insecurity was thus a marriage policy.[2] Another, equally valuable, was the acquisition of a religious sanction, placing the king under the direct protection of God through the unction of the royal coronation. No good study of the French coronation rite exists. Such a study would involve not only an examination of its origins, but also, and more significantly, an investigation of the importance which the kings and their subjects placed upon it. It would certainly show that the Capetians — during the tenth and eleventh centuries at least — held the coronation rite to be the strongest possible guarantee of their position.

Laymen, observing the similarity between the coronation and the ceremony of episcopal consecration, considered that anointing made the king something of a chief-priest. The Capetians were careful to ensure that this 'sacrament', which wedded the king to his kingdom as the bishop was wedded to his diocese, was administered to the heir-designate during his predecessor's lifetime. Between the coronation of Robert the Pious in 987 and the death of Louis VII on 11 September 1180, there were therefore periods of 'bigamy', with two anointed kings ruling at once. In this there lay a distinction between the royal coronation and episcopal

---

[1] *Compte rendu des séances de la Commission royale d'Histoire de Belgique,* 3rd series vol. x (1868), p. 76.

[2] The idea of a prophecy announcing the end of the dynasty reappears in a death-bed statement by St. Louis to his son. It was reported by Bernard Saisset, Bishop of Pamiers, if one of the witnesses in the process against him, Br. Arnaud Jean, a Dominican friar of Toulouse, can be believed: '*Fili, nos sumus prope illam generationem in qua debet regnum Franciae terminare, quia terminabitur in te vel in filio tuo et mutabitur ad aliam generationem, quia in decimam generationem debet magnam mutationem recipere*' (Dupuy, *Différend,* p. 637). The king, however, added that if his successor were faithful to the Church the dynasty might survive to the twelfth generation '*et ultra*'.

consecration, for the Church never allowed the simultaneous occupation of a see by two bishops. Whether or not the Capetians wished this difference to be stressed, it is likely that many churchmen, who had never completely accepted the lay view of the coronation, were not unhappy that it should be so.

The royal house was careful to develop the 'sacred' associations of the anointing. The legends surrounding the anointing oil are early in date. Beginning from the story that it was first provided by a dove to save St. Rémi from embarrassment at the baptism of Clovis, they rapidly became more elaborate. The ampoule holding the holy oil, it was claimed, never emptied; in the fourteenth century it was believed to empty, but to be miraculously refilled before each coronation.

The anointed king could, further, touch for the 'king's evil' (scrofula). This power was claimed by the monarch as early as the reign of Robert the Pious, and although we cannot follow the story in full detail there is sufficient evidence to suggest that every Capetian ruler followed him in this. The gift could, in contemporary opinion, come only from God, who thus showed his particular affection for the descendants of Hugh Capet. Robert II, in a diploma, declared: 'Being assuredly, by the grace of God, superior to other men, it behoves us to be obedient in all things to the will of Him who has made us thus pre-eminent.'[1] It would be unwise to dismiss this as mere verbiage. The respectful phrasing of documents addressed to the king suggests that royal preeminence was no mere formality.

One thing only was lacking: Robert the Pious's chancellor might set his master above other mortals; Cadurc might do even more for his king, Louis VII, and place him on the level of the priesthood; the king might be addressed by his subjects in terms reserved by the faithful today for the Pope — but the royal lineage contained no saint. It was unlikely, in general terms, that the Church would feel disposed to remedy the deficiency. Gregory VII, in his letter of 15 March 1081 to Bishop Herman of Metz, put the papal attitude very clearly: 'Where, amongst emperors and kings, can a man be found to compare through his

---

[1] *R.H.F.*, x, 612.

miracles with St. Martin, St. Anthony, or St. Benedict, not to speak of the apostles and martyrs? What emperor or king has raised the dead, cured the leprous, made the blind to see? Consider Constantine the Emperor, of pious memory, consider Theodoric, Honorius, Charles, Louis, all lovers of justice, zealous for the Christian religion, and protectors of the churches. The Church praises and reveres them, but she has never acknowledged that they were the doers of such miracles.'[1] Though directed at the Emperor, Henry IV, the argument of this letter was equally dangerous for the King of France.

But, on 11 August 1297, a letter of Pope Boniface VIII placed King Louis IX of France amongst the ranks of the saints whom the Church is bound to venerate. The canonisation was no doubt a recognition of the dead king's unique qualities, but it was also the result of the diplomatic pressure exercised by his grandson. There is no mention, either in the letter of canonisation or in the sermon preached by the Pope on the occasion of the act of canonisation itself,[2] of any miracles of the type which Gregory VII had reserved to churchmen. But, for most men, that was of minor importance; for Frenchmen it probably had no importance.[3] What mattered was that the Capetian dynasty had produced a saint.

[1] *Registrum Gregorii VII*, lib. viii, cap. 21 (ed. Caspar, in *M.G.H.*, Epistolae Selectae, Berlin, 1923, vol. ii, p. 559).
[2] *R.H.F.*, xxiii, 148 ff.
[3] King Philip the Fair may have regretted the absence of any striking miracles, to judge from the enthusiasm with which Pierre de Louvois, official of the diocese of Rheims, wrote to him in 1307, announcing miracles performed by the sudary of St. Louis at Rheims, and detailing the healing of those hopelessly ill, and of the deaf, dumb and blind. *v.* Baluze, *Vitae Paparum Avenionensium* (ed. G. Mollat, Paris, 1921), vol. iii, p. 65.

4

The King of France

The first task of Hugh Capet's descendants was to establish their dynasty firmly, to ensure its continuance on the throne, and to win for it a religious prestige and thereby the veneration of the people it had solemnly taken upon itself to govern. Meanwhile they had to organise the practical means of carrying on good government, making use of the prerogatives which the social organisation of mediaeval France put at their disposal.

Feudal society may strike the historian as having been too often anarchical in practice. But in theory it was a rigorously ordered society in which every individual had his fixed place in a strict hierarchy of lords and vassals. The keystone of the system was the king, the suzerain lord of all. In the ninth and tenth centuries the state was unquestionably in eclipse, but this fact did not alter the principles of social and political organisation. Tenth-century France was a patchwork of innumerable nearly independent lordships; but no lord, however powerful, refused to recognise the king's theoretical supremacy. The name 'France' came to mean only a narrow belt of territory around Paris; but the kingdom of France, the ancient *regnum Francorum*, survived not only in theory but even to some extent in practice. The king might be feeble. He might be weaker than some of his great vassals. Nevertheless, the great vassals owed him homage, and it is significant that they performed it. The six great feudatories who at the beginning of the thirteenth century became the six lay peers of the realm, had been in the juridical sense strictly bound to the king for the previous two hundred years and more, and had been his vassals, his 'men', however remarkable in other respects had been their independence of the monarchy.[1] With almost unfailing consistency and success the Capetians insisted on these juridical ties and the rights they conferred on the crown.

In 1002, early in the dynasty's history, when Duke Henry of Burgundy, Hugh Capet's brother, died without leaving an heir, King Robert would not allow the Burgundian bishops and barons to choose a new duke for themselves. He refused to recognise Otto William, the late duke's son-in-law, and waged unremitting warfare in Burgundy for thirteen years, until he was able to put his son Henry in control of the duchy, with the title of duke.

In 1035 Robert the Magnificent, Duke of Normandy, died in the Holy Land, leaving as his only heir his bastard William, the future conqueror of England. When the Norman barons chose William to be their duke, King Henry I ratified their choice and gave his support to William against the nobles of the Bessin and the Cotentin, who were promoting the rival candidature of William's cousin Guy of Burgundy. Juridically, Henry I was William's guardian and trustee, and he used armed force to secure Normandy for the boy.

In 1078 the papal legate, Hugh of Die, summoned to Poitiers in the name of Pope Gregory VII a council which proved to be hostile to the king. Philip I wrote a letter to Duke William VIII of Aquitaine and to the bishops present, declaring that they would be guilty of breaking the fealty they had sworn to the king if they tolerated this 'pseudo-synod'. The upshot was that some of those attending the council were roughly handled by the duke and the townsfolk of Poitiers. In 1101, in similar circumstances, Duke William IX tried to break up another council by sending it word that 'My lord the king has informed me that you — to his dishonour and mine — are threatening to excommunicate him in this city of Poitiers which I hold of him. In the name of the fealty I owe him, he has ordered me to prevent you. Wherefore proceed no further. Otherwise, by the oaths I have sworn to the king, you shall not leave this city unscathed.'[2]

---

[1] Convincing demonstration of this was given by F. Lot in his thesis, *Fidèles ou vassaux? Essai sur la nature juridique du lien qui unissait les grands vassaux à la royauté depuis le milieu du IXe jusqu'à la fin du XIIe siècle* (Paris, 1904).

[2] *R.H.F.*, xi, 108.

In 1127, after the murder of Charles the Good, Count of Flanders, who left no heir, King Louis VI decided that he had the right to be party to the choice of a new count. And so he ordered the *principes* and barons of Flanders to come and meet him on 20 April at Arras, so that he might agree with them on the election of a count. Not surprisingly their choice fell on William Clito, the king's own candidate.

During the years 1162 and 1163, Count Raymond V of Toulouse, who was being attacked by his mighty neighbour Henry II of England, Duke of Aquitaine by his marriage to Eleanor, asked King Louis VII to come to his aid. Powerful vassal though Raymond was, he wrote to the king in these words: 'We have lost our lands, or rather, not our lands but yours, for we are your man, and all that is ours is yours.'[1]

These examples are enough to show that during the period when the Capetians seem to have been infinitely less powerful than their great vassals, they did not hesitate, whenever opportunity arose, to act in such fashion that there could be no shadow of doubt as to their position of suzerainty — a position accepted by their vassals without demur.

The homage which a great vassal performed to the King of France on acquiring his duchy or county illustrates his juridical relationship to the king. The formula of homage varied little during the Capetian dynasty's three centuries. A useful example is the opening words, which formed the essential part, of the homage rendered at Compiègne in June 1196 by Baldwin IX, Count of Flanders and Hainault, to King Philip Augustus, who incidentally, having just been defeated by Richard I of England, was in none too happy a position at that particular time: 'I, Baldwin, Count of Flanders and of Hainault, make known to all men present and to come that I have agreed and sworn to my liege lord Philip, the illustrious King of France, to give him aid, openly and in good faith, all the days of my life, against all mortal men; and moreover to aid him for my land of Hainault both against my lord the Bishop of Liège, if he should ever seek to trouble the king or if the king should wish to proceed against the

[1] *R.H.F.*, xvi, 69–70.

said bishop, and also against the Emperor; and I will never withhold or withdraw such aid from the King of France as long as the said lord king shall be ready to do right to me in his court and to let me be judged by those who ought to be my judges in the court of the King of France.'[1]

The greatest of the feudatories acknowledged themselves to be the king's men when they did homage. None of them ever thought of refusing it. Homage was no mere formula. It created between suzerain and vassal a personal tie, the binding force of which is hard for the modern mind to grasp. It obliged the homager to come with his men, who were bound to him by a tie of the same kind, and rally to the banner of his suzerain when the suzerain called for the military service (or host-service) of his vassals.

The great vassals rarely refused to give military service. They sometimes rendered it in circumstances when to do so involved on the face of things a complete change of front. For instance, King Henry III of England landed with an army at Saint-Malo on 3 May 1230 to support the French barons who had revolted against Blanche of Castile, regent for the young King Louis IX. On Louis' behalf Blanche summoned his vassals to give him armed assistance against the invader. Naturally the barons who were in revolt were summoned like the others, and they came with the others to perform their forty days' military service against the very enemy who had invaded France with their approval, if not at their request. When great vassals of the crown sided with the king's enemies against him, they reserved his rights as their suzerain. On 10 March 1103 Robert of Jerusalem, Count of Flanders, made a treaty at Dover with King Henry I of England against King Philip I of France. The second article of this treaty admirably illustrates the attitude of the great vassals of the Capetians. Homage was a solemn obligation they had freely entered into. It tied them to the king, and they were bound by oath not to break it. The most they were capable of attempting was seeking means to circumvent it. And so the Count of Flanders assured the King of England of his support, 'saving his fealty to Philip, King of France, in such wise that if King Philip shall

[1] *R.H.F.*, xix, 352.

intend to invade the realm of England, Count Robert will seek to prevent King Philip in every way possible, by his counsel and by his prayers, but not by any means incompatible with his fealty, nor by plotting against him, nor by offering him bribes. And if King Philip shall come to England, and shall bring Count Robert with him, Count Robert will take the smallest possible retinue, but not so small that he may thereby incur the forfeiture of his fief to the King of France.'[1]

It is clear that the vassal who rose against the king, even against a king so weak as Philip I, had worries of his own to contend with. The fealty he had sworn to the king acted as a restraint upon him. If he were to violate it, he would set a dangerous example to his own vassals. The whole political system hung indeed by a chain of vassalage running from the humblest tenant to the great feudatory who was the king's immediate vassal. The system also depended on the grant of the fief. It is true that a fief could not be confiscated by the king as long as his own strength was inferior to that of the vassal whom he wished to punish; but he might give the rebellious vassal's fief to some other lord who would be strong enough to seize it by force. The king's position, when confronted by the revolt of a vassal more powerful than himself, was not always easy; but the rebel too ran various dangers, and indubitably knew it. Both king and vassal realised that they could not with impunity cut the ties of homage and fief which so closely bound them together.

For these reasons the Capetian kings, though materially far from strong, were able to hold a continuing if somewhat theoretical sway over great vassals much more powerful than themselves. The very weakness of the dynasty's material resources blinded the great vassals to the dangers latent in rights which the political system allowed the Capetians to exercise in theory but only rarely in practice. For as soon as the crown had acquired a substantial territorial basis, these rights were to enable it to establish an almost immediate mastery over the feudal nobility. The crucial fact of Capetian history — especially of its first two centuries — is that the vassal loyally preserved his fealty to the king.

[1] Rymer, *Foedera* (edition of 1745), i, 2.

Historians have not always grasped this, as a result of mis-understanding the nature of the frequent wars (their frequency incidentally has been exaggerated) between the Capetians and their vassals. Private war, with its concomitant pillaging, arson, devastation and slaughter, strikes a modern eye as simply civil war. To the feudal nobility of Capetian times recourse to it was perfectly legitimate.[1] The vassal who visited his suzerain's property and men with fire and sword genuinely believed himself to be exercising an incontestable right. For a very long time this was also the view of the king. The custom of France recognised the right of a convicted vassal to depart from the royal court and defend his cause sword in hand. This was no more than an exten-sion of the idea of the judicial duel, an appeal to the judgment of God. Since this was the attitude to private war, it is not surprising that reconciliations were frequent, and that neither the great vassals nor the petty feudatories in the royal domain nursed any grudges against the Capetians. They took a long time to learn obedience, but they never made the dynasty an object of lasting hatreds and feuds.

Eudes II, Count of Blois, is deservedly celebrated as one of the most undisciplined of the great vassals in the eleventh century. The history of the time resounds with his quarrels and his wars against Robert the Pious and Henry I. In 1023, having disobeyed a summons to appear at the royal court, Eudes was at war with Robert the Pious. He wrote to the king: 'I am astounded that without having heard me in my own defence, you should hasten to pronounce me unworthy of the fief I hold of you. For consider my ancestry: by dint of it I am, thank God, entitled to succeed to the counties of Meaux and Troyes. Consider the fief you have bestowed on me: it was not granted out of your royal fisc, but is part of the lands which have come down to me by hereditary right and of your royal grace. And consider the feudal services I have done you: you are well aware that for the favours I have had from you I have served you in your household, on your travels, and in your wars. And now you have deprived me of your favour, and seek to take away from me the things you have given

---

[1] Lot has given this proper emphasis in his *Fidèles ou vassaux?*, pp. 4-5.

to me. It may be that in the course of defending myself and my honours (i.e. fiefs) I have committed certain offences against you. I was driven thereto by necessity and the wrongs I have suffered. For is it conceivable that I should hesitate to defend my honour? By God and my immortal soul, I had rather die defending it than live deprived of it. If you will desist from your attempts to take away my honour, there is nothing in the world I should desire more than to be restored to your good graces. For it is very painful for me to quarrel with you, my lord. From the man who is at loggerheads with you are withheld the blessings kingship bestows — justice and peace. Wherefore I implore you to show me that clemency which is as a well-spring within you, and which only evil counsel can cause to dry up. And I pray you to cease persecuting me, and let me be reconciled with you.'[1]

Eudes' letter helps to explain why the Capetian dynasty, feeble and isolated as it was in the midst of a turbulent feudal class, was able to survive. Baronial factions pursued many a vendetta against one another. They never pursued one against the king. During the period of Capetian weakness, the king was the one man who could in certain circumstances mobilise under his banner the entire feudal power of the kingdom. In 1059, for instance, Henry I fielded against William of Normandy an army in which rode knights from Rémois, Soissonais, Laonnais, Vermandois, Flanders, Artois, Amiénois, Ponthieu, Noyonnais, Orléanais, Berry, Bourbonnais, Burgundy, Auvergne, and Gascony; and Suger, with Homeric flourish, calls the roll of the 'battles' which King Louis VI mustered in the plains of Rheims in 1124, when the Emperor Henry V was threatening to invade France. Eudes' declaration also throws light on the strange behaviour of King Henry II of England in 1159, when King Louis VII came to rescue the Count of Toulouse and threw himself into Toulouse town. The King of England, who was also Count of Anjou, Duke of Normandy, and Duke of Aquitaine, and as such a vassal of the French king, decided to abandon the siege for as long as his suzerain should stay in Toulouse. And as Louis VII obstinately

[1] *R.H.F.*, x, 501–2. Eudes' letter has been studied by L. Halphen, in *Revue Historique*, xcvii (1908), pp. 287–96. The same article will be found in Halphen, *À travers l'histoire du moyen âge* (Paris, 1950), pp. 240–50.

refused to budge from the town, Henry II finally withdrew altogether.

Thus, the exercise of their royal functions enhanced the Capetians' prestige among their great vassals. The oaths which their vassals swore to them and which they always took care to insist upon surrounded them with so impressive a rampart that not even the most powerful dared attack it. This is not to say that no one ever made war on the Capetians or that they were never beaten. Few kings have had to suffer so many trouncings on the field of battle as the Capetians up to the time of Philip Augustus. But the king was never totally crushed. For, weak as he was, he was still the king, the Lord's Anointed, the highest suzerain of all; and directly or indirectly all the barons in the realm were his men.

*   *   *   *

The nobility was not alone in its attitude towards the king, which was shared by the heavily feudalised clergy of the time. The Church never refused to put at the monarchy's service the weapons, both spiritual and temporal, in its armoury.

The Capetians were favourites of the Church, more especially of the Church in France. In ecclesiastical eyes the kings of France, if not quite tonsured clerics, had something closely approaching a sacerdotal character.[1] This idea gained strength from the ceremony of consecration, at which the king put on the tunicle of a subdeacon, communicated in both kinds, and was anointed in the manner appropriate to a bishop. The clergy were constantly being reminded of their part in the king's enthronement, for at the Church's great festivals the monarch received his crown anew from the hands of a bishop. There was an occasion when Bishop Ivo of Chartres wrote to Pope Urban II that, in defiance of the papal legate's solemn prohibition, the Archbishop of Tours had crowned King Philip I at the Christmas festivities of 1096.[2]

A clergy well versed in the Scriptures did not readily forget

[1] For instance, the Abbot of La Chaise-Dieu wrote to Louis VII that his monks prayed for the king every day 'for two reasons: first because you are our lord the king; and secondly, because you belong to our order' (R.H.F., xvi, 147).

[2] Ibid., xv, 100.

Melchizedek, King of Salem, the priest of the most high God, who created Heaven and Earth.[1] They hastened to salute the Capetians with the words addressed by the poet Venantius Fortunatus to King Childebert of old:

'Melkisedek noster, merito rex atque sacerdos,
    Complevit laïcus religionis opus.'[2]

In Capetian times the king had the titles, even though he did not perform the functions, of Abbot of Saint-Denis, Abbot of Saint-Martin of Tours, and Abbot of Saint-Aignan of Orléans. Hugh Capet himself had held the title of Abbot of Saint-Germain-des-Prés until 979.

The eyes of the priesthood were fixed on the City of God, where universal order would reign and no one would dream of calling the sovereign's commands in question. To build that city on earth was their earnest hope. And so they idealised the functions of monarchy and invested it with all the attributes of Biblical kingship. Standing as it did for order and justice, it seemed to them to be the one earthly institution to which they could turn for speedy help in realising their great ideal, the one element worth preserving and strengthening in the society which they strove to lead into the paths of Christian peace.

But Church and monarchy did not meet only on the plane of the ideal. Their mutual relationship in the Capetian era cannot be understood if current ideas about the present-day Church are applied to its mediaeval forerunner. The modern conception of the Roman Catholic Church is of an institution with only spiritual and moral functions, and independent of civil authority only in so far as it confines itself to spiritual and moral fields of action. A powerful international organisation, centralised under a supreme head whose authority none of the faithful dare question, the Church has utterly renounced all secular rule over men, and imposes on all those subject to her an absolute unity of faith and doctrine, which takes no heed of the ethnical or intellectual divisions among them. The Church of Capetian times was altogether different. Admittedly the dogma and the morality she

[1] *Genesis*, xiv, 18.
[2] M.G.H., *Auctores Antiquissimi*, vol. iv (1), lib. II, c. 10, vv. 21, 22.

taught were fundamentally at one with those which the Church today teaches. But the centralisation of the Church was a process which had hardly begun before the period of the later Capetians: Innocent III was the contemporary of Philip Augustus. The mediaeval Church's activities extended beyond the spiritual sphere. She owned much of the land. A great many people lived on her estates. Her power was as much temporal as spiritual. In consequence she was profoundly influenced by the secular society in the midst of which she lived.

From as far back as Merovingian times this situation had been developing. In the Gaul which the Franks had conquered the only stable institution was monarchy. The king's power was not defined with any precision. Its origin was an inexorable tradition, not a rationally devised constitution. The Church saw only one aspect of royal power: the clergy believed they were making a definition of kingship when they called the king God's Elect, and a definition of his power when they declared that it had been entrusted to him by God. The truth was that divine right consecrated royal right but did not create it. Royal power had a religious element, but it had other attributes too. The Merovingian king was not only the representative of the state: he was also its owner and master, disposing of his kingdom as if it were private property. His title to reign was personal, irrevocable, and hereditary. Nothing ever tempered his absolutism but the assassin's dagger.

Confronted with Merovingian power, the Church bowed the knee. The king protected and enriched her, he allowed her to retain her internal organisation and her own law, but he did not associate her in the government of his realm. Until the close of the sixth century the Church was contained within the state but was in no way confused with it. Canon law judgments could not look to secular law for any kind of sanction.

A new trend can be traced in the sixth century. It was to declare itself strongly in the seventh. The Church was gradually acquiring a public authority, and some of its canons were incorporated in royal legislation. But the king maintained his supremacy, nowhere better illustrated than in his power over the episcopate. A bishop was obliged to swear the oath of fealty to the king, and therefore to obey his commands. He might not leave his diocese without royal permission. He must ordain to the priesthood candidates who had the king's nomination. As overlord of all the land in the kingdom, the king allowed no one to exercise jurisdiction without his royal consent, and consequently could modify diocesan jurisdiction at will. The Church could not legislate independently of the king: canon law was invalid unless confirmed by him. He nominated to vacant bishoprics whom and when he pleased.

This state of affairs was continued by the Carolingians, under whom, as under their predecessors, no distinction was made between ecclesiastical and civil society. Contemporary legislation — the Edict of Toucy in 865 — and contemporary theory — in the works of Jonas and Sedulius Scottus — affirmed as much.

Once Charlemagne had restored the Empire in the west, each Carolingian Emperor and, after 843, each Carolingian King of France regarded himself as head of the Church. As God's deputy and 'vicar in Church government', according to the formula of Sedulius Scottus, he superintended faith and morals. Church affairs were directed more from the royal palace than from Rome. The bishops became imperial functionaries. They were the counts of the spiritual domain. It was as a servant of the crown that a bishop received the temporalities of his see. The bishopric was in the sovereign's gift. It was a lordship of the *regnum* as well as a high office of the *sacerdotium*. As a royal official, the bishop commended himself to the king, and made a formal request for royal protection. In the king's eyes, this ceremony made the bishop his man, his vassal; and he claimed a special regalian power (*regalis potestas* or *regale*) which was his to exercise over every bishopric during a vacancy, as if it had been a lay fief. The king handed over his regalian rights to the incoming bishop, whom he himself nominated.

The patron saint of a see had from of old been in theory its owner. But this title to ownership was an abstraction, incapable of being upheld or defended, and eventually fell into the hands of the king as the see's sovereign protector. The regalian power was thereby transformed into proprietorship, resting on the king's right to confer the bishopric and on the bishop's vassal status. Thus the king had gained control of the office of bishop, of episcopal election, and of the lands of the bishopric. He had become the proprietor of the see. The homage which bishops performed to him, royal investiture of bishops, and the feudal form of the law governing election all followed from this situation.

During the ninth and tenth centuries the royal rights over the Church suffered the same fate as the other regalian rights, and were divided up among the higher nobility — the descendants of the counts appointed by the Carolingians. For two centuries the old alliance between Church and crown lay in ruins, much to the profit of the great vassals. By the end of the tenth century, when the Capetian dynasty came to power, most of the bishoprics were in the gift and under the suzerainty of the magnates, among whom the king himself must be numbered. Every bishopric, with its cathedral church, lands, and jurisdictions, was conferred by investiture. The grant obliged its recipient to perform homage and swear fealty, which expressed a fairly close personal relationship, ill defined as yet but radically different from the simple relationship between subject and ruler.

Like their great vassals, the Capetians had a number of bishoprics under their direct control. The so-called royal bishoprics during the first two centuries of Capetian rule can be listed as follows: Hugh Capet controlled the sees of Le Mans in the province of Tours; Chartres, Orléans, Paris, Meaux, and Sens in the province of Sens; Beauvais, Senlis, Soissons, Noyon-Tournai, Laon, and Rheims in the province of Rheims; Langres in the province of Lyon; and Le Puy in the province of Bourges. Robert the Pious added the sees of Troyes and Auxerre in the province of Sens; Châlons-sur-Marne in the province of Rheims; Mâcon in the province of Lyon; and the archbishopric of Bourges. Henry I lost the see of Le Mans. Philip I acquired the archbishopric of Tours; the sees of Térouanne and Amiens in the province of Rheims; and Châlon-sur-Saône in the province of Lyon. Louis VI added the see of Arras in the province of Rheims, and Louis VII the sees of Autun in the province of Lyon; Mende in the province of Bourges; and Agde in the province of Narbonne.

What was true of the bishoprics was partly true also of the parish churches and monasteries. During the period 987–1180 there were seventy-nine royal monasteries, though not all of them necessarily had this character for the whole of that time.

From the time of Gregory VII onwards the Papacy was striving to renew its grip on the Church. Even so, in France at least, throughout this same early Capetian period, papal authority was only very relative and was exercised in spiritual matters alone. The oath which a bishop had to take at his consecration did not make him, nor was it intended to make him, spiritually 'the Pope's man'. Of a similar character was the bishop's relationship with his metropolitan or archbishop, as he was later to be called. The bishop received episcopal consecration from his metropolitan and acknowledged him as his ecclesiastical superior but not as his suzerain or sovereign.

In France the bishops and abbots were often recruited from the nobility and naturally shared its ideas. In respect of the private property they might own they formed part of the feudal hierarchy. It is no exaggeration to describe them as having constituted in the Capetian period — especially its first two centuries — an ecclesiastical feudal class, which differed from the lay feudal classes in its inability to acquire great feudal principalities, and over which the king preserved the theoretical rights which had belonged to his predecessors on the throne of France and to the Carolingian emperors.

The Capetians profited all they could from the feudal obligations which their lay subjects owed them. Likewise they steadfastly insisted on clerical respect for royal rights over the Church. In royal bishoprics and monasteries, when a new bishop or abbot was to be elected, the king always saw to it that his own wishes were consulted. Licence to elect a successor to a deceased bishop or abbot had to be obtained from the king. Frequently, if not always, a royal commissioner presided at the election, which had nothing in common with an election of today. There was no voting in secret. A nomination was made, which the electors confirmed. It was in their interest to nominate and elect a candidate favoured by the king, for when a bishopric or abbacy fell vacant, the king took its temporalities into his hand and was wont to make difficulties about restoring them if an election was made which displeased him. He would even refuse to confirm the election.

If the newly elect was acceptable, he bound himself to the king by an oath. For instance, the archbishops of Rheims from the time of Arnoul (who was elected in 989) swore an oath which, with appropriate changes of proper names, invariably ran: 'I, Arnoul, Archbishop of Rheims, promise King Hugh and King Robert that I will maintain unbroken my fealty towards them, giving them aid and counsel in all that concerns them, and that I will not knowingly and faithlessly furnish any manner of aid, help, or counsel to their enemies.'[1]

It is not surprising that under these circumstances the history of the Capetian dynasty came to be closely involved with the history of the Church in France. The king intervened on countless occasions in the affairs of the royal bishoprics. Not all royal bishoprics, it is important to emphasise, lay in the royal domain properly so called. Several of them had the character of Capetian advanced posts inside the domains of the great vassals. Moreover, bishoprics and abbeys frequently came into conflict with local baronial interests which were more or less independent of the king. In this predicament, despairing of effective help from feeble metropolitans or far-away popes, ecclesiastics were only too glad to look to the one lay power which was prepared to assist them.[2] The Capetians could be hard masters, strenuous in upholding their rights over the Church, ruthless at times in exacting respect from the clergy. But they were also generous, and their open-handedness helped to persuade the men of the Church to turn to them the more readily. The catalogues of royal *acta* are crowded with gifts to cathedrals, monasteries, parish churches. This well-spring of favours, privileges, and grants of lands and money

---

[1] *Richeri Historiarum libri iiii*, lib. iv, §. 60 (ed. R. Latouche, *Classiques de l'histoire de France au Moyen Âge*, vol. ii, Paris, 1937, pp. 246–7).

[2] This attitude can be illustrated from a letter addressed in September 1245 by the Chapter of Châlons to the King of France, *qui solus refugium est Ecclesiae, sub cujus solius protectione libertas universalis Ecclesiae constitit, cujus nitor est et patronus, pro quo incessanter et specialiter universalis Ecclesia, tanquam pro rege suo unico, Dominum interpellat* (*L.T.C.*, ii, p. 456, no. 2940).

never, it seems, dried up. The Capetians were genuinely and deeply pious. They invariably treated their clergy with friendliness and respect. Under all these circumstances it is hardly surprising that the alliance between crown and clergy was so close and practical.

It must not be forgotten that the clergy thus won over to the French king's side were a body of important feudal vassals, plentifully supplied with lands, money and men. They owed the king the aid and counsel which every good vassal owed his lord. The feudal services they rendered to the king were a partial compensation for the services he was not able to exact from his lay vassals. Suger tells the story of a certain bald priest — his name is not recorded — who led his flock to tear down the stockade of Le Puiset when Louis VI was besieging it, and thereby made a breach for the royal army to come through: a trivial incident, but a vivid illustration of the Church's general attitude to the struggle the Capetians were waging to win for the monarchy its proper place in the kingdom. The French clergy would never have behaved like this unless they had been satisfied with the way the king treated the Pope, the head of the Church. And the Capetians handled the Pope with outstanding skill. In practice they insisted on their independence, and even showed a certain intransigence when they thought their royal rights were being called in question. But outwardly they were respectful, often sincerely so, and were inclined, almost naturally it seems, to take the side of the Holy See on the many occasions when it ran into any kind of danger. What was even more important was their avoidance of quarrels with the Papacy over issues of principle. It was centuries before they formulated any theory of the relations of the temporal and spiritual powers. Minor conflicts between Church and State were unavoidable, but were never allowed to develop into open war, for successive kings regarded them as mere incidents, which could be smoothed over with a little good will on either side. Whenever the Pope needed a refuge from his enemies, he could rely on a welcome in the Capetian kingdom. There was no Investiture Contest in France. There were no tragic episodes like the murder of Becket in England. No real crisis ever arose in the Capetian monarchy's relations with Church and Papacy before the last years of the thirteenth century.

In short, the French kings usually reigned in harmony with the Papacy. The only rights they claimed over the Church were rights she was ready to concede. They did their best to rally to her defence, and constantly plied her with gifts and privileges. Their reward was success in re-establishing the authority which their Carolingian predecessors had once had over the clergy. The Church failed to keep a careful check on the steps by which this authority was built up. The day was to come when she would have to realise that she had met her master. By then it was too late for her to resist.

* * * *

At first glance it seems as though the royal rights over the lower orders of French society were the most difficult of all for the Capetians to recover. It was practically impossible for the king to establish direct relations with the more lowly of his subjects — if the word may be correctly used at this period — except for the peasants and townspeople of the royal domain itself. He was cut off from them by the intervening strata of the noble and clerical classes. But just as the Capetians had mastered the privileged classes and established the authority of kingship over their feudal vassals, so they achieved their object of imposing it upon peasants and townsmen. Admittedly, before this could be accomplished in a particular territory or fief, the Capetians had to wait until they had annexed it to the royal domain. But the change could not have been brought about so quickly if the king had not had, even in the days when he was confined to an extremely narrow domain, various rights over the common people, of the existence of which they were occasionally reminded. Unluckily, as Luchaire has pointed out, 'with rare exceptions, the rural and urban populace has no recorded history before the beginning of the twelfth century.'[1] Before 1100 the surviving documents say nothing of the monarchy's relations with the ordinary people.

[1] A. Luchaire, *Les communes françaises à l'époque des Capétiens directs* (Paris, 1890), p. 4.

How then did the idea of royal suzerainty survive among people with whom the king never came into direct contact, and for whom paramount authority was represented by the immediate local suzerain, whether duke, count, or baron? Was the idea of royal supremacy totally extinct among them in the eleventh century, only to be miraculously brought back to life in the twelfth? Some historians have been ready to attribute many such 'miracles' to the twelfth century.

Certain popular works of literature such as *The Song of Roland* (to look no further) make it clear beyond question that by the end of the eleventh century, well before the Capetian monarchy rose to its apogee, the idea of the sovereign king was already widespread once more. Indeed, it had never entirely disappeared, to judge from the development of the legend of Charlemagne, the first traces of which appeared long before the end of the eleventh century. It is even arguable that the eclipse of royal power helped to keep the monarchical idea alive, making the king, the supreme upholder of justice, a remote and ideal being to whom men looked eagerly and expectantly to recreate the golden age — a character given to the Carolingian past by an age blind to all qualities in history but the epic.

The clergy, who were closest to the common people, undoubtedly helped to keep alive these ideas about kingship. Whenever the sacrifice of the Eucharist was re-enacted, the Church prayed officially for the king. In the Canon of the Mass, the king was designated by name in the *Te igitur*, as he also was on Easter Saturday in the finale of the *Exultet* and on Easter Eve in one of the *Orationes sollemnes*, which was consecrated to him. No liturgical honours of this kind seem to have been paid to the great vassals. It is hardly likely that the many allusions to the king in the divine offices were altogether lost on the faithful. Obviously it is not clear what happened in church during a service in days when the laity could not follow the office in a book. But conceivably at least some of the congregation attended to what the priest was saying, and perhaps knew enough liturgical Latin to understand him.

There are many examples in public and private charters of the use of the king's regnal year as an element in the date. It follows that notaries knew the name of the reigning monarch and the precise date of his coronation. Possibly the notarial profession jealously kept this knowledge to itself; but it is much more likely that this method of dating indicates that in many parts of the kingdom there was fairly general acquaintance with the fortunes of the monarchy.

The performance of service in the feudal host by the king's great vassals, their attendance at the frequent assemblies of the *curia regis*, and the exercise of royal rights over churches and monasteries were occurrences familiar to the common people, involving much bustle of officials and coming and going of messengers. Even at the period when the king's activities were at their most circumscribed, the common people had many an opportunity of hearing him discussed.

Naturally none of the foregoing applies to the lower orders of society in the royal domain, who knew the king well as their immediate suzerain. The domain centred upon Orléans, Paris and Laon, at the crossroads of the great routes spanning France: and their geographical situation played its part in the spread of the monarchical idea throughout the country. Innumerable travellers crossed the royal domain lands, where they heard the king much spoken of and acknowledged his royal power in the tolls they paid.

The masses of the people, whether they lived in town or countryside, were never allowed to forget the existence of the monarchy, which probably profited from the fact that it stepped out of the past trailing clouds of legendary glory. When Louis VII married Charlemagne's descendant Adela of Champagne he was able to put his dynasty forward successfully as heirs to the great Emperor. The mantle of the Carolingians had at last fallen upon the Capetians. In consequence, despite his many setbacks, Louis VII acquired a prestige which had evaded all his predecessors.

When the communal movement developed among the rural and urban classes in the twelfth century, the Capetians took the opportunity to call attention to and act upon their sovereign rights. The *commune* was a collective lordship intruded into feudal society. It could and indeed was obliged to enter into a relationship of vassalage to the king which was denied to its individual members. Many a *commune* outside the royal domain requested the king, its ultimate suzerain, to confirm its charter. Royal confirmation did not create direct dependence to begin with, but did prepare the ground for it. The day was to come when the king annexed to the royal domain territories where there were *communes* whose charters he had in times past confirmed. To them his suzerainty was already a known fact. It was a role he had assumed in his relations with them long before annexation became a possibility.

5

'Emperor in his own Kingdom'

Feudal suzerainty was not, and could not be, completely effective unless reinforced by the wider authority of a sovereign kingship, recognised and accepted in all France. The Capetian rulers could not hope to draw out the full implications of their undoubted suzerainty without asserting their higher status as the possessors of the crown of France. This, however, presented certain difficulties, always liable to arise in a political and social structure of the kind existing in mediaeval western Europe. The king might thus, for instance, come under the suzerainty of one of his own subjects; he might, again, become subject to the wider sovereignty of the Emperor; yet again, he could be subordinate to the spiritual authority of God, in the person of the Pope, His vicar on earth (and that subordination had certain secular consequences). It would be too much to claim that the Capetians always saw these three possibilities as active dangers. But it is certainly true that many of their policies tended to destroy them, and that, whether of set purpose or not, the kings of France ended by removing all three.

In theory at least the King of France was the most powerful lord in his kingdom. He remained, nevertheless, subject to the normal customs of feudal landholding, and nothing, in the Capetian period, distinguished his fiefs from those held by other lords. The ancient patrimony of the Roman Emperors — the 'fisc' — had disappeared almost completely through Merovingian liberality and the disintegration of Carolingian authority. Properly speaking, there was virtually no 'crown demesne'; the king's lands were the estates he held as a feudal lord. In the case of the family estates inherited from the founder of the dynasty no question of vassalage arose, for there was no superior, after the disappearance of the Carolingians, to whom it could be owed. But the later piecemeal acquisitions created a different situation. Many small fiefs came into royal hands through the substitution of the king for the previous lord. Where such fiefs had previously been held directly from the crown there were no complications. This was not, however, always the case. Often the previous lord had owed homage and services to a superior other than the king, who thus, on acquisition, became the vassal of one of his own vassals.

The situation was paradoxical, and unlikely to survive when the monarchy became more aware of its powers and position. There is evidence, indeed, that from a very early date the Capetian kings were beginning to assert that they could not do homage to any subject. Suger suggests[1] that Louis VI was already taking this standpoint in 1124. The king had the right — by virtue of the county of the Vexin, which he held as a fief of the abbey of Saint-Denis — to bear the standard of the saint. When he received the standard, Louis declared that he was a vassal of the abbey for the county, and would have been bound to do homage for it, *si rex non esset*. The episode is obscure; it is difficult to understand why the declaration should have been made, and the contemporary charter[2] relating to the taking of the standard makes no mention of homage at all. But in one respect at least Suger's story is accurate: as far as we can tell, no King of France ever did homage to the church of Saint-Denis.

A clearer illustration can be found in 1184. In that year Philip Augustus, by acquiring the county of Amiens, became in strict feudal theory the vassal of the Bishop of Amiens. According to a royal charter,[3] the cathedral church of Amiens 'decided and of its own free will consented to allow us to hold the said fief, without doing homage, it being understood that we can neither owe nor do homage to anyone'. In compensation, the king surrendered to the church his right of hospitality (procurations, *gîte*), with the reservations that 'if the said lands should in the future come into the hands of anyone who can do homage to the church of Amiens,

---

[1] *De rebus in administratione sua gestis* (*Oeuvres*, ed. Lecoy de la Marche, Paris, 1867, pp. 161–2).
[2] E. J. Tardif, *Monuments historiques, Cartons des rois* (Paris, 1866), p. 217, no. 391.
[3] *Receuil des actes de Philippe Auguste* (Paris, 1916), vol. i, pp. 169–70, no. 139.

homage shall once again be taken' and that the *gîte* should in that case be returned to the king. A similar agreement was reached in 1192 with the Bishop of Térouanne, after Philip had acquired Hesdin.

After Louis VIII had taken possession of the vast lands confiscated from the Albigensian heretics, the Archbishop of Narbonne received in October 1228 a royal grant of a perpetual annual rent of 400 *livres tournois;*[1] this was in place of the homage and services which he had formerly received from certain of the former holders of these lands. It was accepted that Louis could not do homage: *et ipse nemini homagium facere teneatur.* Again, there survives an *arrêt* of the *Parlement,* issued at Candlemas and executed in April 1270,[2] relating to the county of Mortain. Although by this the king was not declared incapable of doing homage to the Bishop of Coutances for the county, it was, however, stated that he had refused to perform the homage, despite repeated requests by the bishop. It was further laid down that, with the bishop's consent, the *bailli* of the Cotentin would in future do the necessary homage on entering upon his term of office. We may perhaps detect in this a certain weakening of the royal attitude, but the date of the *arrêt* (at the very close of the reign of St. Louis) forbids us to lay too much weight on this.

The marriage of the heir-apparent Philip, son of Philip III, on 20 February 1285 to Joan of Navarre, Countess of Champagne and Brie, made him liable to do homage, as her husband, to the Bishop of Langres for certain fiefs in Champagne. This he did, but a document recording the act[3] specified that the homage was done 'on condition that, should we become King of France, the homage will disappear and become of no account; provided always that we shall be bound to provide to the said bishop or his successor a vassal able to hold the fief, or at the least to come to a peaceful settlement with him concerning the matter'.

All the above instances relate to homage owed to churchmen.

---

[1] *L.T.C.,* ii, p. 94, no. 1808.

[2] *Olim,* ed. Beugnot (Paris, 1839), vol. i, pp. 327–8. Cf. L. Delisle, *Cartulaire Normand,* no. 778, in *Mémoires de la Société des Antiquaires de Normandie,* vol. xvi (1852), p. 178.

[3] A. Longnon, *Documents relatifs aux comtés de Champagne et de Brie* (Paris, 1901), vol. i, p. 486, no. 61.

It is unlikely, however, that lay lords were treated differently. Certainly Philip the Fair's great ordinance of March 1303 on the reformation of the kingdom does not suggest it. Without re-asserting that the king could do no homage, this ordinance laid down rules to be followed in cases where he did in fact acquire a fief which could involve him in doing it. When such a fief came to the king by confiscation it was stipulated that he could 'either place the fief in the hands of a man capable of doing homage, or give adequate and reasonable compensation to the lord of the fief'.[1] No distinction was made between lay and ecclesiastical lords, and a clarifying *arrêt* of the *Parlement*, given on 22 October 1314, removed any doubt by declaring that the kings of France were not accustomed to do homage to their subjects: *cum reges Franciae subditis suis homagium ferre nunquam fuerit consultum*.[2]

The king had thus escaped from the common law and custom of his kingdom. He could have vassals, but could never be one.[3]

*   *   *   *

There were, however, wider horizons. The ultimate temporal authority in mediaeval western Europe was, in theory at least, in the hands of the Emperor. There was fairly general agreement on this, although it should be remembered that the theory only reached its full height in the thirteenth century, under the impulse of the revived Roman Law and the work of the glossators of Bologna. In earlier times a rather different idea of the Empire prevailed. Otto I's restoration of the Empire was primarily a return to the state of Charlemagne, not to that of the Roman Emperors. It was complicated by the survival of the Carolingian dynasty, not in Germany, but in France. Abbot Adso of Montiér-ender, in the *Libellus de Antichristo* which he dedicated to Gerberga, the queen of the Carolingian Louis IV d'Outremer,

---

[1] *Ordonnances des rois de France*, ed. de Laurière (Paris, 1723), vol. i, p. 358. A more accurate text is given by E. Boutaric, *Rapport sur une communication de M. Beauchet-Filleau*, in *Revue des Sociétés savantes*, 1866, 2nd term, p. 446.

[2] *Olim*, vol. ii, p. 616, no. 5.

[3] Some princes of the blood royal appear to have successfully claimed the same privilege, to judge by two documents relating to homage and services due from Alphonse of Poitiers, the brother of St. Louis, to the Bishop of Poitiers for the castle of Civray and the lordship of Angle. *Cf.* Boutaric, *loc. cit.*, p. 446.

King of France (936–54), wrote: 'The kingdom of the Romans is in great part destroyed, but as long as the kings of France survive, who ought to rule the Roman Empire, then its dignity will not perish entirely, but will live in them.'[1]

This persistence of Carolingian claims is a partial explanation of the lack of German displeasure at the change of dynasty in France. There may even have been hopes in the imperial court that the Capetians might become imperial vassals. Gerbert (who became Pope, as Sylvester II, in 998) may even have been involved in plans to achieve this, but it is doubtful whether any action was ever taken. Certainly no positive results were achieved. The Capetians were anxious to live on good terms with the Empire, in view of their domestic difficulties in France, but even so they were never prepared to admit to being imperial vassals. For their part, the Emperors of the eleventh and early twelfth centuries never sought to treat the rulers of France as inferiors. As a German historian has pointed out,[2] the King of France was the only European ruler whom the King of Germany was prepared to meet on terms of equality.

Descriptions of the meeting of the Emperor Henry II and King Robert the Pious in August 1023 illustrate this.[3] The two rulers met on the 6th of the month on the banks of the Meuse, the Emperor camping at Ivois and the king at Mouzon on the opposite bank, each with a considerable entourage. A large crowd of spectators had gathered, to see which would make the first move. After four days the Emperor (calling to mind the precept, 'the more exalted you are, the more humbly you should behave') decided to cross the river with a small retinue, and to visit the French king. The latter returned the visit on the following day. Similarly, there is no suggestion that the Emperor Henry III and King Henry I met as lord and vassal at Ivois in 1056. On this occasion the interview ended stormily, but the cause was a French demand for the return of Lorraine, which King Henry alleged had

---

[1] Migne, *Patrologia latina*, vol. 101, col. 1295.

[2] W. Michael, *Die Formen des unmittelbaren Verkehrs zwischen den deutschen Kaisern und souveränen Fürsten, vornehmlich in X, XI und XII Jahrhundert* (Hamburg, 1888), pp. 17–18.

[3] Raoul Glaber, *Historiarum sui temporis libri v*, lib. iii, c. 2 (ed. M. Prou, Paris, 1886), pp. 58–9); and *Gesta episcoporum Cameracensium*, lib. iii, c. 37 (*Monumenta Germaniae Historica Scriptores*, vol. vii), p. 480.

been unjustly seized by the German crown; the Emperor ended by making a formal defiance.

The quarrel with the Papacy took all the attention of the Emperors after the middle of the eleventh century. The French kings took no part in this, beyond giving refuge to several Popes when imperial successes made it impossible for them to remain in Rome or Italy. Philip I received several imperial requests for support, although never in the terms used in summoning a vassal; he took no effective action in response. Indeed, the long-standing friendship between the French crown and the Papacy was inaugurated during his reign, and led to a certain coolness in Imperial-French relations. The Emperor Henry V even attempted to invade Champagne in 1124, but his army never encountered that assembled by Louis VI. The letters allegedly exchanged by the two rulers at this time are of extremely doubtful authenticity, and prove nothing more than that the English writer Walter Map, who recorded them,[1] did not consider that the king admitted to being an imperial vassal.

The accession of Frederick Barbarossa brought a change. The house of Hohenstaufen had ambitions to reign in the succession of Augustus, Constantine and Theodosius, and its Italian successes made these ambitions more positive. Frederick felt able to write to the Eastern Emperor in Constantinople that France, Spain, England, Denmark and the other kingdoms bordering on the Empire were constantly sending ambassadors to his court, to show their respect and obedience, and to offer oaths of loyalty and hostages. As far as France was concerned, this was more a statement of hopes than of facts. Frederick styled himself *Romanorum Imperator Augustus*, and claimed to hold in his hands the government of Rome and of the entire world — *urbis et orbis gubernacula* — in virtue of his duty to watch over the destinies of Christendom — *sacro Imperio et divae Reipublicae consulere debemus*. To him, the Roman Empire was as superior to kingdoms and principalities as was the sun to the stars. Such high-sounding generalities did not stand alone. At the diet of Saint-Jean-de-Losne the Emperor (or perhaps his chancellor, Rainald of Dassel)

[1] *De nugis curialium*, ed. M. R. James (Oxford, 1914), p. 229.

spoke disdainfully of the kinglets (*reguli*) of imperial provinces who dared to meddle in the affairs of the Church of Rome.[1] This was an obvious reference to the action of Louis VII in taking the side of Pope Alexander III against his imperially-supported rival. Contemporaries certainly took this view. A satirical poem[2] credited the Emperor with the intention of sending an embassy to the King of France, to affirm imperial supremacy, to remind him of his subjection to Roman Law, and to summon him to serve the Empire.

The Hohenstaufen Emperor Henry VI and the Welf Emperor Otto IV followed Frederick's lead. The lawyers of Bologna, not surprisingly, were enthusiastic supporters of the Hohenstaufen thesis, seeing reborn in Frederick and his successors the universal ruler whose law they studied. But the other rulers of the West, placed thus under imperial suzerainty without their consent, reacted very differently. The King of France, for one, had no intention of becoming an imperial vassal — in which determination he was abetted by the Papacy.

The Capetians, therefore, were careful to forge marriage links with the lineage of Charlemagne. Louis VII married a princess of Carolingian descent, Adela of Champagne, and his son Philip — the *Carolide* of Guillaume le Breton — followed his example. Philip was never prepared to bow to the imperial pretensions; Pope Innocent III could recall the failure of the Emperor Henry VI's attempt to secure the French king's homage.[3] The epithet *Augustus* given to Philip by his biographer, and retained by history, is a sharp reflection of his attitude to the imperial daydreams. Public opinion in France, such as it was, followed the king, and it is significant that, led by the minstrels, men thought of Charlemagne as a King of France rather than as an Emperor.

Further, and more significantly, the French crown, with papal assistance, took steps to settle the whole question of its own independence. The bull *Per venerabilem* of 1202, issued by

[1] Saxo Grammaticus, *Gesta Danorum* (ed. Watterich, *Pontificum Romanorum Vitae*, Leipzig, 1862, vol. ii, p. 532).
[2] Ed. J. Acher, *Le jubilé de M. Hermann Fitting*, in *Revue générale de Droit*, vol. xxxii (1908), p. 152.
[3] *Registrum de negocio Imperii*, epist. 64 (Migne, *Patrologia Latina*, vol. 216, col. 1071).

Innocent III in the case of the legitimation of the children of Count William VIII of Montpellier, declared that the King of France recognised no temporal superior: *cum rex superiorem in temporalitatibus minime recognoscat*.[1] In 1219, at the request of Philip Augustus, Pope Honorius III forbade the teaching of the Civil Law in the University of Paris.[2] This was a precaution, lest the Emperor and his supporters should claim that the *regnum Francorum* was part of their new Roman Empire simply because the Civil Law was in use in southern France. St. Louis, in 1254, had the same possibility in mind when he authorised the inhabitants of the seneschalcies of Beaucaire and Nîmes (part of the royal domain) to continue to use the Civil Law. He was careful to emphasise that the King of France did not hold himself bound either by it or by Roman legislation: *non quod earum obligat nos auctoritas*.[3] Philip the Fair, in organising the teaching of the Civil Law in the University of Orleans in 1314, repeated the reservation, stating that the Roman customs of the South did not possess the force of properly established law, but were simply local customs in the image of the written (Roman) law, depending upon royal approval for their validity.[4] Canonists and lawyers echoed the argument. Sinibaldo de' Fieschi, later to become Pope as Innocent IV, strongly rejected the idea that the King of France could be subordinate to the Emperor,[5] and French lawyers developed a well-known brocard as a summary of the position: *li rois ne tient de nului, fors Dieu et lui.*

The theoretical attractions of the idea of imperial supremacy retained supporters in France even in the last days of the Capetian dynasty. Some of the most determined upholders of the absolute independence of the French crown, such as Jean de Paris and Guillaume de Mende, paid intellectual court to the Emperor's claims, if without any illusions about their practical relevance. Events had long overtaken the Hohenstaufen pretensions. Otto of Brunswick was defeated by Philip Augustus at Bouvines in

[1] *Registrum de negocio Imperii*, epist. 128 (Migne, *op. cit.*, col. 1132).
[2] Decretal *Super specula* of 16 November 1219 (Denifle and Chatelain, *Chartularium Universitatis Parisiensis* (Paris, 1889), vol. i, no. 32, p. 92).
[3] Isambert, *Recueil des anciennes lois françaises* (Paris, 1821), vol. i, p. 264.
[4] *Ordonnances des rois de France*, vol. i, p. 502.
[5] *Apparatus in quinque libros Decretalium*, on c. 13, IV, 7.

July 1214. His rival Frederick of Swabia, the future Emperor Frederick II, crowned King of the Romans in the following year at Aachen, embroiled the Empire again in Italian adventures and conflict with the Holy See. In his efforts to unite the kings of the West on his side, Frederick tried hard to persuade them that his cause was theirs also, whilst attempting to maintain a shadowy supremacy over them at the same time. His death on 13 December 1250 brought on the Great Interregnum. For virtually an entire century the imperial crown lay disused, except for the single year (24 June 1312 — 24 August 1313) when it was worn by Henry VII of Luxemburg. There were Kings of the Romans, chosen by the imperial electors, but none of them received the papal anointing which alone could create an Emperor.

Contemporaries saw these rulers for what they were — no more than kings of Germany, and weak kings at that, preoccupied with challenges to their authority and unable to establish an hereditary right to the crown. They had more pressing tasks than that of asserting a general supremacy over all other rulers. In any case, they lacked the necessary sanction of imperial coronation. Some of them, such as Albert of Austria and Henry of Luxemburg, so far from treating the King of France as an inferior, sought his aid in their quest for the imperial throne. In one sense it might even be said that the King of France was, from the death of Frederick II until the accession of the Valois, the real 'Emperor' in the West.

There were those who hoped that the descendants of Charlemagne would once again wear the imperial crown themselves. In 1272, in 1308, in 1313 and in 1324 attempts were made to draw the Capetians into such an adventure, either in their own interests or those of junior members of the royal family. All these attempts failed: the kings of France were too sober to dream such heady imperial dreams. They remained indifferent to the offers made to them, and never even took seriously the various candidatures of princes of the blood royal. The description given by Marino Sanudo of the reaction of the court of Charles IV to the schemes of John of Luxemburg, King of Bohemia, might sum up the fate of all such suggestions. John wished to set the imperial crown on the head of his brother-in-law, the King of France, but his dazzling proposals were unavailing. As far as the Capetians were concerned, it was sufficient to have destroyed for ever all imperial claims to suzerainty over France, and to have secured a papal declaration that the French crown had no temporal superior. There was no need for them to aim at the Empire when they were already, as it was being put at the French court as early as 1300, 'Emperors in their own kingdom'.

$$*\qquad*\qquad*\qquad*$$

The Capetian kings, free as they were from all temporal overlordship, were always good Christians and faithful servants of the Church. They never challenged the spiritual sovereignty of the Pope, as Head of the Church and God's vicar on earth. Recognition of papal authority, however, implied certain potential dangers for the monarchy, particularly in a society in which the boundaries between the spiritual and temporal powers were difficult to draw. We must therefore examine the interaction of the spiritual authority of the Pope and the temporal sovereignty of the King of France.

This interaction caused no difficulties during the first two hundred years of the dynasty's existence. At first the king was too weak to allow clashes to develop into real conflicts; later, the Holy See was too much in need of French support against the Empire to magnify inevitable differences over details into more fundamental disagreements.

The thirteenth century saw a change. Increasing royal power made the king less acquiescent, and more inclined to resent any challenge to his sovereignty. At the same time the Papacy, fresh from its triumph over the Empire, was steadily developing a political doctrine which made the Pope the temporal as well as the spiritual ruler of Christendom. Inaugurated by Gregory VII during his struggle with the Emperor Henry IV, the doctrine was taken up again, in a subtly modified form, in the decretal *Novit* of Innocent III. It was proclaimed without any reservations in the encyclical letter *Eger cui levia* of Innocent IV, published in the course of the final struggle with Frederick II. The doctrine was directed primarily against the Emperor, whom it endeavoured to relegate to the position of a papal creation; it could, however, also affect the status of all monarchs, including the King of France, as Frederick was careful to point out to his fellow-rulers. The Capetians, nevertheless, took no action against it; most probably they dismissed the whole concept as a purely intellectual specu- lation — and no Capetian before Philip the Fair ever showed much interest in such theoretical questions. As long as the new papal doctrines stopped short at the frontiers of royal authority they met no opposition in France. As long as the Pope was careful to intervene only with moderation in affairs of the state and allowed the king to treat the French Church as his ancestors had done, the Capetians were content to follow their traditional church policy, to be obedient within certain limits, to draw sub- stantial benefits from their connection with the Church in France, to settle differences with it amicably, and above all to avoid any discussion of principles.

In this way a conflict could be, and was, postponed: it could not be avoided indefinitely. The king could not be completely sovereign as long as an outside authority could intervene in the name of moral justice — *ratione peccati* — to limit or even to suspend royal actions. The Popes of the thirteenth century claimed to be able to do precisely this. As early as the reign of Philip Augustus, the crown had found it necessary to issue a warning. Philip had made it clear to Pope Innocent III that his dispute with King John of England was a dispute between lord and vassal, and that no one had any right to interfere in such a question, involving as it did a fief.[1] Innocent had maintained his right to intervene, but had been careful to limit it to the moral sphere, and to add: 'Let it not be imagined that we intend in any way to disturb or diminish the jurisdiction of the illustrious King of France. . . . We can scarcely sustain the burden of our own posi- tion, and why should we therefore seek to usurp that of another?'[2]

As far as France was concerned, Pope Innocent IV's theories remained theories only, and there was peace between the two

---

[1] *Registrum Innocentii III*, lib. vii, ep. 42 (Migne, *Pat. Lat.*, vol. 215, col. 326).
[2] *Loc. cit.*

powers until the close of the century, apart from some minor incidents. But then Pope Boniface VIII and King Philip IV came face to face on the formidable and dangerous ground of first principles, after three centuries during which both sides had been careful to avoid it. Although there is no place in this study for a detailed history of their conflict, we must, for our own purposes, attempt to define the respective positions of the two adversaries, examine some of their statements and actions, and consider the outcome of their quarrel.

Financial reasons lay behind the first episode. To further his struggle against his rebellious vassal of Aquitaine, Edward I of England, Philip the Fair demanded a contribution from the clergy and churches of the kingdom. It had already been acknowledged that, *pro defensione regni*, the king was entitled to demand an aid from all his subjects, and as far as their personal property was concerned the clergy raised no objection. But taxation of the property of churches had never been seriously considered before. In practice, despite a refusal by Pope Nicholas IV in 1292, the Papacy had always during the thirteenth century allowed the king the tenths which he requested, usually accompanying the concession by a statement that the royal purposes were useful to the Church.

Between July 1294 and February 1295 a series of provincial synods granted Philip a tenth for two successive years, without any reference to the Holy See; no protest came from Rome. The papal silence is probably to be explained by the long vacancy preceding the election of Pope Celestine V, the latter's short pontificate, and his resignation. In 1295 the king raised a hundredth and then a fiftieth, both of which affected the goods of the clergy. There were some local protests, but none from Rome. In the following year, he demanded and obtained a new tenth from an assembly of prelates, but this time the protests were more numerous and energetic. Edward I of England was treating his clergy in similar fashion, and Boniface VIII felt compelled to intervene. The bull *Clericis Laicos*[1] of 24 February 1296 was directed against both kings; by it the Pope prohibited the levying

[1] *Les registres de Boniface VIII*, ed. Thomas, Faucon, Digard and Fawtier, vol. i, c. 584–5, no. 1567.

of any imposition upon the clergy by any lay power without the authorisation of the Holy See, and forbade the clergy to pay or assent to any aids or subsidies to any lay authority without the same authorisation.

This bull should not be viewed in too modern a light. Compulsory general taxation did not yet exist, and therefore no question arose of wilful refusal to perform a duty owed to the king. The latter would have been the first to admit that the clergy of his kingdom could not be compelled to give him financial aid without their consent. But it was, from the royal point of view, very serious if the Pope should prohibit the giving of such consent; such a prohibition could be construed as an intolerable interference in the affairs of the kingdom, and a derogation from the king's sovereignty. Despite his disavowals in the bull *Ineffabilis amoris* of 20 September 1296, Boniface's intentions were perhaps accurately expressed by those who — on the Pope's own admission — told Philip: 'The prelates and clergy of your kingdom cannot perform the services due from their fiefs, nor pay aids due by reason of these fiefs, . . . nor can they make a gift to their king of a cup or a horse.'[1]

In the upshot, the Pope beat a precipitate retreat, and on 31 July 1297 surrendered by authorising the king to obtain financial aid from the clergy of his kingdom in cases of necessity, even without papal authorisation — *inconsulto etiam Romano pontifice*.[2] A significant aspect of the clash had been the general loyalty of the clergy to the crown. Boniface had tried to frighten Philip by threatening to put the strength of the Church at the service of the foreign enemies of France, and to call to his aid internal opposition to the crown; in other words, he had menaced the king with both foreign and civil war. The struggle, further, had brought about a revival of the verbal violence which had marked the conflict between Innocent IV and Frederick II. Pamphleteers had made threats which were disturbing to the Church — the more so as the writers may well have had the approval of members of the royal court, or even have been instigated by them. Thus, the

---

[1] *Ibid.*, vol. i, c. 619, no. 1653.
[2] *Ibid.*, vol. i, c. 942, no. 2354.

unknown author of the *Dialogue between a cleric and a knight*
declared that ecclesiastical franchises granted by princes could be
revoked or suspended in the public interest; that the right of
revocation was not limited to the Emperor, but belonged to kings
also; and that the King of France had the right to modify imperial
legislation.[1] The anonymous treatise known from its first words
as *Antequam essent clerici* maintained that the kings of France had
protected their kingdom before there were any clergy, and defined
the Church in terms hostile to the claims of the priesthood: 'Holy
Mother Church, the spouse of Christ, is not made up of clerks
alone, but of laymen also, and Christ was not raised again to save
the clerks alone.'[2]

This dispute over clerical taxation was settled without reference
to first principles; that produced by the arrest of Bernard Saisset,
Bishop of Pamiers, led to a more decisive collision. In this case
events followed an exactly contrary course: the immediate cause
of dispute dropped rapidly into the background, and the basic
issues came to the forefront. In the bull *Ausculta, fili* of 5 December
1301 Boniface VIII declared that the Head of the Church was
raised 'above kings and kingdoms' as was formerly Jeremiah. He
continued: 'Let no person therefore persuade you, most dear son,
that you have no superior and that you are not subject to the
supreme head of the Church's hierarchy. Anyone who thinks thus
is insane, and anyone who persists in maintaining it is an un-
believer who has strayed from the Saviour's fold.' The Pope
reproached Philip on numerous counts, not confined to his
behaviour in matters spiritual, and, to demonstrate that his claims
were no mere theories, announced to the king his intention of
summoning a council of the prelates of the French Church to
meet at Rome — outside the kingdom of France — on 1 November 1302: 'To bring you back to the straight road of virtue, we
should be justified in employing force against you, in using the
bow and the quiver. But we love rather to take counsel with the
churchmen of your kingdom before making order concerning the
peace, safety and prosperity thereof. You may assist at this

---

[1] Goldast, *Monarchia sancti Romani imperii* (Hanau, 1612), vol. i, p. 17.
[2] Dupuy, *Différend*, p. 12.

assembly either in person or through representatives, but we shall not hesitate to proceed in your absence. And you shall hear what God shall show forth by our mouth.'[1]

Less than a year later, in the bull *Unam Sanctam* of 18 November 1302, Boniface defined the relative positions of the spiritual and lay powers thus: 'The Holy Catholic Church is single and apostolic; that is a dogma which faith enjoins us to believe and to maintain; outside the Church there is neither salvation nor remission of sins. . . . This Church, single and unique, has but one body and one head — not two heads, which would make it a monster; that one head is Christ, and the vicar of Christ, Peter and his successor. . . . In this Church there are two swords, the spiritual and the temporal, as we are told by the Evangelist. . . . And of a surety he who denies that the temporal sword is Peter's to wield forgets the words of our Lord: put up your sword in its sheath. The two swords are thus in the hands of the Church, both the spiritual and the temporal, the one to be wielded for the Church, and the other to be wielded by it — the latter by the hands of priests, the former by the hands of kings and knights, but always on the order of the priesthood and only so far as allowed by it. For it is necessary that the one sword be under the other and that temporal authority be subject to spiritual authority. . . . The spiritual authority is bound to establish temporal power and to judge it whenever it errs. . . . If a temporal authority should err, it is to be judged by the spiritual authority; but if an inferior spiritual authority should err, it is to be judged by its own superior authority. The supreme spiritual authority has no judge but God. . . . And therefore we declare, pronounce and make plain that it is absolutely necessary for every human creature who wishes to attain salvation, to be subject to the authority of the Roman Pontiff.'[2]

Finally, in a consistory held on 24 June 1302 — between the dates of these two bulls — the Pope held forth to the members of the College of Cardinals, and endeavoured to justify himself against the reproaches addressed to him by the French court. He

---

[1] *Les registres de Boniface VIII*, vol. iii, c. 328–35, no. 4424.
[2] *Ibid.*, vol. iii, c. 888–90, no. 5382.

said: 'If ... the king does not wish to return to the paths of wisdom, let him not attempt to drive us to the brink, for we shall not suffer it, but shall in time to come reply fittingly to his folly. We know the feelings of the Germans, the men of Languedoc and the Burgundians towards the French.... Let me remind you, my brethren, that our predecessors deposed three kings of France, as the French may read in their chronicles as well as we may in ours, and as may be seen—for one case at least — in the Decretum. And though we are unworthy to unlatch the sandals of our forerunners, yet since the king has committed all the abuses of which his ancestors were guilty who were deposed, therefore we shall cast him down as we would a servant.'[1]

The papal position was thus stated quite unambiguously. The Pope was claiming to be the king's superior inside his kingdom; he was summoning French bishops and prelates to Rome to judge their king; he was threatening him with deposition, and not with spiritual punishments alone. The striking feature of the whole attack was that it grew out of an idea which was universally accepted in western Christendom. There was no dispute about the spiritual pre-eminence of papal authority. No one, however, had foreseen the possible temporal implications of that pre-eminence.

The counter-attack depended upon the discovery of a spiritual authority superior to that of Rome, but less immediately dangerous to the monarchy. Such an authority Philip and his counsellors found in the idea of the Church Universal, composed (in the words of the pamphleteer quoted above) 'not of clerks alone, but of laymen also'. The Pope might in truth be the Head of the Church, but his authority must bow before that of the Church assembled, before the canons of Councils of the Church. If the Pope accepted the authority of a Council, then the Council was superior to him. He had accused the king of maltreating the French Church, and of being a disobedient son: the king replied by denouncing him as an intruder, a heretic, a wolf making use of a wrongfully-acquired apostolic dignity to spread death in the sheepfold, and — most decisively — by appealing against him to a General Council of the Church.

[1] Dupuy, *Différend*, p. 79.

Philip was careful to give this appeal the greatest possible impetus. By a series of meetings, held throughout France from 15 June 1303 onwards, he secured almost unanimous support. Thus fortified, he moved forward; following the inquisitorial procedure of the Roman Law, he attempted to secure the person of the accused. On 7 September 1303, Guillaume de Nogaret arrested the Pope at Anagni. His success was short-lived, for the townspeople changed sides and rescued Boniface. But the blow had been struck. The Pope died a month later — on 11 October — in Rome, to which his supporters had taken him.

The most significant part of the sequel, for our purposes, was the Church's disavowal of Boniface's stand. On 27 August 1311 Pope Clement V, in the bull *Rex gloriae*,[1] ordered the deletion from the registers of the Papal Chancery of all matter that could be injurious to the King of France. Under this order, the bulls *Unam sanctam, Salvator mundi, Ausculta, fili* and others were removed. The king's action against Boniface was declared 'good, sincere and just', he himself being declared to be 'absolutely innocent and without fault'.

The bull *Rex gloriae* marked the emergence of the King of France as complete sovereign of his kingdom. Thereafter he recognised no superior, and was indeed 'emperor in his kingdom', holding his crown only by his own right and from God alone. This position had been reached without any formal proclamation of principles. The Capetians had preferred to have their sovereignty recognised by those who might have been tempted to challenge it. It was the bishops involved who declared the king incapable of doing homage. It was the Pope who proclaimed the independence of France from the Empire. If the Papacy did in fact remain silent on the complete temporal independence of the crown and the superiority of the temporal authority over the spiritual, nevertheless the Church recognised and proclaimed that independence and superiority when it destroyed the acts by which a foolhardy pope had challenged them, and when it blackened the memory of Boniface VIII with the compliments which it paid to the zeal of his conqueror.

[1] Dupuy, *Différend*, p. 600.

D2

6

The Capetian Patrimony

The Capetians needed three centuries before they could call themselves 'emperors in their own kingdom' without appearing ridiculous. They succeeded in the end because, in a society in which the possession of land was the only source of power, they were able to build up a domain greater than that of any of their great vassals or of any contemporary ruler in Europe. In 1328, the last year of Capetian rule, an official document drawn up at the close of a scrupulously exact enquiry estimated that the domain included 23,671 parishes and 2,469,987 hearths. Its total area appears to have been 313,663 square kilometres. This was about three times the area of the appanages and the great fiefs outside the domain, which amounted to 110,721 square kilometres.[1]

It would be interesting to have similarly precise figures for the royal domain at the accession of Hugh Capet in 987 and at regular intervals thereafter. That is unfortunately impossible. Exact information only begins with the *État des paroisses et des feux* of 1328 and similar documents, and their appearance coincides with the dying out of the dynasty. But it is possible to trace the development of the royal domain with the help of the maps in Auguste Longnon's historical atlas[2] and the same author's admirable and now classic account of the formation of French unity.[3] There is, however, a danger that Longnon's maps and commentary, if used by the uninitiated, will create the illusion that when the king

[1] F. Lot, '*L'État des paroisses et des feux* de 1328', in *Bibliothèque de l'École des Chartes*, xc (1929), pp. 51–107, 256–315.
[2] A. Longnon, *Atlas historique de la France* (Paris, 1885–9).
[3] A. Longnon, *La formation de l'unité française* (Paris, 1922). It must be remembered that this admirable book was published posthumously, and is a reconstruction of Longnon's lectures made by one of his most distinguished pupils, not the book which he himself would have published had he been alive in 1922.

acquired a county, a town, or a castellany, he got absolute possession of all its lands. The fact was that he succeeded to the rights of the former lord into whose shoes he had stepped, and those rights did not necessarily carry a more than theoretical authority or imply total possession or extend to every quarter of the county, town, or castellany. An excellent illustration of this state of affairs is provided by the royal domain itself under Philip I and Louis VI, who had to spend most of their reigns enforcing at the point of the sword their rights and authority over lands which had for generations formed part of the Capetian patrimony.

A feudal lord's domain — and the royal domain, during the eleventh and twelfth centuries at least, was no exception — had a territorial character. But it was even more a collection of rights. By the thirteenth century certain seigneurial domains had come to be composed of little more than rights, and their lords became known as 'landless lords'. It would be interesting to discover precisely how the royal domain evolved and whether the increase of the royal rights was not more important and advantageous than territorial growth. Unfortunately the history of the royal domain as a whole has still to be written. The only scholar to have embarked on the task is an American, W. M. Newman, who has published a valuable monograph on the domain from 987 to 1180, the period which is poorest in documentation.[1] His example might well be followed for later periods.

Mr. Newman takes an economic standpoint. He counts as part of the domain only territories and localities where the documents incontrovertibly prove the king to have exercised some right which yielded a profit. Whatever the limitations of this definition, he applies it impeccably. His book offers a marked contrast to the work of Longnon, especially in the section in which, following in his predecessor's steps, though in a different spirit, he outlines the historical geography of the domain between 987 and 1180. The contrast is even more striking when Newman's maps of the domain under Henry I and again under Louis VII are compared with the corresponding maps in Longnon's atlas: not that one of the two

---

[1] W. M. Newman, *Le domaine royal sous les premiers Capétiens (987–1180)* (Paris, 1937): a University of Strasbourg thesis.

historians is wrong and the other right — they have looked at the
problem from different angles. Longnon is concerned with the
political aspects of the domain; Newman sees it as an economic
entity. In fact it had both a political and an economic character,
each with its own particular importance and its own limits.

Economically, the domain was a collection of lands and rights
which the king exploited directly, as their proprietor. This,
incidentally, was how the contemporaries of the Capetians and
the Valois thought of the domain. Hence the revenues collected
by the king as sovereign were called 'extraordinary', and quickly
came to be handled by a special administration, separate from that
responsible for the domain properly so called.

Politically, the domain included not only the *corpus* of lands
and rights identified by Newman but also what was known as the
mouvance, the fiefs over which the king exercised his more or less
immediate suzerainty. It is even logical to add to these the lands
over which the king could exercise only his sovereign rights. It
must be pointed out that an economic fact, such as the payment of
a due or a fine or the ability to levy a financial *aide* is often the
only clue to the existence of suzerainty and sometimes to that
of sovereignty.

The problem is indeed more complex than the study of any
historical map would suggest. Nor does it seem possible to draw
a map of the royal domain in its wider sense. That difficulty was
encountered as early as the beginning of the fourteenth century
when the newly created *Chambre des Comptes* conducted large-
scale investigations into the royal rights and their extent, thus
continuing the work which had originated with the enquiries
under Philip the Fair or perhaps even as far back as those undertaken by St. Louis.

It must be added that the Capetian kings were very generous.
They granted a good deal of land away at random, and the time
came when they had little idea of what they had deliberately
alienated and what had been filched from them. In the absence of
an authoritative survey of the domain lands and of a complete
register of the royal rights, usurpations (or *soupprises*, as they
were called in the thirteenth century) were frequent; and the

Capetian dynasty died out just as the monarchy was starting a vigorous drive to stabilise the domain.

From the domain in its economic sense the king drew the means of supporting a household and a policy. It also gave him initially the resources he required to make his suzerainty effective and profitable. Only with the increasingly powerful exercise of suzerainty did sovereignty acquire reality and the Capetians become fully kings of France. The early stages of this process are unfortunately lost in obscurity. For nearly two centuries the Capetians struggled with the feudal barons, great and small, who surrounded them. The petty lords of the domain proper were the most difficult of all to subdue. But once they had been reduced to submission, the monarchy swept on to master the entire kingdom in a single century.

The clues to the monarchy's resources from Hugh Capet's accession in 987 to Louis VII's death in 1180 are scanty and vague. It seems unlikely that Hugh Capet's domain did not extend beyond the few miserable fragments which Newman has painstakingly identified. He himself does not believe them to be a complete list. Nor is it likely that the longer lists he has compiled for the next five reigns, from 996 to 1180, give a full picture.

The question has been raised whether the so-called ecclesiastical domain was the real source of such royal power as existed. One difficulty has been to decide on the exact meaning of the terms 'royal bishopric' and 'royal monastery'. Lack of unanimity on this score has led historians into remarkable disagreement over the numbers of royal bishoprics and monasteries. Lot maintains that of the 77 bishoprics in his kingdom, King Hugh had the nomination to between 20 and 25 and, by exercising his regalian right, drew their revenues during vacancies; and that he had the same kind of patronage over 51 monasteries of varying importance.[1] For the reign of King Hugh, Newman counts only 6 bishoprics as royal for certain, another 6 as very probable, and 2 as probable: giving a maximum of 14. He counts 9 monasteries as certain, and 2, possibly 4, as probable: giving a maximum of 13.[2]

[1] Lot, *Études sur le règne de Hugues Capet*, pp. 222-3, 226-32. Lot produces his figure for royal monasteries with certain reservations.

[2] Newman, *Domaine royal*, pp. 202-4.

But even if agreement could be reached as to the exact number of royal bishoprics and monasteries, it would still be necessary to determine their precise value to the king — an almost impossible task.

However we approach it, the problem of the early history of the royal domain seems insoluble. All we can say with confidence is that the first Capetians had a domain off which they were able to live, but that we have no precise information about the revenues they were deriving from it before the end of the twelfth century, when some concrete facts at last emerge. In 1223 a certain Conon, *prévôt* of Lausanne, happened to be in Paris. Philip Augustus had died that year, and Conon heard some royal officials boasting about their late master's power, and claiming that Philip's father, Louis VII, had little short of 19,000 *livres parisis* to spend every month: in other words an annual revenue of 228,000 *livres parisis*. Happily for historians, Conon wrote down these figures, and his note of them has survived.[1] They may stand for gross revenue or alternatively for the sum which came into the royal coffers once the local expenses of administration and collection had been met. In fact it is not clear how they should be interpreted. Nevertheless, they throw some light on a subject which is utterly obscure for earlier reigns. While little is known of the extent of the royal domain in the very early Capetian period, considerably more information has survived about the acquisitions to the royal domain made by the first six Capetian kings between 987 and 1180. With the help of a study of these acquisitions it is possible to trace the domain's growth at this period and the methods by which the earlier Capetians aggrandised themselves; and, taking Conon's figures into account as well, to obtain a clearer notion of the royal revenues.

Gautier, Count of Dreux, who died some time before 980, was survived by his widow Eva, who died on 23 December of either 991 or a slightly earlier year. Gautier had no heir of his body. Hereditary succession to fiefs was not yet firmly established, and King Hugh Capet took the county of Dreux into his own possession; or more probably one-half of the county, the other half

---

[1] *Monumenta Germaniae Historica, Scriptores*, xxiv, 782.

having gone to the Duke of Normandy, doubtless as the result of an agreement with Hugh. But, possibly as early as 991, Hugh granted his new acquisition to Count Eudes I of Chartres as a reward for his help in Hugh's struggle with the Carolingian pretender Charles of Lorraine. This is the only acquisition, ephemeral as it was, which can be ascribed with certainty to the first Capetian king. Hugh also possessed the Abbey of Corbie, which may have been a second and more permanent acquisition of his, although there is no knowing whether he acquired it before or after his accession in 987.

The reign of Robert the Pious saw by contrast a considerable expansion of the domain in its widest sense. Robert was the king who annexed Burgundy. Its duke, Henry, third son of Hugh the Great and hence Robert's uncle, died at Pouilly-sur-Loire on 15 October 1002, leaving no direct heir. But he had married in 974 Gerberga, Countess of Mâcon, who had had a son, named Otto William, by her first husband Adalbert, son and co-monarch of King Berengar of Italy. Gerberga and OttoWilliam persuaded Henry of Burgundy to adopt OttoWilliam and designate him his successor in the duchy and also in his own two counties of Auxerre and Autun, which lay within the duchy and which he held directly himself. Robert the Pious, however, intervened, for it was by no means certain that a great fief like the duchy of Burgundy could lawfully be given to a new duke without the king's consent. Royal investiture was necessary to put a great vassal's heir in legitimate possession of his fief. Nor had Henry left an heir of his body. The practice of adopting an heir, as he had adopted Otto William, was rapidly dying out in contemporary French society. If Burgundy were indeed an hereditary duchy and an adopted heir's claims were held to be invalid, the King of France, Duke Henry's nephew, could put himself forward as rightful heir to the duchy.

The story is obscure, but it is known that OttoWilliam refused to give way to Robert's claims, and that the king had to wage war for thirteen years (1003–16) before he won control of the duchy. The crown did not keep Burgundy for long. Robert administered it for the rest of his reign, but as soon as Henry I became king he gave away all his father's conquests in Burgundy to his own younger brother Robert, in 1032.

As Burgundy was only won after a prolonged struggle and was so soon disposed of, it is hard to believe that the crown made much profit out of it. But the episode is important because it reveals that the Capetian monarchy was from the very beginning capable of a far more vigorous and protracted military effort than is suggested by the tale of the royal lands and rights, in so far as it can be reconstructed from the texts. True, King Robert was assisted by Duke Richard II of Normandy, but it may be doubted whether Richard's aid would have been proffered if the king had been as weak as the documents seem to imply.

In addition to his temporary acquisition of Burgundy, Robert the Pious re-established his authority over the counties of Dreux and Melun and prepared the ground for the crown to recover the county of Sens. Dreux came to him through the retrocession which Count Eudes I of Chartres made him, it is not known how or why or when. Melun, a county forming part of the Capetian family estates, had been granted by Hugh Capet, before his accession, to Bouchard the Venerable, Count of Vendôme. When Bouchard died in 1007, Melun passed to his son, Bishop Renaud of Paris, and when Renaud himself died in 1016, the county naturally reverted to the crown.

At Sens the count, Fromont, was at loggerheads with the archbishop, Lietry, whom he could not forgive for having got the archbishopric over the head of his son Bruno. After Fromont's death in 1012, relations were even more difficult between the archbishop and the new count, Renaud, brother to Lietry's old rival. The chronicle of Saint-Pierre-le-Vif records that one day at mass the archbishop was just going to give Count Renaud the kiss of peace when *ille, vultum avertens, in posterioribus suis pacem ei offerebat*.[1] In the end the archbishop asked for royal protection and Robert the Pious made a surprise descent on Sens and seized the town on 22 April 1015. After some desultory military operations a bargain was struck, whereby Renaud was to keep the county for life, and at his death half the town of Sens and the

---

[1] *R.H.F.*, x, 223.

entire county were to revert to the crown. The archbishop was to have the other half of the town. This agreement was carried out on Renaud's death in 1055. Henry I was then on the throne, and Sens was his one acquisition. As already explained, Henry handed over to his brother Robert the conquests their father had made in Burgundy, keeping only the homage of the counties of Auxerre and Nevers. The lordship of Corbie was subtracted from the royal domain when Henry granted it as dower to his sister Adela at the time of her marriage to Count Baldwin V of Flanders. To Duke Robert of Normandy Henry gave up the suzerainty over the French Vexin — the region lying between the River Oise and the River Epte.

The losses to the domain incurred under Henry I were in part made good under Philip I. On 14 November 1060 Geoffrey Martel, Count of Anjou, died without issue, and his lands were divided between his two nephews, Fulk Réchin and Geoffrey the Bearded. The heritability of fiefs had now become part of French feudal custom. Fulk was discontented with his share of the lands and attacked his brother. The story is obscure and the chroniclers contradict one another but they are at least unanimous that Fulk gave the Gâtinais to King Philip I. Historians have generally assumed that Fulk was purchasing the king's neutrality. It is clear that in 1069, the approximate date of this transaction, the Capetian monarchy was already a force to be reckoned with, since its neutrality cost so much to buy. The precise limits of Philip's new acquisition are hard to determine, but as Louis VI was in his turn to acquire in 1120 certain castellanies in the Gâtinais, it is reasonable to suppose that Fulk's grant was confined to the four castellanies of Château-Landon, La-Chapelle-la-Reine, and Lorrez-le-Bocage, in the present Department of Seine-et-Marne, and Lorris in the Department of the Loiret.

Raoul de Crépy, Count of the Vexin, Valois, Amiens, Bar-sur-Aube, and Vitry, and stepfather of Philip I by his marriage to Anna of Kiev, Henry I's widow, died in 1074, leaving by his previous marriage a son, Simon, and two married daughters, of whom one was the wife of Barthélemy de Broyes, son of Hugh Bardoul, lord of Pithiviers, and the other the wife of Herbert of

Vermandois. Raoul's heritage was now disputed between King Philip I and Hugh Bardoul. Simon, his heir, found himself pestered with matrimonial advances made on behalf of the daughter of Count Hildebert of Auvergne and the daughter of Duke William the Conqueror of Normandy. To escape these embarrassments he fled to the cloister and became a monk, probably in April 1077. What happened next was that Philip I acquired the county of the Vexin. It is not known how or why, but it was certainly with Simon's consent.

At some time between June 1097 and October 1102 Eudes Arpin, Viscount of Bourges, who was anxious to go on crusade but could not afford to, raised some money by selling to King Philip his viscounty, which consisted mainly of the town of Bourges and its banlieu (the *septaine*). The chronicles which mention the sale give various figures for the price paid to Eudes Arpin: 60,000 *livres*, which seems too much;[1] 6000 *sous* (about 300 *livres*), which seems too little;[2] and 60,000 *sous* (about 3000 *livres*), which is the most plausible sum, but cannot be verified.[3] Mediaeval chroniclers produce extremely vague and inaccurate figures for sums of money, the size of armies, and so forth. But it is at least clear from the conflicting amounts given as the price of Bourges that contemporary writers believed a notable quantity of cash had changed hands. Colour is lent to their belief by the fact that the *prévôté* of Bourges, admittedly augmented by the lordship of Issoudun, yielded the royal treasury for the financial year 1202–3 the appreciable revenue of 1977 *livres* and 4 *sous*.[4] It is interesting that Philip I, who is rightly regarded as one of the least powerful of the early Capetians, could find the money to buy Bourges out of his revenues, which have been estimated as very slender.

Philip I was also responsible for the return of Corbie to the royal domain. The circumstances are obscure, but may plausibly be reconstructed as follows: Count Baldwin V of Flanders, who

---

[1] *Chronicon Regum Francorum*, in *R.H.F.*, xi, 394.
[2] *Chronicon Vizeliacense*, in *ibid.*, xi, 385.
[3] Aimoin, *De gestis Francorum*, in *ibid.*, xi, 157.
[4] F. Lot and R. Fawtier, *Le premier budget de la monarchie française* (Paris, 1932), pp. 142, 144, 146.

acquired the lordship of Corbie by his marriage to Adela, sister of King Henry I, left two sons — Robert the Frisian, who was excluded from the succession and set himself up with a fief by his marriage to the widow of Florence, Count of Holland; and Baldwin VI, who succeeded his father and acquired Corbie with the rest of the inheritance. Baldwin VI's wife Richilda bore him two sons. The elder, Arnoul, succeeded to Flanders on his father's death in 1070, and the younger, Baldwin, received Hainault at that time. The two heirs were mere boys. Their mother Richilda governed in their name, to the disgruntlement of the nobility; and Robert the Frisian seized his chance to claim the patrimony, although he had been debarred from the succession. Richilda, who was his sister-in-law, threatened to clap him into prison, and Robert appealed for justice to the suzerain of Flanders, his uncle King Philip I. With a timely bribe of 4000 *livres* Richilda persuaded Philip to abandon any thought of intervention on Robert the Frisian's behalf. The king in fact took up arms against his nephew and on 22 February 1071 defeated him at the battle of Cassel in Flanders, in which the young Count Arnoul was killed. A few days later Robert the Frisian was made prisoner and handed over to the king, who, now that Arnoul was dead, came to terms with his captive. Philip recognised Robert as Count of Flanders and married his step-daughter, Bertha of Frisia. The various texts which mention the return of Corbie to the royal possession make it plain that Arnoul had been concerned in the transaction; and as Corbie was not brought into the terms of the final peace between King Philip and Robert the Frisian, it seems probable that it had been the price of the king's fruitless intervention on Arnoul's behalf. If so, once Arnoul had been killed, Robert the Frisian appears to have confirmed the grant of Corbie to Philip I.

In 1104 Prince Philip, elder son of Philip I by Bertrada de Montfort, married Elizabeth, daughter of Guy Troussel, lord of Montlhéry. Arrangements highly favourable to Prince Philip were made on this occasion, and they paved the way for the cession by the lord of Montlhéry at the beginning of 1108 — shortly before his death — of all his lands to the heir to the throne, Prince Louis — the future Louis VI, who had been associated in the kingship with his father since 1100, and succeeded him on 3 August 1108, a few months after the cession of Montlhéry.

Louis VI carried on an energetic struggle with the feudal nobility of the Île-de-France and it is consequently tempting to assume that he made important additions to the royal domain. But his acquisitions were few. The continuator of Aimoin is able to dispose of them in three short sentences: 'From Fulk, Viscount of Gâtinais, he bought Moret and Le Châtelet-en-Brie, Boësses, Yèvre-le-Châtel and Chambon. He fortified Monchauvet, Lorrez-le-Bocage and Grès, and also Corbeil, and La Ferté-Alais. And he also acquired Montlhéry and Châteaufort.'[1] Louis' real work was to re-establish royal authority in the royal domain lands of the Île-de-France and the Orléanais. This process is difficult to trace in detail. Suger's account of it in his biography of Louis VI is confused, and its chronology is dubious. As a result of this obscurity what were probably only more effective enfeoffments sometimes appear as new acquisitions.

Louis VI handed on to his successor a domain which was better policed and more submissive to royal authority; but he had almost certainly made no substantial additions to its territory. To police was not to conquer. The lords he disciplined kept their lands and titles and soon became members of the royal entourage. The monarchy had led them back to the path of feudal duty, and they or in some cases their immediate descendants became the principal agents of royal power.

When discussing the royal domain under Louis VI it is customary to mention the marriage of the heir to the throne with Eleanor and to speak of the 'acquisition' of Aquitaine. But Aquitaine never became part of the royal domain. It constituted Eleanor's dower, and when she left Louis VII for her second husband Henry Plantagenet she took Aquitaine with her. Only if a son had been born of her marriage to Louis VII and had succeeded Louis on the French throne would Aquitaine have become part of the royal domain. It is questionable whether the duchy added much to the revenues of the royal household while Louis' marriage with Eleanor lasted. Louis' generous grants to the

[1] *R.H.F.*, xii, 123.

churches of Aquitaine on the occasion of their wedding suggest a doubt; and although the Plantagenets had a much more highly developed administration in Aquitaine than Louis VII, they do not seem to have extracted any considerable revenue from the duchy. Thus while there is a case for crediting Louis VI with having tried to prepare the way for the annexation of Aquitaine to the royal domain, that is the most that can be claimed, and it is false to suppose that annexation was ever brought about, even during the short period of Eleanor's marriage to Louis VII.

There is no serious monograph on the reign of Louis VII, and the history of the royal domain is cloudy for his forty-three years as king. It is at least clear that there were no important acquisitions. The domain grew only in the sense that, as under Louis VI, royal authority was enforced anew in places where it had previously become a dead letter. A few ecclesiastical homages were acquired, especially in the south of France, at the cost of making over regalian rights to the bishoprics and abbeys — not that the king had as a rule been in a position to exercise them.

To sum up: although it cannot be denied that advances were made by the Capetian kings who ruled from 987 to 1180, it is more difficult to decide whether the royal domain increased significantly during these two centuries. The few acquisitions which were not of a merely temporary nature seem to have been largely offset by the granting away of innumerable petty fragments of the domain. It is certain that record of only a small fraction of these alienations has survived. Newman has collected and tabulated all the documentary information about the domain between 987 and 1180. His explanatory notes make it plain that a considerable proportion of the lands and rights which the Capetians possessed can only be traced in documents dealing with the alienation of these assets by the crown. His tables convey not so much the state of the royal domain at this period as the extent of the losses it suffered. Perhaps it would not be a paradox to claim that from Hugh Capet to Louis VII the royal domain and the royal revenues varied little.

It must now be decided what was the extent, at the time of Hugh Capet, of the royal domain in its wider sense — the lands over which the king directly or indirectly exercised an effective authority yielding him a profit. According to Lot,[1] the remnants of the patrimony which had come down from Robert the Strong formed the nucleus: Parisis, Orléanais, Étampais, Châtrais, Pincerais, Melunais, a few alods in Berry, the port of Montreuil and the abbey of Saint-Riquier-en-Ponthieu, and the abbey of Corbie in the Amiénois. Next there was what the Capetians had taken over from their Carolingian predecessors: a few royal palaces in the valleys of the Aisne and the Oise — Attigny, Compiègne, and Verberie; and the patronage of the bishoprics of Rheims, Laon, Noyon, Châlons, Langres, and Le Puy.

Around this domain there lay a ring of counties held directly of the king: Vendômois, Corbonnais, Gâtinais, Melunais, Arcésais, Valois, Soissonnais, the counties of Pontoise-Meulan and Beaumont-sur-Oise, Beauvaisis, the counties of Breteuil, Amiénois, Vermandois, Ponthieu, and Vimeu. To these must be added the counties of Sens and Joigny, the viscounty of Bourges, and probably the lordship of Bourbon.

Over Hugh Capet's heterogeneous domain his successors maintained a fluctuating yet enduring body of rights. The documents are unfortunately too meagre to allow the vicissitudes which royal authority underwent to be followed in detail. But it is clear that the royal rights came to provide the crown with the revenues and resources which the Capetians needed to keep themselves in power during the first two hundred years of their history. Under these conditions there was possibly small difference between the revenues of Hugh Capet and those of Louis VII. On the other hand, the 19,000 *livres parisis* a month which Conon's informants said Louis VII received would have had a far greater value at the end of the tenth century, a time of lower prices. Conon's figures cannot perhaps be accepted for the monarchy of two centuries earlier without the risk of serious error; and yet most of the royal revenues were fixed by tradition or by long-term contracts which were automatically renewed.

If the present writer is not mistaken, the early Capetians were powerful lords. To regard them as the '*petits seigneurs*' of the Île-de-France is to perpetuate a myth. They were wise enough

[1] Lot, *Études sur le règne de Hugues Capet*, pp. 187–91.

not to nurse excessive territorial ambitions: presumably circumstances thrust this wisdom upon them. Their domain was less attenuated than has sometimes been supposed and it gave them the wherewithal to live and to make their power felt within its own boundaries and the lands which neighboured it. The office of king gave them by no means negligible rights over the great fiefs, and the Capetians were consequently able to achieve more than their great vassals. But before the king could lay hands on what the great vassals had to give, he had first to establish full control over the royal domain proper, the true seat of Capetian power. The police operations of Robert the Pious, Philip I, Louis VI, and Louis VII were all directed to this end. By 1180 the task was nearly accomplished. Thenceforward, though the Capetians did not refrain from making small additions to the domain as opportunity arose, their principal achievement was to bring a steady pressure to bear on the great fiefs and in due course carry out the huge territorial acquisitions which made them within a century truly sovereign over the entire kingdom of France.

7

The Great Fiefs

The consolidation of the royal domain in the twelfth century was matched by a similar process in the great feudal principalities of Flanders, Anjou, Brittany, Champagne, Burgundy, and (to a lesser degree) Aquitaine and Toulouse in the south. The leaders, and possible models, were the Dukes of Normandy, who on their own account also applied the new methods in their conquests across the English Channel. The process made for stability. As a result of it, France ceased to be a conglomeration of petty lordships over which individual adventurers tried to establish a rule of force. Instead, hereditary succession to fiefs became the rule, dynasties were consolidated, and the greater families were able to build up considerable domains. More regular administrative methods followed, in Flanders, Anjou and Champagne. Philip Augustus was, in consequence, confronted in 1180 by a ring of feudal principalities as well organised as his own — if not more so.

In the long run, the crown was the gainer. When a great lordship fell into royal hands — as many did after 1180 — it brought to the king a complex of lands and legal rights, and new followers and dependents, without any need to repeat the laborious task of pacification. It was not surprising that as a result the standing and resources of the crown increased far more rapidly after Philip Augustus than they had done under his predecessors. There was no radical change of policy involved. If royal power had a new strength in the thirteenth century, it still continued to be exercised in support and vindication of legal rights. It was these legal rights which made the Capetians the masters of their kingdom, and enabled them to acquire lands and jurisdictions in a permanent and definitive manner, without creating the ambiguities and hatreds which would have accompanied the use of force alone.

The first step towards an understanding of this momentous process is a study of the relations of the royal house with the counties of Flanders, Toulouse and Champagne, and the duchies of Burgundy and Brittany, from 1180 onwards. This must be followed by an examination of the problems posed by the enormous principality created in the west of France by the Angevin rulers of England, in order to discover if the methods so successful elsewhere required any modification there. Finally, after examining the minor acquisitions made in the period, it should be possible to determine whether or not any clear-cut principles lay behind the individual acts of Capetian policy. The inconvenience of this method, with its disregard for strict chronology, is offset by its value in reducing a complicated series of events into some sort of order. It would be unwise, however, to infer from an analysis of this sort that the Capetians and their contemporaries looked at events in this particular way; any impression of a continuous and conscious policy would be historically misleading, however satisfying it might be intellectually.

★   ★   ★   ★

The reduction of the county of Flanders, the first of the great fiefs to be brought to heel, began at the very start of Philip Augustus' reign. It was touched off by his marriage at Bapaume, on 28 April 1180, to Isabella, daughter of Count Baldwin V of Hainault and niece of Philip of Alsace, Count of Flanders. The last-named held as part of his county of Flanders not only Flanders proper, but also 'the lands beyond the New Dyke', which were already occasionally called Artois, and which included Arras, Bapaume, Ruhout, Saint-Omer, Aire, the suzerainty of the county of Boulogne, Lens, Guines, Saint-Pol, Lilliers and Hesdin. Philip of Alsace had married, in 1159, Elizabeth of Vermandois, daughter of Raoul of Vermandois (brother of King Philip I) and of Petronilla, sister of Louis VII's first queen, Eleanor of Aquitaine. In 1164, on the death of her brother, Raoul the Leprous, Count of Vermandois, the Countess of Flanders inherited

Vermandois (the counties of Ribemont, Péronne, and Montdidier), the Amiénois (the small county of Amiens, a fief of the bishopric of Amiens, together with a considerable number of fiefs held from it) and Valois (of which the county of Crépy formed the core). At some unknown date — possibly in 1175 — Count Philip compelled his wife to make him a gift of these three provinces; Elizabeth had been unfaithful, and the gift may well have been the price of peace with her husband. The count had the gift confirmed by King Louis VII in 1179, and later by King Philip Augustus, most probably on the occasion of the latter's marriage to Isabella of Hainault. At the same time he gave Artois to Isabella as her dowry, but reserved to himself the life-rent.

Countess Elizabeth died between 14 and 16 April 1183. The succession was claimed by her sister, Eleanora, for Elizabeth left no direct heir. Eleanora at first refused to recognise the gift of Vermandois, the Amiénois and Valois to Count Philip, but eventually came to an agreement with him, by which she received Valois and an annual rent from Roye. At this point, however, the crown intervened. Philip Augustus, claiming to be Elizabeth's heir, also refused to recognise the gift which she had made to her husband. He claimed that his own confirmation of the transaction had been forced on him by his tutor, the self-same Philip of Alsace, who was very much an interested party. There has been much debate over the grounds of the king's intervention, but it is most probable that he acted to fulfil his royal duty to protect the rights of a legitimate heir. But a political purpose lay in the background. With only a problematical hold on the queen's dowry — for the royal couple had as yet no child, and the retention of Isabella's dowry depended on the existence of an heir — the king was alive to the danger that Philip of Alsace might create a power more formidable than his own. Further, the marriage of the claimant Eleanora to Count Matthew of Beaumont was childless; the count was the grand chamberlain of France, and King Philip had not unreasonable hopes that their possessions might eventually find their way into royal hands.

Philip of Alsace took up arms to defend what he considered to be his rights, and was supported by several great feudatories who had their own reasons to suspect the king's ambitions. Against them Philip Augustus acted with skill. He detached the Count of Hainault from the coalition by threatening to repudiate his daughter, came to terms with the Count of Champagne, and gained the support of Henry II of England, always closely involved in the affairs of the great French vassals. There was no great battle, and Philip Augustus never used the army of 2000 knights and 14,000 serjeants with which the chroniclers generously credited him. An agreement was concluded at Amiens, on 20 March 1186, by which Philip of Alsace retained seisin of the counties of Saint-Quentin and Péronne only, together with the town of Ham, out of all his wife's lands. The king became the legal owner of these parts of Vermandois, with the right to secure seisin at will by the payment of a fixed price to the count. Philip Augustus also received the county of Montdidier, Tourotte and Choisy, and the county of Amiens (augmented by Roye), with the homage and services due for the sixty-five castles held from it, whilst the remainder of Vermandois went to Eleanora of Beaumont. She was not required to pay the normal *rachat* which accompanied a new enfeoffment; in her case the lands ceded to the king were held to be his compensation. Artois remained as before, but the birth of Prince Louis on 5 September 1187 made it more likely that the queen's dowry would become a permanent part of the domain. Two years later, after his mother's death, the prince inherited her rights over the province.

Philip of Alsace went on the Third Crusade with his king, and died at Ptolemais on 1 June 1191. Philip Augustus at once sent messages to the nobles and townspeople of Péronne and Saint-Quentin, demanding an oath of fealty. Meanwhile the regent Adela of Champagne and the Archbishop of Rheims, the king's lieutenant, occupied Artois in the name of Prince Louis. The province was thus united *de facto* to the royal domain, a position legalised by the prince's accession as Louis VIII in 1223.

Philip Augustus returned from the East soon after the death of the Count of Flanders. It has been suggested that he planned to seize the county, but the absence of any legal grounds makes it unlikely that he had any such designs. He was always careful to have a good case in law before he acted, and on this occasion there was an heiress to be considered. She was Count Philip's sister Margaret, the wife of the Count of Hainault, and she had a son to succeed her. By the time Philip Augustus returned to France Baldwin of Hainault had taken possession of the county of Flanders in right of his wife. The king did not, as far as we can tell, raise any objection, and in March 1192 he received Baldwin's homage for Flanders. If anyone had ambitions, it was the new count, for as early as 1198 he laid claim to Artois and to the part of Vermandois which had been surrendered at the Treaty of Amiens in 1186. His son, Baldwin X of Flanders, took up the claim on his succession, but without any success. He finally ceded Artois, the Amiénois, and the counties of Péronne and Saint-Quentin to the French crown by a treaty concluded at Péronne on 2 January 1200. However, Guines, Ardres, Lilliers and Richebourg were permanently detached from Artois by this treaty; Aire and Saint-Omer, also separated, were reunited to the province when the crown acquired them in 1212.

Philip had meanwhile come to a new agreement with Eleanora of Beaumont. In 1192, on payment of a *rachat* of 5000 gold marks, she was confirmed in her possession of Valois, and of Chauny, Ribemont, Ressons, Lassigny and Origny; she was also given the county of Saint-Quentin and annual rents from Péronne and Roye. Further, for a payment of 13,000 *livres tournois* and the remission of the *rachat* already mentioned, she renounced any title to the remainder of Vermandois and to the county of Amiens. She and her husband were to hold the lands ceded to her as fiefs, doing liege homage to the king, who was to inherit the lands if Eleanora died without children. Should Philip, on the other hand, leave no heir, then the countess was to resume the lands that she had abandoned. In the event, Matthew of Beaumont died in 1208 and his wife in 1213, leaving only collateral heirs, and Philip Augustus was able to take the last remnants of Valois and Vermandois into his own hands. A complex series of transactions (of which the account given above is only the barest outline) had thus augmented the royal domain by the Amiénois, Artois,

Vermandois and Valois — and all without violence and without leaving any loophole in law for a future counter-claim.

Flanders itself, stripped of its former accretions, now came into contact with the royal domain. Count Baldwin X, soon after his accession, went to the East, where he became ruler of the Latin Empire of Constantinople, and died in 1205 outside the walls of Adrianople. His heiresses in Flanders were two daughters, Joan and Margaret, who came under the guardianship of their uncle, Philip of Namur. Philip was a weak man, with interests of his own at stake, and readily became the liege vassal of the King of France, promising not to marry off his nieces without Philip Augustus' permission. In 1208 the king demanded, and secured, the direct wardship of the two young girls. In 1212 he gave the elder, Joan, in marriage to Ferrand of Portugal, a nephew of his own daughter-in-law Blanche of Castile. But before Ferrand and his young wife were able to take possession of Flanders, Prince Louis seized Aire and Saint-Omer, claiming that they had been his mother's property and had been unjustly detained by the Count of Flanders at Péronne in 1200. Ferrand had no option but to submit to this, and by an agreement at Lens on 25 February 1212 the lands were ceded to the prince.

It was a humiliating experience, which the new count did not forget, and which outweighed in his mind the fact that he owed his advancement to his kinship with the prince's wife. It was consequently not surprising that after some hesitation he let himself be drawn into the negotiations leading up to King John of England's great coalition of 1213 (which we shall discuss later). When Philip Augustus, aware of what was happening, invaded Flanders, Ferrand openly took the Angevin side — with disastrous consequences.

The French victories at La Roche-aux-Moines on 2 July and at Bouvines on 27 July 1214 destroyed the coalition. Ferrand was taken prisoner at Bouvines, and spent thirteen years as a captive in the Louvre palace. But he was not deprived of his fief, which in any case he held only as the husband of Countess Joan. His helpless wife was forced to come to a provisional agreement with the king on 24 October 1214, and to accept a certain degree of

royal supervision. In 1224 she was compelled to accept the jurisdiction of the king's court, and it was not until 1226 that she was
able to make her final peace with the new King Louis VIII.
Ferrand was then freed, at a price of 50,000 *livres parisis*, to be
paid in two instalments, the second of which was guaranteed by
the pledging of Lille, Douai and Sluys. He and his countess
became liege vassals of the king, their loyalty being assured by
the threat of excommunication and by an oath taken by the
knights and towns of the county, who promised aid and counsel
to the king as overlord, should the count and countess break faith.

Royal sovereignty was unchallenged in Flanders until Joan's
death in 1244. Count Ferrand was one of the few great feudatories
who gave the regent Blanche of Castile no trouble during the
minority of St. Louis. When the countess died, she was succeeded
by her sister Margaret, who had married Bouchard of Avesnes in
1212; by him she had two sons, John and Baldwin. On Bouchard's
death she married again; her second husband was William of
Dampierre, to whom she bore three sons and two daughters. The
validity of her first marriage — and in consequence the legitimacy
of her two elder sons — was open to some doubt, for Bouchard
had previously been ordained subdeacon. This awkward fact
became important after Margaret's succession to Flanders, for by
that date both her husbands were dead, and the question of her
inheritance loomed up. Her children, unable to agree, called on
St. Louis, the suzerain, to decide between them. In 1246, at
Amiens, the king pronounced in favour of William of Dampierre,
the eldest son of Margaret's second marriage. The children of her
first marriage were compensated; John of Avesnes, the elder, was
given the county of Hainault, which was detached from Flanders
for his benefit.

From the royal point of view, this award had more than strict
justice to commend it. The separation of Hainault (an imperial
fief) from Flanders removed the danger of a double allegiance,
and threw Flanders more decisively under French influence.
Further, it gave future counts of Flanders dangerous neighbours,
for the Avesnes family never abandoned their claim to the entire
inheritance of their mother. There was also the possibility that

Hainault might become, if not a French fief, at least an ally of the French crown. Philip the Fair actually achieved this in 1293; he even received the Count of Hainault's homage for the Ostrevent, a part of the county over which suzerainty had been previously undetermined.

French suzerainty over Flanders, unopposed after Bouvines, became still more evident after the award of 1246. The Dampierre family were driven to rely upon royal support against the claims of their Avesnes relations. That support had to be paid for, and as a result direct royal authority became more and more obvious. The development of a deliberate policy, directed towards under-mining the authority of the great vassals inside their fiefs, was powerfully aided in Flanders by the particular social conditions of the county. The prosperous Flemish industrial towns, products of a precocious economic growth, were the home of a rich urban patriciate, jealous of any attempt to limit its independence, and ready — as the counts of Flanders were — to appeal to the king when a dispute arose.

In such circumstances the Capetians were able to restrict the freedom of action of their Flemish vassals. They summoned all cases involving royal rights before the royal courts, and particu-larly before the highest court of all — the *Parlement*. All appeals to royal justice were received; and, by custom, in cases of appeal the appellant was removed from the jurisdiction of his immediate lord during the interval between the lodging of the appeal and the pronouncing of sentence, and came instead under the protection of the appellate authority. In this role of appellate judge, the French king was able to impose the use of the French language in the courts of Flanders when a royal agent was present, and to have the royal banner flown over towns under his temporary protection.

This precise and inexorable policy drove the counts of Flanders to resistance. Count Guy of Dampierre allied with another victim of the same policy, Edward I of England, Duke of Aquitaine, and came into open conflict with King Philip the Fair. But Edward could not do much for his ally in 1297, and abandoned him two years later. As a result Count Guy, with his two sons, Robert of Béthune and William of Crévecoeur, surrendered to Philip in

May 1300; all three were imprisoned. Flanders was not, however, annexed to the royal domain, but came under royal administration, to await the time when it could be returned to a count who would give proof of good behaviour. This is shown by the peace of Athis-sur-Orge (23 June 1305), which followed a series of conflicts in which the king had been opposed not so much by the other sons of Count Guy, who were still at liberty, as by the Flemish towns, which had become increasingly resentful of royal maladministration. By the peace Robert of Béthune, as heir to the deceased Guy, recovered the whole of Flanders. Philip the Fair contented himself with destroying the walls of the towns, and with an oath of fealty — renewable every five years — from all the inhabitants of the county; this oath contained an engagement not to enter into any alliance without the king's consent.

One territorial acquisition arose from the complicated financial provisions of the settlement. An agreement reached at Pontoise on 11 July 1312 commuted the annual payment of 20,000 *livres* which the count owed to the crown as compensation for his wrongdoing. In its place he ceded the castellanies of Lille, Douai and Béthune — the so-called *transport* of Flanders.

*   *   *   *

The most powerful feudal principality in southern France was the county of Toulouse. It had been isolated for two centuries from any direct contact with the royal domain, and seemed destined to be the last of the great fiefs to be absorbed by the crown. There had certainly been some faint signs of royal interest before the reign of Philip Augustus. Louis VII had been assiduous in building up friendships and loyalties within the boundaries of the principality, and the crown had for some time been securing new vassals — mostly ecclesiastical — along the routes leading towards Toulouse. Philip himself, towards the end of his reign, annexed the important county of Auvergne to the domain. He had acted on an appeal by the Bishop of Clermont, using the lord of Bourbon as instrument; Count Guy II had been brought to heel, and the suzerainty over his county, surrendered to the crown by Henry II of England at Azay-le-Rideau in June 1189, had been made effective. But even the final annexation of Auvergne hardly suggested that the crown was about to exert pressure on the county of Toulouse itself. In fact, an ecclesiastical crisis started the process before Philip's reign was out.

At the beginning of the thirteenth century, the county of Toulouse comprised a considerable territory. Besides the county proper, it included the duchy of Narbonne, Quercy, Rouergue, Agenais, Albigeois, the viscounty of Nîmes, and the Comtat Venaissin; its vassals included the Viscounts of Béziers and Carcassonne, the Count of Foix, and the lord of Montpellier. The ruling count was Raymond VI, a member of the old house of Saint-Gilles.

During the twelfth century, Manichaean doctrines, known to history under the name of Catharism, had won over a large proportion of the nobility of Languedoc and of the general population also. At the Council of Bourges (1163) Pope Alexander III had given a warning of what was happening; King Louis VII may have prompted him to do so. But it was not until after the Lateran Council of 1179 that the Church took more positive action. Then missions, recruited from the Cistercian Order, were sent into Languedoc. Their success, however, was very limited, and by the accession of Pope Innocent III it was clear that new steps were necessary.

Pope Innocent was determined to solve the problem. Papal legates were sent, St. Dominic and his companions preached and argued. But these efforts were inadequate, possibly because the nobility protected the Cathari and because Raymond VI was a friend of the opponents of the Church. Innocent therefore turned to force. The murder of the legate Peter of Castelnau in 1208 gave the opportunity, and a crusade was preached against the heretics of Languedoc.

Philip Augustus did not oppose this step, although he declined an invitation to take part. He pointed out, however, that a crusade against the Count of Toulouse himself would be unjustified unless he had first been convicted of heresy. Allegedly, Philip said: 'Condemn him as a heretic. Then, and only then, will you have the right to publish the sentence and to invite me, his

E

suzerain, to confiscate my vassal's lands in a legal manner.'
Despite these reservations, however, Philip accepted the action of
the Lateran Council of 1216, which deprived Raymond VI of his
lands and conferred them on Simon de Montfort. The only
exception made was the northern part of the county of Toulouse
proper, which was placed under custody for the count's young
son, Raymond VII. At an assembly at Melun in April 1216 Philip
formally accepted Simon de Montfort's homage for the conquered
lands.

When Simon was killed outside the walls of Toulouse early in
1218 the royal attitude changed. The war with John of England
was over, and Philip may well have felt more free to take positive
action in the south. So, when Amaury de Montfort, Simon's son
and heir, was in difficulties in 1219, threatened by Count Raymond
and his son, backed by something of a popular insurrection in
Languedoc, the king authorised his son, Prince Louis, to enter
the county of Toulouse with an army. Three years later Philip
Augustus sent 200 knights and 10,000 serjeants to help Amaury
against the menace of the new Count Raymond VII (who had
succeeded his father in 1221) and the Viscount of Carcassonne,
Raymond Trencavel, another victim of the crusade. On the other
hand, the king refused Amaury's proferred cession of Albigeois.

Louis VIII, who succeeded to the throne in 1223, had more
decided views. He realised that the cause of orthodoxy would be
lost in Languedoc unless the crown came to its rescue, and he
decided to support it with all his might, provided that his intervention could be made to furnish a profit. He was, in fact, looking
for an opportunity to establish royal authority in Languedoc on a
permanent basis.

In January 1226, at Paris, a papal legate excommunicated Count
Raymond VII, although he had made his submission and sought
absolution at Bourges in the preceding year. The Church confirmed the possession of Raymond's lands to the king, with the
right to hold them and to bequeath them to his successors.
Amaury de Montfort, for his part, surrendered all title to his
father's conquests, and his uncle, Gui de Montfort, confirmed
the cession. King Louis then took the Cross. He received from

the Church the normal crusader's indulgences and privileges for himself and his kingdom, and also the promise of a tenth from the revenues of the churches of France; this last was to be spread over five years.

It was further put on record that twenty-nine of the chief barons of France had advised the king in the Albigensian affair, and had promised to aid him faithfully in the enterprise.[1] Different constructions can be put on this document. It may have been a simple guarantee against baronial desertion; if so, it was to prove inadequate. It may equally well have been a precautionary measure to ensure the permanence of any royal conquests in the south. The king was proposing to seize the fief of one of his great vassals. The vassal in question, the Count of Toulouse, had been excommunicated, but only *after* making his submission; and he had never been declared a heretic. In these circumstances, could confiscation of his lands and goods by his suzerain be legal? To judge by his remark quoted above, Philip Augustus would not have thought so. But a different situation would arise if twenty-nine great barons were to counsel the king to proceed with the conquest of Toulouse. Confiscation would then take on something of the character of a judgment of peers in the king's court; it would, feudally speaking, become legal.

Louis invaded Languedoc with a large army, and as early as March 1226 submissions began to come in. They increased with the siege of Avignon and its fall on 9 September, despite the defection of some of the great vassals, who left the army on the completion of their normal forty days' service. The crusade became a mere military promenade, and the king was able to press on with the organisation of royal government in the conquered lands. He retained the administrative system set up by Simon de Montfort, and established a firm alliance with the local clergy. He died on his homeward journey north, at Montpensier, on 8 November 1226.

Capetian occupation of the county of Toulouse was thus a fact. The dynasty's legal title was less certain. In this instance an unconditional act of cession by the former proprietor did not

[1] *L.T.C.*, ii, pp. 68–9, no. 1742.

exist — and the evidence shows that the kings always set great store by such surrenders. With circumspection, Raymond VII need not have despaired of recovering his lands. Unfortunately for himself, he preferred to use force, and joined the baronial revolt against the regent Blanche of Castile. With considerable local support, he made some headway at first. But the papal legate, Cardinal Romano Frangipani, supported the regent, and secured the payment of the tenth granted in 1226. This provided the money needed to supply Imbert de Baujeu with forces for the defence of the royal lands in Languedoc. By the end of 1228 Raymond was suing for peace, and a treaty drawn up at Paris on 12 April 1229 finally settled the fate of Languedoc.[1]

The clauses of this treaty which affected the crown are of interest to us. Count Raymond acknowledged that he had done liege homage and sworn fealty to the king for the fiefs which were left to him. He further acknowledged that he had abandoned to the king all his other lands to the west of the Rhône (the seneschalcies of Beaucaire-Nîmes and Carcassonne-Béziers), as well as the suzerainty of a number of fiefs; these fiefs were now to be held directly from the crown. One of King Louis' brothers was to marry the count's daughter, Joan of Toulouse, who was to be given into the king's custody. She and her husband were to receive Toulouse and its bishopric[2] after Raymond's death; if she and her husband should die childless, Toulouse and the bishopric of Toulouse were to come to the king. Finally, should Raymond die without any legitimate child but Joan, then the remainder of his lands were to pass to her and her heirs.

This document, one of major importance, was the legal establishment of the royal conquest. By it the crown secured an unchallengeable title to the seneschalcies of Beaucaire and Carcassonne, and — of even greater importance — the possibility of a future annexation of the entire Toulouse fief.

After 1229 Blanche of Castile was careful to improve Raymond's position, and to protect him against an avaricious clergy. She obtained for him a postponement of his crusader's vow, and tried

---

[1] *L.T.C.*, ii, pp. 147–52, no. 1992.
[2] '*Tholosa et episcopatus Tholosanus erunt fratris domini Regis qui habebit filiam nostram.*'

unsuccessfully to have the marquisate of Provence, which had been given to the Church by the 1229 treaty, restored to him. But kindness was lost on the count. His attitude was ambiguous during the revolt of the dispossessed Raymond Trencavel in 1240, which seriously threatened Capetian authority in Languedoc. In 1242 he joined a new feudal coalition, which was supported by Henry III of England. The coalition, however, collapsed, and on 20 October 1242 Raymond was again seeking mercy from Louis IX. He was pardoned by the treaty of Lorris in January 1243, but only on condition that he executed a clause of the 1229 treaty which guaranteed his loyalty by an oath taken directly to the king by his rear-vassals. He also lost the suzerainty of the county of Foix, which passed under direct royal lordship.

Count Raymond died on 27 September 1249. His daughter Joan was his sole heiress. She had been married in 1236 or 1237 to Louis VIII's third son, Alphonse; since 1241 he had been Count of Poitiers and lord of part of Auvergne. Both he and his wife were on their way to Egypt with St. Louis' crusade when Count Raymond died.

The succession was an important matter. It involved the county of Toulouse, Albigeois (north of the river Tarn), Rouergue, the Comtat Venaissin (returned to Raymond in 1234), Agenais, and Quercy (in which royal authority had made important advances). Moreover Raymond's cartulary shows that since 1229 he had considerably increased his personal domain inside these fiefs by a policy of purchase.

Blanche of Castile, acting in the absence of her son, sent two knights, Gui and Hervé de Chevreuse, and a cleric, Philip, treasurer of Saint-Hilaire, to receive the inheritance in Alphonse's name. A long letter from these commissioners to their master survives,[1] describing in detail their actions and their difficulties. It has been correctly pointed out that seisin was taken in conformity with the treaty of 1229, and not under the terms of Raymond VII's will. Indeed, after his return from the east, Alphonse in 1251 had the will set aside, and took possession of the endowments

---

[1] E. Boutaric, *Saint Louis et Alphonse de Poitiers, Étude sur la réunion des provinces du Midi et de l'Ouest à la couronne* (Paris, 1870), pp. 69–77.

of a number of pious foundations provided for in it, being himself unwilling to give effect to the dead count's intentions.

For the remaining twenty years of his life, the new count conducted an effective personal administration of his own inheritance and the lands acquired through his marriage. The fortunate survival of his archives has enabled a scholar[1] to show clearly that his system and methods were identical with those of the crown. Alphonse's rule thus prepared the way for the day when the Capetians would assume direct control of the whole of the former principality of Toulouse.

St. Louis probably had this eventuality in mind when he concluded the treaty of Corbeil with James I of Aragon on 11 May 1258. By this treaty, he abandoned the suzerainty of Catalonia and Roussillon, which dated from the earliest Capetian period but had never been effective. In return, James renounced all claims over the county of Toulouse, and limited his rights in France to the lordship of Montpellier only.[2]

Count Alphonse and his wife died at Savona within three days of each other (21 and 24 August 1271), shortly after their return from the disastrous crusade to Tunis. By 5 October 1271 Guillaume de Cohardon, seneschal of Carcassonne, was taking seisin of their lands in the name of King Philip III, under the terms of the treaty of 1229. There was no resistance. After his return from Africa the king made a demonstration of force in Languedoc, and quickly brought to heel the counts of Foix and Armagnac, who tried to take the opportunity to recover their independence of action. The process of substituting the king for the dead count went slowly on until 1285; it was carried through with a circumspection which avoided any strain on a populace only too likely to associate this new rule with their memories of crusade and massacre.

Care was taken to ensure that the royal possession was firmly based in law. All possible claimants to a share in the inheritance of Alphonse and his wife had their cases examined and settled.

[1] E. Boutaric, *ibid.*
[2] Joan of Toulouse considered herself as the owner of the lands she had inherited from her father and gave them away by her will, the original of which is preserved in the *Archives Nationales* (J. 406, no. 4). Philippa of Lomagne was to receive Joan's lands in Albigeois, Agenais, Rouergue and Quercy. The will was quashed by sentence of the *Parlement* in 1274 (*Olim*, vol. ii, p. 55, no. v).

Philippa of Lomagne, a cousin of Countess Joan, to whom the latter had left what she considered as her personal inheritance,[1] was deprived of it by a decision of the *Parlement*, but indemnified. Charles of Anjou, Alphonse's brother, who laid claim to the dead prince's *apanage* of Poitiers and Auvergne, was confronted with another decision of the *Parlement* — that the possessions of the holder of an *apanage* who died without heir should return to the crown. The Papacy received the Comtat Venaissin, which Raymond VII had surrendered in 1229 and had taken back as a fief in 1234 from Pope Gregory X; there being no heir, the fief naturally escheated to the overlord. Lastly, the claims of the King of England to Agenais and Quercy were dealt with. Agenais had been part of the dowry given to Joan of England, the wife of Count Raymond VI, by her brother, King Richard I. It had been agreed at Paris in 1259, when St. Louis and King Henry III came to terms, that the territory should return to its original proprietor, the Duke of Aquitaine, should Alphonse and Joan die childless; this was in fact done, by a treaty concluded at Amiens in 1279. Edward I of England claimed Quercy on the same terms, but in this case it was decided in 1279 that there should be an inquest as to whether or not the province had been a part of Joan of England's dowry. In 1286 it was finally settled that Quercy should belong to the King of France, but should be burdened with an annual payment of 3000 *livres tournois* to the King of England.

The great principality of Toulouse thus fell into royal hands, thanks to a well-manipulated crusade and a convenient marriage. But it would be wrong to assume that this result had been planned from the start. It is quite conceivable that the marriage of Alphonse and Joan of Toulouse might have turned out to be the first step in the creation of a new feudal state in Languedoc, powerful enough to be a threat to the monarchy. Only the accident of their lack of heirs turned a potential danger into a source of additional strength. Once again, fortune was on the side of the Capetians.

* * * *

A fortunate marriage was also the decisive factor in bringing to

[1] *L.T.C.*, iii, pp. 405–8, no. 4411.

the Capetians another potentially dangerous fief, this time to the east of the royal domain: the counties of Champagne and Brie.[1] During the eleventh and twelfth centuries the royal possessions had been at times virtually encircled by those of the house of Champagne; the kings had been forced to take up a defensive attitude which on occasion verged on submission. This situation, however, began to change after the marriage of King Louis VII to Adela of Champagne. Succeeding kings found it possible to intervene in Champagne in new and altered circumstances. On the surface at least this was a peaceful offensive, with the apparent aim of helping the counts of Champagne in an increasingly difficult domestic situation. Underneath, however, it had a deeper purpose; the crown was aiming at bringing these great vassals into a real dependence.

Count Thibaud III of Champagne died in 1201, on the eve of his departure on crusade. He left his fief, consisting of the counties of Champagne and Brie, with their dependent fiefs, in the hands of his young Countess Blanche, the daughter of King Sancho VI of Navarre. She was expecting a child. The barons of Champagne, anxious to leave for the east, saw no particular danger in allowing the overlord, the King of France, to take a hand in the administration of the fief. At the end of May the countess was received as the liege-woman of the king at Sens. She promised not to remarry without his consent, and to hand over to his care her one daughter and her expected child. Philip Augustus, for his part, promised to bring up his cousin, and to give her in marriage, when she reached the age of twelve, with the consent of the queen-mother Adela of Champagne and ten named barons of Champagne. The promises were guaranteed by the king's receipt of the towns of Bray-sur-Seine and Montereau as security.

When the expected child, the future Count Thibaud IV, was born, his mother had to promise not to have him declared of age before he became 21. Further, when Thibaud was twelve years

---

[1] H. d'Arbois de Jubainville, *Histoire des ducs et des comtes de Champagne* (Paris, 1859–66), stops with the marriage of Joan of Navarre to King Philip the Fair. For events subsequent to this date a little-known *mémoire* by Secousse (*Mémoire sur l'union de la Champagne et de la Brie à la couronne de France*, in *Mémoires de Littérature tirés des registres de l'Académie des Inscriptions*, vol. xvii (1743), pp. 295–315) is useful.

old, he and his mother, by a new treaty (21 November 1213), swore to serve the king faithfully; the promise was guaranteed by an oath taken by the barons of Champagne. Philip Augustus was able, as a result, to exercise unchallenged authority in the fief until his death.

After the old king's death Thibaud IV attempted to shake off royal control; his efforts became more serious during the regency of Blanche of Castile, which followed the death of Louis VIII. He was involved in all the intrigues against the regent, and joined all the feudal coalitions. But he was a better poet than a politician, and was in any case hampered by a platonic affection for the regent. He also had ambitions in Navarre, which was bequeathed to him by his grandfather Sancho VI in 1234. He was further troubled by opposition to his title to Champagne from his two cousins, Queen Alix of Cyprus and Philippine, the wife of the adventurous Érard de Brienne, who were daughters of his uncle, Count Henry II. It was the regent who eventually rescued Thibaud from his difficulties, and saved him when his former allies in the coalition of 1230 turned on him as a traitor. She settled the succession to Champagne in his favour, and advanced him money to buy off the claim of the Queen of Cyprus. The debt was repaid by the cession to the crown of the counties of Blois, Chartres and Sancerre, and the viscounty of Châteaudun, which thus became direct fiefs.

Count Thibaud was succeeded in 1253 by Thibaud V, who was also forced to rely upon royal support against a rival claimant, Count John of Brittany, who claimed in the name of his wife Blanche of Champagne, the daughter of Thibaud IV. The young Thibaud V and his mother Margaret of Bourbon (the third wife of Thibaud IV) were driven to become close supporters of St. Louis. Thibaud himself married the king's daughter, Isabella, and his brother, Henry the Fat, who later succeeded him, married the king's niece, Blanche of Artois. Neither brother lived long, Thibaud dying on his return from the crusade of Tunis, on 4 December 1270, and Henry on 22 July 1274. The succession to the kingdom of Navarre and the fief of Champagne then passed to Henry's daughter, the young Joan of Navarre.

E2

There were numerous suitors for the hand of so important an heiress. Her mother, Blanche of Artois, promised her first to a son of the King of England, then to a son of the King of Aragon, but eventually — at Orléans in May 1275 — concluded an agreement which favoured the French crown. In it we can detect the handiwork of the counsellors of the dead St. Louis, still in power under his son. By the agreement, Blanche surrendered the guardianship of Navarre to the King of France. She and her new husband, Edmund, the brother of Edward I of England (whom she married immediately after the agreement), were to administer Champagne until the heiress Joan came of age or was married. Joan was to marry a son of Philip III; as she and her future husband were related within the prohibited degrees, a papal dispensation would be necessary.

The name of the countess's future husband was not specified, possibly from fear of arousing local resentments in Champagne. But we may surmise that the royal advisers had in mind the heir to the throne himself, Louis, the eldest son of the king and his late wife Isabella of Aragon. The Papacy certainly suspected this and had no wish to see the power of the crown increased in this way. When Pope Gregory X gave the requested dispensation, therefore, he gave it in favour of the king's second son, Prince Philip.

Events made the precaution useless. Within a year Prince Louis was dead, and the future Philip the Fair thus became the heir-apparent to the throne, in addition to being the betrothed of Joan of Navarre. The marriage took place in 1284, when the countess reached the permitted age. On 17 May of the same year Blanche of Artois and her husband relinquished their guardianship; Blanche received 60,000 *livres tournois* in compensation and had a considerable dower confirmed to her. Thereafter Prince Philip styled himself King of Navarre and Count of Champagne and Brie. In the following year he succeeded his father as King of France.

The counties of the Champagne fief were not, however, annexed to the royal domain. Philip ceased to use the title of count when he became king, while his wife continued to call herself Countess of Champagne and Brie, and also Queen of Navarre. The king acted as lord of Champagne, but he was always

careful to have his acts confirmed by his wife, under the style of
Countess Palatine of Champagne and Brie. Philip, legally, was
acting as had Blanche of Artois' husband, as administrator of his
wife's lands on her behalf.

Joan's death on 4 April 1305 did not change the position. Her
eldest son, Prince Louis, inherited his mother's property, and in
his turn styled himself King of Navarre and Count Palatine of
Champagne and Brie. When he came of age, documents concerning the administration of Champagne were issued in his name,
and that of his father no longer appeared. After he became king in
1314 the fief was again united to the royal domain, but for his
lifetime only. As events were to show, the annexation was not
necessarily permanent.

King Louis X died on 5 June 1316. He left a daughter Joan —
of doubtful legitimacy after the disgrace of her mother, Margaret
of Burgundy — and a young widow, Clémence of Hungary,
whose expected child would, it was hoped, be an heir to the throne.
In expectation of a long minority, Count Philip of Poitiers, the
brother of the dead king, established his right to be regent of the
kingdom. But the young heir, the baby John I, died only five days
after his birth on 14 November 1316. His half-sister Joan, the
daughter of Louis X and Margaret of Burgundy, became the
heiress to the crowns of France and Navarre, and to the counties
of Champagne and Brie. This time a final annexation of Champagne to the royal domain seemed imminent.

The regent Philip, however, displaced the legitimate heiress,
and had himself crowned at Rheims on 9 January 1317. The last
two Capetian rulers may have been good fathers, good sons, good
husbands, and perhaps even good brothers, but they certainly
qualified for the title of wicked uncles. Joan of Champagne
therefore lost the crown of France. The barons of Champagne
were not prepared to agree that she should lose Navarre,
Champagne and Brie also. They may well have been fortified in
this opinion by the consideration that a countess aged seven
would be a less troublesome lord than the King of France. In the
upshot, they expressed their views by what the chroniclers called
the *commoçion et rebellion des nobles de Champagne* — a last

flare-up of feudal anarchy. The fate of the revolt was that of most similar feudal outbreaks — a complete failure.

Philip V might well have made use of the agreements reached when he became regent, which authorised him — should King John I die — to retain Champagne and Brie. He thought it wiser to obtain a title by negotiation with the young heiress herself, or rather with her tutors, her grandmother, Duchess Anne of Burgundy, and her uncle, Duke Eudes IV of Burgundy. By a treaty on 27 March 1318 Joan's rights to the counties of Champagne and Brie were renounced in return for an annual rent of 15,000 *livres tournois* and a cash payment of 50,000 *livres*. However, one article of the agreement declared that the countess's title to Champagne and Brie would revive should Philip die with 'it a male heir.

When the king died on 2 January 1322 he left only daughters to succeed him. His brother, Charles of La Marche, overturned their claims and seized the throne. Joan of Champagne, who had married Count Philip of Évreux on 18 June 1318, then claimed Champagne and Brie in terms of the treaty of 1318. King Charles protracted the resulting negotiations, and a new agreement was not reached until 1328, at the very end of his reign. By this the annual rent of 15,000 *livres tournois* was raised to 15,000 *livres parisis*, and the cash payment to 70,000 *livres tournois* (from 50,000). Joan's final renunciation was not made until 1335, and the two counties, which had been under effective royal control since 1285, were not annexed definitively to the domain until November 1361.

The instances which we have examined in detail show how the Capetians set about these great annexations. They did not proceed by conquest, but by a slow insinuation of royal authority, losing no opportunity to use the rights arising from their dual position as kings and overlords, creating new opportunities where none had existed, and following a careful policy of marriage-alliances. The whole process was carried through with infinite patience, and in the end wore out all resistance. The final achievement was to secure the legal titles to confirm a *de facto* possession which was in some cases almost a century old.

But the dynasty did not set out to annex every great fief, as the history of two other principalities — Burgundy and Brittany — will prove.

*   *   *   *

The dukes of Burgundy were descended from Robert, brother of King Henry I, which probably explains much of the good relations which normally existed between the two houses. The serious difficulties which faced the dukes in their attempt to control a powerful baronage may also have had something to do with their reluctance to set the crown against them, and with their anxiety to use in their own support the powers of intervention which feudal custom allowed to their suzerains. The duchy was the only great fief over which royal suzerainty was never contested. The dukes regularly did homage and performed their due services to the king. They appear to have been the first great vassals to be prepared to appear in the king's court to have their differences with their own vassals settled there; no doubt they were often happy to have the support of their royal cousins.

As a result, the rise of royal authority had an increasing impact on Burgundy. For all that, Duke Hugh III was rash enough, on one occasion, to join the enemies of Philip Augustus. The king immediately took the side of one of the most troublesome and recalcitrant Burgundian vassals, the lord of Vergy. In 1186 a royal army entered Burgundy, took Châtillon-sur-Seine, and made prisoner the duke's heir. Hugh speedily made his peace with his king, and accompanied him shortly afterwards on crusade, to take his part in the complicated royal manoeuvres against Richard of England.

Thereafter the dukes of Burgundy were always loyal vassals of the crown. Royal judicial and financial power made itself more and more felt in the duchy. There was little opposition, as long as the forms of ducal authority were respected. Even Philip the Fair's acquisition in 1295 of the imperial county of Burgundy — better known as Franche-Comté — did not alarm Duke Robert II unduly. More accurately, what apprehensions the duke did have were quickly removed by the gift of an annual rent of 1000 *livres*, and a promise that Prince Philip (who became Count of Burgundy by his marriage) would do homage for those parts of the county which were held as fiefs from the dukes of Burgundy. Later, the king's eldest son was betrothed to Duke Robert's daughter, and the duke, in January 1297, undertook the custody of the county on the king's behalf.

As is well known, the last years of the reign of Philip the Fair and the short reign of his eldest son saw a general movement of protest amongst the nobles of the kingdom. It was directed against royal encroachment on the rights and privileges of the noble class, and gives an interesting indication of the extent to which royal authority had penetrated into the duchy of Burgundy. A protest against the action of the crown was natural enough in the domain; equally, any agitation in a great fief should, on the face of matters, have been directed against its lord. But the movement in Burgundy was not a protest against ducal rule. When an assembly of the Burgundian league met at Dijon on 31 March 1315, and 110 nobles appeared, together with the representatives of 18 abbeys, 11 chapters and 11 towns, it was against the crown that they took action. The two *Chartes aux Bourguignons* of April and May 1315 were secured from King Louis X. Even without a detailed study of these documents, it is clear, from the demands made and the answers given, that the king's power had been almost absolute in the duchy. The charters, indeed, show that the complaints were almost identical with those of the nobles of the royal domain, and that the Burgundians looked to the king rather than to the duke for redress of their grievances; the duke was no longer considered competent to prevent excesses of government in his own fief.

Understandably enough, the Capetians made no attempt to disrupt the territorial integrity of the duchy of Burgundy. There would have been little point in attempting to annex to the royal domain a great fief which the king could already treat as a part of his own estates; what made the situation even more favourable was that the holder of the fief behaved more as a royal lieutenant than a great independent noble.

Shortly before the first *Charte aux Bourguignons*, Louis X granted another ordinance at Saint-Germain-en-Laye. It was given at the request of the Duke of Brittany, and has been described as similar in character to the provincial charters granted to the leagues of the nobility of the royal domain.[1] But there was one significant difference. This ordinance — of March 1315 — was, in form at least, given at the request of the duke, who presented the complaints of his vassals to the king. As Artonne emphasises, 'the duke and the king were the only two parties concerned'. Although the undertakings given by the king were very similar to those contained in the provincial charters, and in many cases identical, the difference is still important.

It would be dangerous, however, to infer from this one fact that Brittany had escaped the fate of the other great fiefs in the thirteenth century, and had remained unaffected by the growth in royal power. It is certainly true that the Capetians had to wait a long time before they could make their influence felt in this remote land, which throughout its history has always been resentful of outside supervision. By the treaty of Gisors of 1113, Louis VI had abandoned direct overlordship of the county of Brittany to Henry I of England, Duke of Normandy. At no time was the crown able in Brittany, any more than in Burgundy, to develop the technique of territorial dismemberment. Despite all these facts, however, the Capetians were able eventually to make their sovereignty effective.

Even after the surrender at Gisors, the kings never completely lost interest in Brittany. Only ten years later, in 1123, Louis VI confirmed the Carolingian privileges of the bishopric of Nantes, proclaimed its *libertas*, and declared that the bishop owed the same services to the king as did other royal bishops.[2] For part of his reign Louis VII supported the claim of the Viscount of Porhoet to the county, and so maintained a local centre of opposition to the expanding power of the English kings.

The marriage of Henry II's son Geoffrey to Constance, the daughter of Count Conan, made English rule effective in Brittany, and put severe restraints on the turbulent local feudalists. In such

[1] A. Artonne, *Le mouvement de 1314 et les chartes provinciales de 1315* (Paris, 1912), p. 48.

[2] Dom Morice, *Histoire ecclésiastique et civile de la Bretagne* (Paris, 1750), preuves, vol. i, pp. 544–7.

a situation it was easy for Philip Augustus to pose as the champion of Breton liberties when, after the death of Geoffrey, he took the part of Constance and her son Arthur against Henry II and Richard I. But this was purely a political move, as was demonstrated when Arthur claimed the crown of England in succession to his uncle Richard. Philip at first supported the claim, but then abandoned Arthur at the peace of Le Goulet on 22 May 1200; by this Arthur was left in possession of Brittany only, to be held as a fief of his uncle King John. It was not until two years later that Philip was able to secure his real objective. Then John's disinheritance by the royal court, and the seizure of his possessions, enabled the king to confer Brittany on Arthur as a royal fief. The county thus returned under direct royal lordship, and the treaty of Gisors was set aside.

The next step came when Arthur was murdered by his uncle in April 1203. The heiress to Brittany was his sister Eleanor, the only surviving child of Geoffrey and Constance. But Eleanor was at Bristol in England, in the wardship of her uncle King John, who claimed the right to administer her inheritance as guardian. To recognise her right to Brittany would be to deliver the county to the King of England — which was desired neither by the Breton nobles nor by the King of France. However, Eleanor's mother Constance, after the annulment of what had been virtually a forced remarriage to an English earl, Ranulf of Chester, had taken a third husband, the Poitevin Guy of Thouars. She bore him several daughters before her death in 1201. An assembly of Breton lords and prelates at Vannes, in 1203, declared that Eleanor's captivity invalidated her right of succession, and set in her place her half-sister Alix, the eldest of the daughters of Constance and Guy of Thouars. Her father was given the wardship of the fief; in 1206 he was involved in pro-English intrigues amongst the Poitevin barons, and Philip took the government of Brittany into his own hands.

The king's first intention was to marry the heiress Alix to a Breton lord, Henry of Penthièvre, but eventually he gave her hand to a member of the royal family, Peter of Dreux, great-grandson of Louis VI — better known to history as Peter

Mauclerc. On 27 January 1213 Peter did liege homage to the king for Brittany; the formula used stated explicitly that, should the new count fail in his duty to the king, then his vassals would be bound to take the suzerain's side against him.[1] Brittany thus found itself in a situation similar to that of Burgundy, governed by a member of the royal house, and Philip Augustus may well have imagined that the new count would be drawn to the crown by ties of both blood and gratitude. Events were to prove him wrong.

Peter Mauclerc had enough to do in establishing his authority in his county to cause any trouble before the death of Louis VIII. But the regency of Blanche of Castile gave him an opportunity to show exactly how far the bonds of blood and gratitude constrained him, and to show also the extent of his ambitions. He was involved in all the rebellious feudal coalitions; he did homage to Henry III of England for Brittany in 1229, and supported him against his own rightful lord. All his adventures came to nothing, and eventually he had to make his final submission in November 1234. When his son, Count John I the Red, came of age in 1237 Peter had to relinquish the government of Brittany; he went East and died there.

John I (1237–86), John II (1286–1305), Arthur II (1305–12) and John III (1312–41) were all obedient vassals of the French crown. They were sufficiently adroit to be able to retain their honour of Richmond in England, which the rulers of Brittany had possessed since 1156. But their loyalty to the Capetians was sufficiently unquestioned for Philip the Fair to confer the rank of duke on John II in 1297, and to admit him as one of the peers of France; previous rulers of the province had borne no higher title than count. The ordinance of 1315 shows that, in fact, this loyalty allowed the king to intervene as freely in Brittany as in Burgundy.

So, without any need for actual conquest, the crown had reached a position which enabled it to treat both Burgundy and Brittany as if they were parts of the royal domain. By observing certain formalities and making certain arrangements, the king could obtain service in men and money from both duchies whenever he required it. His appellate justice was admitted

[1] *L.T.C.*, i, p. 387, no. 1033.

without difficulty inside each fief. The two great feudatories showed themselves to be faithful vassals, took their full part in important decisions, and gave tangible proof of their loyalty when the occasion arose.

Their examples demonstrate clearly why the Capetians did not, even when they had the opportunity, follow a uniform policy towards the great fiefs of France. They help to explain why all fiefs were not annexed, and why those that were annexed tended to be given out again to members of the royal family. And certainly the results were not unimpressive. When dukes of Burgundy and Brittany acted as (and were sometimes even called) royal lieutenants, and when the principality of Toulouse returned to the crown on the death of Alphonse — then the concept of a feudal monarchy did not appear unworkable. With loyal and devoted members in possession of every fief — by no means an impossible situation — then the feudal bond might well be sufficient to unite the entire kingdom, at least as far as the age understood unity.

The dangers inherent in the idea had not shown themselves clearly by 1328. The Capetians saw only its advantages, and above all the assistance it gave in dealing with recalcitrant local loyalties. But a warning of these dangers had already been given. The history of the one great fief that remains to be considered, the lands of the house of Anjou, had already shown the perils of a system of government built on feudal rights and loyalties.

8
The Lands of the House of Anjou

The reduction of the Flemish principality, the acquisition of Champagne and Languedoc, and the peaceful penetration of the duchies of Burgundy and Brittany were all vital steps towards the territorial unification of France. Before any of them could be accomplished it was necessary to remove the danger — at least in its more acute form — presented by the existence in western France of the great conglomeration of fiefs controlled by the Angevin kings of England.

The power of the House of Anjou had been founded in the eleventh century by Fulk Nerra and Geoffrey Martel. It had been firmly consolidated in the twelfth by Fulk the Young and Geoffrey the Fair. In 1127 Fulk the Young, Count of Anjou, Maine, and Touraine, married his son Geoffrey the Fair to Matilda, widow of the Emperor Henry V and daughter and heiress to King Henry I, who had ruled England since 1100 and Normandy since 1106. When Stephen of Blois, Henry I's nephew, forestalled Matilda and seized the throne of England in 1135, Geoffrey the Fair pressed his wife's claim to Normandy, and after a confused and protracted struggle got himself installed Duke of Normandy at Rouen on 19 January 1144. When he died in September 1151, Geoffrey left his son Henry Plantagenet a vast principality made up of the best organised fiefs in the French kingdom — Anjou, Maine, Touraine, and Normandy.

In May 1152 Henry Plantagenet married Eleanor of Aquitaine, whose marriage to King Louis VII had just been annulled. Eleanor brought her new husband the inheritance left her by her father, Duke William X of Aquitaine. Her heritage comprised the duchies of Guyenne and Gascony; the counties of Poitiers, Saintes, and Bordeaux; and the overlordship of the viscounties of

Thouars and Châtellerault, the lordships of Mauléon, Parthenay, and Lusignan in Poitou, the lordships of Châteauroux and Issoudun in Berry, the counties of La Marche and the Auvergne, the viscounties of Limoges, Turenne, and Ventadour in the Limousin, the counties of Angoulême, Périgord, Fézensac, Armagnac, Astarac, Pardiac, Comminges, and Bigorre, and the viscounties of Béarn, Oloron, and Gabardan (with its dependencies the viscounties of Lomagne, Dax, Labourd (Bayonne), and La Soule). The marriage also allowed Eleanor's new husband to claim the county of Toulouse in her name. This is what Louis VII had done in 1141. For Eleanor, through her mother Philippa of Toulouse, was a direct descendant of Count William IV of Toulouse, whose inheritance had passed to his younger brother Raymond of Saint-Gilles, overriding the rights of the elder branch of the family.

Thus in the west of the French kingdom there had arisen a principality stretching from the Channel to the Pyrenees and from the Atlantic to the Rhône Valley. Moreover, Stephen of Blois, Matilda's successful rival for the throne of England, died on 25 October 1154, having previously recognised Henry Plantagenet as his heir. Hence Henry, who was already Duke of Normandy and Aquitaine, and Count of Anjou, Maine, and Touraine, became King of England; and in 1158 Conan, the legitimate heir to the county of Nantes in Brittany, resigned his fief into Henry's hands. The county of Nantes, commanding the mouth of the Loire, was the gateway of Brittany. Possession of it had been withheld from Conan since 1156 by its hostile baronage.

The 'Angevin Empire' created by these means was a formidable power. The Capetians had only one instrument for detaching and absorbing those parts of it which lay within the kingdom of France — their rights of suzerainty and sovereignty. The King of England was the French king's vassal for his continental lands, owing him the homage and services of his French duchies and counties. He was justiciable in the royal court of France for any breach of feudal custom. Infringements of its complex rules inevitably occurred and played into the French king's hands. Time was on the side of the Capetians: both time past — for the dynasty had a tradition two hundred years old, and its disappearance was inconceivable; and time to come — for the Capetians could afford to wait, while their Angevin rivals could not. The crown of France might be weak; but it was indivisible. The Angevin Empire was a collection of fiefs which luck had brought together under the rule of a single family, and which luck and the laws of inheritance might again split up. Henry II was king in England, but in Anjou, Maine, and Touraine he was no more than one of the great vassals of the crown, and in Aquitaine he was merely the Duchess Eleanor's husband and the administrator of her property. Eleanor survived her husband, and until her death at the age of eighty on 31 March 1204 she retained a voice in the policies in which her marriage had involved her great inheritance. Her relations with Henry, a husband of notorious infidelity, were by no means harmonious; and the very extent of the lands of which she would one day dispose by will gave her considerable influence over her sons, which she used in a manner often displeasing to Henry.

The conflict between the Capetians and the House of Anjou lasted for nearly a century. This first 'Hundred Years' War' has already been fully dealt with by several eminent historians,[1] and there is no point in recounting its course in the present work. It will only be necessary to explain how the Capetians gradually succeeded in breaking up the Angevin continental empire and annexing the greater part of it to the crown. They employed methods they had been using ever since William the Conqueror had added a foreign kingdom to his duchy of Normandy. They played on the deep differences between the two halves of the Anglo-Norman state. They exploited the family quarrels over the possession of England and Normandy which broke out whenever a Norman king grew old or died. And they made effective use of their suzerainty.

Henry II had married Eleanor without asking Louis VII's permission. As feudal suzerain the King of France had the

[1] Meticulous accounts for the period 1183–1226 are to be found in the works of Cartellieri and Petit-Dutaillis. The latter has published an illuminating synthesis of the whole conflict in *Histoire Générale: Histoire du Moyen Âge*, ed. G. Glotz, vol. iv, part 2, pp. 127–63.

wardship of the daughters and widows of his vassals, who could not marry or remarry without his consent. And King Louis, declaring Henry to be guilty of violating feudal custom, summoned him to the royal court to answer for his disobedience. When Henry neglected the summons, the royal court pronounced his property forfeit as that of a rebel vassal.[1] But there were difficulties in the path of executing the sentence. Louis failed to give vigorous leadership to the feudal coalition he had organised; and in August 1154 the king made a treaty with his rival, under which he renounced the title of Duke of Aquitaine (which he had been using conjointly with that of King of France), gave back the only two castles he had been able to capture, and accepted an indemnity of 2000 *livres*. There was no longer any question of trying to enforce the sentence of confiscation pronounced by the royal court.

A few years later Louis VII tried again, with only partial success, to stop the aggrandisement of Henry II. In May 1159 Henry invaded the Toulousain, which he was claiming in right of his wife. Count Raymond V appealed to King Louis, who negotiated for the calling off of the Angevin attack. But Henry and his army pressed on with their campaign, and Louis came in person to his vassal's assistance and heroically joined Raymond in the threatened city of Toulouse. The move succeeded. Henry recalled in time that he was Louis' vassal and withdrew, not daring to besiege his suzerain. By exercising his suzerainty, the King of France had administered an important check to the King of England. The following year Louis VII had to give up supporting Raymond V. In 1173 the count did liege homage to Richard, third son to Henry II and by now Duke of Aquitaine; and the county of Toulouse remained a feudal dependency of the

---

[1] Henry II's condemnation by the Court of France was accepted by Luchaire (*Lavisse*, vol. iii, part 1, pp. 29–30) and Kate Norgate (*England under the Angevin Kings* (London, 1887), i, 393–4), but questioned by Lot (*Fidèles ou vassaux?*, pp. 205–12). It is true that the delays necessary for the citations which preceded the assembly of the court could not be respected, but the citation itself presents no difficulty; Lot does not deny the presence of the great vassals at the royal court at the end of June; and it is a fact that they set out on campaign in the king's company. It would be surprising if there had not been even the semblance of condemning the great vassal against whom the king was mounting his expedition. The interpretation accepted by Lot of the words *defecit a justicia*, used by the author of the *Historia gloriosi regis Ludovici*, is perhaps a little over-subtle.

duchy of Aquitaine until 1202. But all that did not matter much, as a clause inserted into the homage reserved the fealty due to the King of France and (rather platonically) affirmed the superior status of the king in the county of Toulouse. Thus the royal rights were safeguarded for the future.

It was also his position as suzerain which gave Louis VII the chance of interfering in and inflaming the quarrels which raged in the Angevin family. This was an effective means of weakening his great antagonist. Henry II and Eleanor produced a large family, and reared four of their sons to the age at which custom demanded that they should be provided for. Their eldest son Henry was granted Normandy in October 1160 and was associated with his father on the throne of England in 1170. Richard was given Aquitaine in 1169 and Geoffrey Brittany in 1175. John, the youngest child of Henry and Eleanor, was not old enough to be entrusted with any estates until the very last years of his father's reign, and by the time he came of age all the available lands had been given away. As Duke of Normandy, Duke of Aquitaine, Count of Poitiers, the sons of Henry II came to perform homage to the King of France and became his men. It was in vain that Henry II sought to utilise the Norman procedure of *pariage* to maintain the unity of his continental territories in favour of his eldest son, the 'Young King' Henry. (Under *pariage* the eldest son succeeded to all the heritable property and was alone answerable for it to the suzerain; each of his brothers received a share, but held it of him). This device could not be put into full operation in Aquitaine, which was not part of Henry's heritage but Eleanor's. And when she granted it to Richard, he owed homage not to his father or his eldest brother, but to the King of France. The Young King Henry had done homage as Duke of Normandy to Louis VII in October 1160. When he repeated his homage in 1170, it was made to embrace Anjou, Maine, and Brittany as well. At the same time Richard did homage to Louis for Aquitaine.

It is true that in 1174 Henry II compelled his sons to perform homage to him after their rebellion, but this new homage did not necessarily annul their homages to the King of France. Henry II himself had done homage to Louis VII in 1151 and again in 1169, and was to perform it yet again to Louis' successor, Philip Augustus, in 1180. Thus throughout the conflict between Louis VII and Henry II the French king's suzerainty was affirmed and recognised. This did not save Louis from defeats at his vassal's hands. Nevertheless, to judge from the Toulouse affair in 1159, Louis' suzerainty occasionally cramped Henry's style, and put him in the wrong in the eyes of contemporaries, including the barons of his continental fiefs. To play the rebel vassal was hardly prudent for a king when many of his own vassals were rebelliously inclined. It was not that the idea of rebellion itself shocked feudal society. On the contrary, it was one of the legitimate courses open to a vassal needing to safeguard his rights against the encroachments of his suzerain. But in the disputes between Louis VII and Henry II, Henry was the law-breaker as well as the vassal in revolt. For his rebelliousness against an impeccable suzerain there could be no justification.

It may be objected that Louis VII was constantly intriguing with Eleanor of Aquitaine and with Henry II's sons. But after all Eleanor, as Duchess of Aquitaine, was herself a royal vassal. Two of Henry's sons had done homage to Louis. Another, Geoffrey, by dint of his father's vassalage, was the French king's rear-vassal. And the king had, as suzerain, not merely the right but the duty to concern himself with the welfare and harmony of his great vassal's family, to ensure that a proper settlement was made on the sons. It would be unfair to accuse Louis of hypocrisy; nor did Henry ever complain that the French king was making trouble in his family. Louis' own grievances against Henry were many and varied, and Henry never made a serious effort to deny their validity.

Thus from 1154 to 1180 Henry II had the appearance of a vassal engaged in unjustifiable revolt against his suzerain. This line of conduct undermined his own position. It constantly reminded the baronage of the Angevin fiefs that the King of France was Henry's suzerain — if only because his suzerainty was so often invoked. And it helped to prevent the fusion of the individual elements of the Angevin empire on the continent. Provincial separatism, already too strong for Angevin rule to subdue, was reinforced.

Nevertheless, the reign of Louis VII saw no Capetian territorial expansion at Angevin expense. On the contrary, the French Vexin, which Louis had named in 1159 as his daughter Margaret's dowry against her forthcoming marriage to the Young King Henry, was seized by Henry II long before the marriage had been consummated. But Louis cannot fairly be said to have had the worst of the conflict with his vassal. He admittedly encountered setbacks, but they did not detract from his position as suzerain, nor did Henry take advantage of them to escape the implications of his vassal status. Louis handed on the French crown to his successors with its rights unimpaired. Only the appropriate opportunity was needed to make them highly effective. Philip Augustus was to see it and take it.

Philip's policy towards the Angevin kings of his day underlines the importance of law in this contest between the French crown and its great vassal. Between Philip's accession in 1180 and Henry II's death in 1189 the relations between suzerain and vassal were unchanged, except that the suzerain was now an unscrupulous young man, while his prematurely ageing vassal grew ever more irascible with the years. To begin with Philip profited from Henry's loyalty. Early in his reign, first his kinsmen of the House of Champagne, then a coalition of the northern and eastern barons ranged themselves against him. Henry stood aloof. Had he intervened on the side of Philip's foes, the French monarchy's plight would have been desperate.

Henry II got small thanks for his loyalty, for Philip upheld the cause of his sons. The Young King Henry died on 11 June 1183, and Geoffrey on 19 August 1186, but Richard was still left to claim a suzerain's support from Philip, who accompanied him to the tragic meeting with Henry at Bonmoulins on 18 November 1188, where the English king was requested to enfeoff Richard — who already had Aquitaine — with Poitou, Touraine, Maine, and Anjou, and to recognise him as his heir by making his barons take an oath to him. Richard's fear was that he would be passed over for the succession to the throne of England in favour of John, and would be left with nothing but Aquitaine. Henry II rejected Philip's request, and Richard thereupon flung himself on his knees before the French king, clasped his hands, and in a loud voice proclaimed himself Philip's vassal for Normandy, Poitou, Anjou, Maine, Berry, and the Toulousain, and called upon Philip to help him make good his rights. The scene, which Richard and Philip had doubtless rehearsed beforehand, throws a clear light on the French king's position. Richard's request affirmed Philip's suzerainty over the Angevin lands and his right to regulate the succession to them; and it provided a justification for Philip's intervention in Henry's family affairs.

The intervention did not go unrewarded. When Henry II capitulated at Ballan on 4 July 1189, he renounced the suzerainty of the Auvergne, the restoration of which to the crown had been vainly claimed in the past by Louis VII. Henry also gave up the lordships of Graçay and Issoudun. The House of Capet had made its first territorial acquisition at the expense of the House of Anjou.

Henry II died of grief on 6 July 1189. Philip II now seems to have conceived a savage hatred for the new King of England, Richard. Whatever his reasons — and they remain obscure — the result was an abandonment of the policy which until then had served the Capetians so well. Philip ceased to put himself forward as the champion of the rule of law. He broke his own solemn engagements to Richard. And he violated not only feudal law but also canon law, which declared the lands of a vassal who had gone on crusade exempt from attack by his suzerain.

Philip's behaviour profited him little. Richard returned from the captivity in which he had been kept in violation of all existing conventions, and took a terrible revenge on the felonious King of France. Only his death at the siege of the castle of Chalus on 6 April 1199 saved Philip Augustus and, it seems, brought him to his senses. Philip now returned for good to the old Capetian policy of making the law his principal ally — the policy of judicial conquest.

Circumstances favoured the change. The death of Richard without a direct heir had raised the sort of problem in which a suzerain invariably had a voice. Two of Richard's kinsmen had claims on his inheritance. The better and arguably the only true claim was that of Arthur, whose parents were Constance of Brittany and Henry II's son Geoffrey, a younger brother of Richard's. Geoffrey was dead, and his claim on the Angevin inheritance had been replaced by Arthur's. The other claimant was John, whom Richard had created Count of Mortain and Lord of Ireland, and who could claim a closer relationship to the *de cujus* whether this was taken to be Richard or Henry II.

The English barons, under the influence of Henry II's faithful counsellor William Marshal, decided in favour of John, who was created Duke of Normandy at Rouen on 25 April 1199 and crowned King of England at Westminster on 27 May of the same year. The reasons for their choice are obscure. The official explanation was apparently that Arthur's youth and the influence upon him of King Philip's 'felonious counsel' tipped the scales in favour of John. It is conceivable, however, that the selection of John marked a reaction among the English barons against the excessive preoccupation of their previous kings with their continental possessions. John had never held extensive territories on the continent, and the barons seem to have assumed that he would be unlikely to cling so tenaciously to the Angevin patrimony across the Channel or to demand their services so importunately for its defence against the King of France. The artificial union brought about by Henry II, just strong enough to hold together in his own lifetime, was proving to be a brittle thing in the hands of his heirs. The insularity of the English barons, and their lack of enthusiasm for the continental territories, made a vital contribution towards Capetian victory over the House of Anjou. Neither Philip Augustus nor St. Louis was to have a more effective weapon.

John Lackland made the mistake of not asking Philip Augustus to invest him with Normandy, and Philip declared himself for Arthur, who had been put under the royal guardianship by his mother. Arthur did homage to Philip for Normandy, Brittany, Anjou, Poitou, Maine, and Touraine. But what support Philip gave him was short-lived and of little use. On 22 May 1200 the Kings of France and England came to terms at Le Goulet. John, as his brother Richard's legitimate heir, was to hold 'of the lord

King of France all his fiefs as his father and his brother King Richard held them of the lord King of France and as fiefs ought to be held'.[1] Despite the silence of the texts on this topic, it is probable that on this occasion John did homage to Philip Augustus for his fiefs. In addition he surrendered to the King of France Évreux and the Évrecin, paid Philip as suzerain a relief of 20,000 marks, and married his niece, Blanche of Castile, to Philip's son Louis. John gave Blanche for her dowry the fiefs of Graçay and Issoudun,[2] and the suzerainty of certain fiefs in Berry. Philip was to have a life-interest in all these properties. Arthur was to have nothing except Brittany, to be held of John as a fief.

Thus Philip's first clash with John Lackland ended by giving him an important gain. John solemnly recognised that he was the French king's vassal. In addition the annexation of Évreux and the Évrecin gave Philip a base for future operations against Normandy. Yet the Angevin Empire remained intact and Brittany stayed outside the royal sphere of influence.

But John's folly was to play into Philip's hands and to give him the chance to make the fullest use of his suzerainty and deal Angevin power on the continent a deadly blow. On 20 August 1200 John married Isabella, daughter of Audemar, Count of Angoulême. Isabella was already betrothed to Hugh the Brown of Lusignan, Count of La Marche. It need not be supposed that John married Isabella merely to gratify his passion for her. A deeper cause of the match was that John expected it would eventually give him the chance to seize La Marche and Angoulême. The two counties had always cherished a strong spirit of independence, and the counts of Angoulême regarded themselves as holding their fief directly of the French crown.

John made no move to offer Hugh the Brown the compensation for stealing his betrothed to which he was entitled in law. The Lusignans waited in vain for this until Easter 1201. They then levied war against their offending suzerain. John replied by confiscating the property of the rebels, offered to settle the dispute by judicial combat, and even sent for various brawny

[1] *L.T.C.*, i, p. 218, no. 578.
[2] These two last fiefs, abandoned by Henry II in 1189 to Philip Augustus, had returned to the Angevin kings in Richard's time.

champions to represent him. The Lusignans preferred to appeal to their ultimate suzerain, the King of France.

Philip Augustus took great care to act in accordance with law. He advised John to make certain concessions to the Lusignans, but in vain. Philip consequently ordered the dispute to be settled in the royal court, summoning John to attend on 28 April 1202. John failed to come; and so, according to the English chronicler Ralph of Coggeshall, the best and almost the only authority on the whole affair, 'the court of France, being assembled, adjudged the King of England to have forfeited all the lands which he and his ancestors had before that time held of the King of France, for the reason that he and they had long neglected to render all the services due from those lands, and had nearly always disobeyed the summonses of their lord the king.'[1] Philip then defied his great vassal, thereby breaking the feudal bond between them. It would now be perfectly lawful for Philip to conquer all the Angevin lands, for they had escheated to the crown as the fiefs of a recalcitrant vassal.

But Philip apparently did not overrate the opportunities offered him by the sentence which his court had pronounced. To conquer the Angevin lands he needed the help of the entire nobility of his kingdom. It was doubtful whether the barons would be ready to help the king to add to a power which some of them were already beginning to find excessive and dangerous. There was the further question of whether escheat to the crown implied downright annexation or temporary confiscation until such time as the vassal condemned should make amends to the king. Finally, Arthur of Brittany was a problem. In 1199 Philip had acknowledged Arthur's rights over the Angevin lands. At the time of John's condemnation he regarded Arthur as John's legitimate heir. And Arthur's supporters had rallied to the royal banner to execute the royal court's sentence.

At Gournay in July 1202 Arthur did liege homage to Philip Augustus for Brittany, Anjou, Maine, and Touraine, agreeing that if he should ever break the homage, his vassals and their fiefs

[1] Ralph of Coggeshall, *Chronicon Anglicanum* (ed. J. Stevenson, Rolls Series, London, 1875), p. 135.

should be taken over by the king to be used against him.[1] With regard to Poitou, 'if God shall permit us to conquer it by any means soever', Arthur was to perform liege homage for it to the king, but it was specified that the Poitevin barons belonging to the king's party and the others whom the king wanted to join it should do liege homage to the king and then, at the royal command, repeat the homage to Arthur, 'saving the fealty due to the king'. It was also agreed that the royal court should settle certain disputes relating to the lands of the duchy of Aquitaine, to which the King of Castile was advancing claims, if the disputants could not come to an agreement on their own. But the crucial part of Arthur's declaration dealt with Normandy: 'Concerning Normandy, it shall be ordered as follows; namely, that our lord the King of France shall retain to his own use as much as he shall please of all acquisitions which he shall make and God shall permit him to make in Normandy; and that he shall give such lands in Normandy as he pleases to those of his men who have lost their lands through serving him.'

The agreement of Gournay throws a good deal of light on Philip's policies and methods. Troublesome as the Angevins had been to him and his dynasty, he had no desire to see the liquidation of their vast holding in the west. He wanted only Normandy for himself. Of all the Angevin fiefs it was the richest, and the biggest thorn in the side of the Capetian monarchy as long as it stayed in alien hands. Even so, Philip did not wish to acquire it without the consent of its lawful owner. As for the rest of the Angevin lands, Philip merely took precautions against the possibility that Arthur might turn on him, and asserted or reinforced his direct suzerainty. Over Aquitaine his suzerainty was still rather tenuous; for he accepted the right of its duke and the King of Castile to reach an agreement on Gascony without submitting the terms for his approval, and reserved only his right to intervene in and settle any disputes which the two parties could not decide for themselves.

Three weeks later, however, on 1 August 1202, Arthur was made a prisoner by King John at Mirebeau, and was never seen again. By 1206 his death began to be assumed. In 1210 it became

[1] *L.T.C.*, i, p. 236, no. 647.

known for certain. In fact Arthur had been murdered by John at Rouen on 3 April 1203. But his disappearance, possibly because there was prolonged uncertainty as to his fate, did not check Philip's progress. With the capitulation of Rouen to Philip on 24 June 1204, Normandy may be regarded as entirely conquered. Abandoned by John, the barons surrendered and the towns opened their gates to the King of France to save their property and their privileges. But there was no formal proclamation of the annexation of Normandy to the royal domain. The ducal domain yielded a considerable revenue, and as it had escheated to the crown, Philip had the right to exploit it, which he proceeded to do without modifying the provisional nature of the situation. The door was left open for a restoration of the *status quo* should John or his eventual heir ever be pardoned. John, for his part, refused to recognise Philip's *fait accompli*. Until the end of his reign he continued to lay claim to his lost lands and titles. Even after the battle of Bouvines in September 1214 he was still calling himself Duke of Normandy and Aquitaine and Count of Anjou. His son Henry III used all these titles until 1259.

Touraine and Anjou, where the baronage deserted John, were swiftly conquered. By 1206, when Philip and John made a truce, the two counties seem to have been decisively lost to the English king. But on Poitou Philip's forces made little permanent impression. By 1206 it was still almost entirely under John's control. It continued to be governed by an English seneschal until the end of Philip's reign.

Philip's forces nowhere penetrated Aquitaine. It was in the lands of Eleanor's inheritance that Capetian influence took longest to find a foothold. Eleanor's longevity — she lived on until 1204 — may well have strengthened Aquitaine's resistance. The duchy's feudal nobility shed no tears for the decline of Angevin power. Nevertheless their preference was for an Angevin suzerain as against a Capetian. John to them was now a remote and enfeebled figure. But Philip had come alarmingly close. His power seemed to be expanding illimitably. His energies matched those of the forceful Angevins in their heyday.

Philip appears to have grasped this situation. He appointed

Amaury de Thouars, a great Poitevin baron, as a sort of viceroy
for Poitou and Aquitaine. But he did not press for the firm
establishment of his authority there, and showed a much greater
concern to build up his power in Anjou and Touraine. The
administration of Brittany he entrusted first to Gui de Thouars,
third husband of Countess Constance, and then to his own cousin
Peter Mauclerc, together with the hand in marriage of Alix,
daughter and heiress to Constance and Gui.

To sum up: Philip Augustus ruined the Angevin continental
empire, but he did not try to incorporate the whole of it into the
royal domain or bring it all under his personal sway. He occupied
Normandy, Anjou, Maine, and Touraine, and firmly intended to
keep them. He brought Brittany and the Auvergne under direct
royal suzerainty, and ultimately annexed the Auvergne. But
Poitou, Aunis, Saintonge, Guyenne, and Gascony remained
outside his control, and their escheat, ordered by the royal court
in 1202, was never carried out.

Why was this? Lack of means can hardly have been the
explanation. The resources put at Prince Louis' disposal for his
invasion of England in 1215–16 and his expeditions into Languedoc
in 1215 and 1219 could have been diverted to the task of conquering Poitou and Aquitaine. There is no need to suppose that
Philip was any longer afraid of alarming and offending the French
baronage. After Bouvines he was able to do as he liked. Possibly
the death of John in 1216 and the accession of his nine-year-old
son Henry III made it harder to complete the execution of the
sentence of 1202. It was a moot point whether a sentence passed
on a vassal should be carried out after his death at his son's
expense. In this case, moreover, sentence had been pronounced
years before Henry III was born, a fact which could admittedly
be used to support arguments against him as well as in his favour.
Henry III himself did not accept the validity of the sentence of
1202. After Philip II's death he appealed to Rome and tried to
procure the suspension of Louis VIII's coronation until justice
should have been accorded to him. Even at the Capetian court
opinion was that the sentence had probably been excessive.
During the negotiations in 1217 for the withdrawal of the French

invaders from England, Louis had apparently promised to inter-
cede with his father for the restoration to Henry III of the
Angevin continental fiefs. Henry was a mere boy. His disinheriting
by the French king could easily be made to appear an odious
business, especially by contrast with the generous behaviour of
his grandfather Henry II towards Philip Augustus as a boy-king.
Lastly, the King of England was now a vassal of the Holy See.
John had surrendered his kingdom to Innocent III's feudal
custody. Faithful to its age-old principles, the Church preached
that mercy be shown to the fatherless and put public opinion on
Henry's side.

Presumably all these considerations weighed heavily with
Philip Augustus; and his own good sense must have warned him
of the overwhelming difficulties a still immature monarchy would
have to face in trying to absorb in a single generation the whole
of the huge Angevin holdings. And so, whatever the full truth
about his motives, he died leaving the Angevin power shattered
but a considerable part of the Angevin fiefs still not under
Capetian control. In practice, his conquest had not been entirely
clinched. In law, the rights and wrongs of it all were still an open
question.

Louis VIII's reign was short, but long enough for him to
conquer Poitou. The minority of Louis IX gave Henry III the
chance to make an armed attempt at the recovery of his inheritance.
But his expedition of 1230 and Taillebourg-Saintes campaigns
of 1242 failed to win back Poitou, and the situation remained
unchanged. Henry had lost Poitou, but he kept the duchy of
Aquitaine, which Louis IX was powerless to conquer. Henry held
Aquitaine free of all obligation to the King of France, for the
sentence of 1202 and the defiance with which Philip II had
accompanied it had broken the bond of vassalage which had so
long attached the House of Anjou to the French crown. Should
Louis IX wish to settle his dispute with the Angevins by following
Capetian tradition and treating it as a feudal question — and it
was by insisting that this was its character that Philip II had kept
the Papacy from intervening — Henry III would have to be
recognised as a royal vassal and persuaded to make a formal

F

surrender, by due process of law, of the fiefs the French king had conquered.

That was what St. Louis achieved by the treaty concluded at Paris on 28 May 1258.[1] This agreement has been heavily criticised. Louis' contemporaries believed he had been tricked. Modern French historians have usually thought that he was the victim of his own misplaced generosity. But it is too often forgotten that Henry III was also censured by his subjects for agreeing to the Treaty of Paris. Under its terms Henry and his son Edward renounced in favour of the King of France all their rights in Normandy, Anjou, Maine, Touraine and elsewhere in the kingdom of France, except for certain rights which were reserved to them in Quercy and the Agenais. The King of England was to hold the duchy of Aquitaine of the King of France by liege homage, and to perform the services for it. The services for Bigorre, Fézensac, and Astarac, which were dependencies of the duchy of Aquitaine, were to be the subject of a judgment in the royal court of France. Henry's brother and sister were to ratify the treaty. Every ten years the inhabitants of Aquitaine were to swear on oath to the King of France that they would give neither aid nor counsel nor subsidy to the King of England to enable him to break the treaty. If the duke, their suzerain, refused amends to the King of France for any offence he had committed, they were to be bound to aid the King of France against him.

The King of France for his part handed over to the King of England all fiefs and domains held by him in the dioceses of Limoges, Cahors, and Périgueux. He was to indemnify the King of England for any such fiefs enjoying the privilege that they were not to be taken out of the hand of the King of France, in case the holders of those fiefs should refuse to surrender that privilege. The Agenais and Quercy, which were held by Joan of Toulouse, wife of Alphonse of Poitiers, Louis IX's brother, were to revert to the King of England if the marriage of Joan and Alphonse should turn out to be childless. The same condition was to apply to Saintonge 'beyond the River Charente'.

---

[1] L.T.C., iii, pp. 411–13, no. 4416. The Treaty of Paris was not ratified and published until 1259.

Thus St. Louis had obtained from the Plantagenets the juridical surrender of their rights over the lands which he and his predecessors had conquered from them. He had brought the great fief of Aquitaine back to its vassal status, taking what he judged to be the precautions necessary to maintain his suzerainty and to ensure that the holder of the fief respected it. He had also whittled down Angevin power in the west of his kingdom by reducing it, with Henry III's consent, to Aquitaine only. On the other hand he had permitted the survival of a great fief without asking himself whether it would not give the English king — the one ruler capable of dealing with the King of France on equal terms — a formidable base for operations into the heart of France.

It is true that by granting Henry III such generous conditions as those of the Treaty of Paris Louis IX was hoping, as he himself said, to 'foster love' between his own descendants and Henry's.[1] In this he failed. But his example strongly influenced later Capetian policy towards the dukes of Aquitaine until the dynasty died out.

Louis IX's son, grandson, and great-grandsons all attempted to increase their authority over Aquitaine and to make use, for this purpose, of the suzerainty re-established in 1258. Their behaviour in the south-west of France was similar to their behaviour, already discussed, in the north. Appeals from Aquitaine to the *Parlement* of Paris became the occasion of increasing royal encroachment. But the Duke of Aquitaine was more than a mere Count of Flanders: he was also King of England. Should he decide that his suzerain was abusing his position, he could call upon great resources of men and money and, as King of England, enlist against the French king, without committing treason, the aid of allies outside France.

From time to time the King of France found his relationship with his overmighty vassal intolerable, and the conflict between them, always smouldering, flared up. Twice — in 1294 and 1324 — the royal court of France repeated its action of 1202 and declared Aquitaine confiscated. Twice royal armies successfully invaded the duchy. But the Capetians reaped no lasting profit. They seem to have shrunk from following their energetic action

[1] Joinville, *Histoire de saint Louis* (ed. Wailly), p. 245.

to its logical conclusion, and on each occasion a peace treaty was arranged at Paris: on 22 May 1303 after the first breach; and on 31 March 1327 after the second. By the terms of each of these treaties the King of England kept Aquitaine — which was considerably reduced in size in 1327 — and the situation, despite its intense difficulties, remained unaltered.

There was another approach to the problem — by way of the marriage-alliances so dear to the Capetians. Louis IX and Henry III were related, each having married a daughter of Count Raymond Berengar of Provence. In 1303 it was decided that King Edward I of England should marry Philip IV's sister Margaret and that Edward's son and heir should marry Philip's daughter Isabella. Before the conclusion of the Treaty of Paris in 1258 and while Edward I was still only heir to the English throne he had been granted his father's lands in Aquitaine on the occasion of his marriage to Eleanor of Castile. When he became King of England he retained control of Ataine,qui distrusting his son Edward too much to hand it over to him. But it was the young Prince Edward who did homage to Philip IV for Aquitaine on his father's behalf in 1305; and it should be remembered that at this time he was King Philip's prospective son-in-law. Between his accession to the throne of England as Edward II in 1307 and Philip IV's death in 1314 Aquitaine was consequently in the hands of the French king's son-in-law; thereafter Edward II's relationship to the French kings — Louis X, Philip V, and Charles IV — was that of brother-in-law. When Edward II quarrelled with Charles IV in 1324 and it became necessary to patch up a peace, one solution envisaged was to grant the duchy to Edward's son, the future King Edward III.

Thus perhaps from as early as 1258 and certainly after 1303 the Capetians were aiming to resolve the difficulties created by the continuing Plantagenet possession of Aquitaine by making the duchy an *apanage* for the heir to the English throne. In theory he would be easier than his father to confine to a vassal's role. Marriage-alliances and the bonds of kinship they established would make him more amenable to the suzerainty of a French king who was also his kinsman. The chronic and time-honoured quarrelling within the Plantagenet family would make him prone to accept French royal interference in his duchy in return for help against his father. Aquitaine, governed by a duke who was really one of the Capetian family himself, would be no more troublesome to the crown than the other great fiefs ruled over by royal cadets who cheerfully served the king more or less as provincial viceroys.

This policy offered immediate advantages, but it held dangers for the future. It led, though the monarchy seems hardly to have realised it, to the creation of a new magnate class, more formidable than the old by virtue of its royal blood, and capable of challenging the position of the established dynasty, as events were soon to show. In 1328 Charles IV died, leaving only one child, a daughter. Edward III, King of England, Duke of Aquitaine, and grandson of Philip IV through his mother Isabella, was now to appeal to the precedents of 1316 and 1322, which had debarred women from the throne, and to put forward a perfectly legitimate claim to be King of France. He would assuredly not have dared to advance this claim if he had not been a great French baron and one of the twelve Peers of France as well as King of England.

9

Territorial Gains and Losses

Any picture of Capetian policy towards the great fiefs which represents it as one of continuous pressure — as a war of attrition almost — is somewhat misleading. No positive intention of consolidation lay behind the royal acquisitions and annexations, and no consistent plan of campaign produced the advances which we have described. Chance opportunities often precipitated actions of which the consequences were far from clearly envisaged. There is no evidence of any sort to suggest that the Capetians had any clear idea of the course that they were following, beyond a general conviction that no occasion of possible aggrandisement should be neglected.

This lack of consequence emerges in full clarity from a study in detail of their actual acquisitions. At the same time as the dynasty was solving its political problems by a policy directed, however intermittently, against the great fiefs, it was also missing no opportunity of laying its hands on lands and jurisdictions of any and every sort, without any geographical preconceptions or any reservations as to the methods used.

These acquisitions cannot now be listed completely. A prior necessity — a feudal geography of France — is still wanting, and is likely long to remain so. Given such a work, it would be possible to examine individual fiefs in detail (as far as the evidence allows), which in its turn would make it easy to put precise dates on all royal gains. But this last task is far from easy. As we have seen, the fourteenth-century royal officials themselves had no very exact idea of the nature and extent of the royal rights. It is unfortunate that only fragments survive of the enquiries which they carried out to remedy their ignorance. These, in any case, do not always provide satisfactory answers for our purposes; whilst they determine the extent of royal lands and rights, they do so by reference to documents which are not necessarily always those recording the original cessions to the crown.

Greater precision is possible in some of the more important cases. Longnon, in his lectures on *La formation de l'unité française*, set out the principal additions to the royal domain reign by reign. But he was limited by the fact that he was speaking to an audience, rather than writing a book, and he therefore forbore to enter into great detail in cases of minor importance. As a result, the reader of his work might be tempted to imagine that the Capetians built up their domain in a series of large-scale operations; he might even find it somewhat difficult to discover why these took place at all. It would be not easy for him to see that often the purchase of a small estate or of petty rights of jurisdiction was the first step on the road to an acquisition of much greater importance.

The methods used bore a considerable similarity to those employed in dealing with the great fiefs. The Capetians rarely used force. Where possible they preferred to secure a complete or partial renunciation from the previous holder, and to have it recorded in properly legal manner, free from any conditions or restrictions which might leave the royal title open to challenge in the future. But even a cautious policy of this sort owed much to the crown's strength, however discreetly it might be employed. The stronger the kings became, the more they were able to increase their domain, and the less reluctantly possessors of lands and rights turned towards them, sought their suzerainty, and fell in with their search for fresh acquisitions.

Although the magnitude of this piecemeal process increased sharply from the reign of Philip Augustus onwards, it had begun at a much earlier date. The comparatively brief catalogue of earlier gains is merely a reflection of the scarcity of all written evidence for the eleventh and twelfth centuries.

It is hardly surprising that the earliest recorded instances involved the churches of the realm, and in particular those situated in the great fiefs of central and southern France. Surrounded by covetous enemies, these churches were ready and eager to turn to their natural protector, the King of France, and to remind him of the duty of protection which his office obliged him to fulfil. Such appeals were answered. For example, Louis VII intervened several times to protect churches in Auvergne, at a time when royal suzerainty in that province was being actively challenged by the House of Anjou. Such churches often received royal diplomas, confirming the privileges given by the Carolingian rulers and abandoning regalian rights which the king himself had long been unable to exercise. Contacts of this type made it possible for the Capetians, and in particular Louis VII, to make the monarchy again a real force in regions where it had become a name only.

The results were not long to seek. In 1161 Bishop Aldebert of Mende came to Paris to do homage and fealty to King Louis VII. The bishop was also Count of the Gévaudan, and so his homage meant not only that another see had become a 'royal bishopric', but also that another county had become a direct royal fief; this gain turned out to be a permanent one. The Count-Bishop of Cahors followed suit in 1211, and the Bishop of Viviers, Count of the Vivarais, in 1305.

Laymen, too, sought royal lordship. A few years after the Bishop of Mende, the Count of Forez — recommended to the king by the dying wish of his father, Guigue III — did homage to Louis VII for his county. In 1172–3 he was followed by Girard, younger brother of the Count-Bishop of Mâcon, and Humbert, lord of Beaujeu, after a royal intervention in their quarrel with the abbey of Vézelai and other Burgundian churches; the act recording their homage mentions that other lords of the province became royal vassals also, though in a less binding fashion.

The process of *pariage* contributed further to the growth of the royal domain. By it the king became associated in the administration of a lordship held by a subject, on a footing of complete equality. Such an agreement placed the non-royal partner under the king's direct protection, and gave offences against him the character of *lèse-majesté*. Its usual result, sooner or later, was the annexation of the lordship to the royal domain, most frequently by the king's purchase of his partner's share of the revenues.

There is no adequate modern study of the historical aspects of *pariage*.[1] It served the crown extremely well, and remained in use all through the Capetian era. Most often, though not always, it applied to ecclesiastical lordships. It was by no means confined to complete *seigneuries*. For example, in 1171 Louis VII became associated in *pariage* with one Girard Lefèvre, of Joigny, in the exploitation of four mills on the river Vanne; the king provided a guaranteed stream of customers by obliging his burgesses of Sens, and others under the jurisdiction of the local *prévôt*, to bring their grain there for milling. Again, he made an agreement in 1177 with Hugh Lenoir, of Marolles-sur-Seine, the occupier of the lands of Flagi (*département* Seine-et-Marne, *canton* Lorrez-le-Bocage) and Bichereau (*commune* Thouri-Ferottes).

The list of thirteenth-century *pariage* agreements is a long one, even although not every reign has been systematically investigated. The increasing frequency of the agreements is a clear indication that the crown found them progressively more advantageous. They were useful opening moves in the familiar Capetian campaigns of peaceful penetration. More accurately, perhaps, *pariage* was a second rather than an opening move, for it was normally entered into with subjects who were already royal vassals. Its eventual result was the disappearance of private lordships through annexation into the royal domain.

Of a different character was the *sauvegarde*, which introduced royal authority into areas where it had not previously existed. The great attraction of the *sauvegarde* for subjects was that, in theory at least, it created a royal obligation without demanding any reciprocal duty. It implied that the king would intervene to protect a monastery or town which came under the royal *sauvegarde*. Any attack on his *protégés* was construed as an attack on the king's majesty; therefore it came within the jurisdiction of the king's courts. The right was a valuable one. Through it the Capetians made their authority felt outside their domain, and even outside their kingdom. The Ostrevent and part of the Barrois—lands bordering on France but not part of it — came under royal authority through the use of the *sauvegarde*, as did Verdun, Toul and Lyon.

---

[1] M. L. Gallet, *Les traités de pariage dans la France féodale* (Paris, 1935), concentrates unduly for our purposes on the legal aspects of the institution.

But neither *pariage* nor *sauvegarde* was more than a preparatory step towards absorption into the royal domain. The thirteenth-century Capetians increasingly made use of purchase as a means of adding lordships of all sizes, and even small parcels of land, to their family possessions. In this they were undoubtedly helped by the contemporary crisis in the fortunes of so many noble families, whose ability to resist was progressively weakening in the face of the growing wealth of the crown. Thus, when Count John of Beaumont-sur-Oise died without direct heirs, his succession was disputed between Thibaud d'Ulli, son of his cousin-german Ives de Beaumont, and Ives' two sisters, Beatrice and Mary. Thibaud was awarded the fief by a decision of the royal court in 1223; it may have been in token of gratitude that he shortly afterwards sold a considerable part of the county to Philip Augustus for 7000 *livres parisis*. Characteristically, Louis VIII took care to obtain a renunciation from the dead count's nephew, the Archbishop of Rheims, who might have claimed both the royal purchase and the part of the county retained by Thibaud.

The position of the county of Ponthieu was regularised at much the same time and by the same means. Philip Augustus had confiscated it in 1221, after Simon of Dammartin, the husband of the heiress of the county, had joined the Bouvines coalition. By the feudal custom of France, Louis VIII was entitled to retain Ponthieu during Simon's lifetime. At the latter's death, his children could hope to recover their inheritance, but only by the king's clemency; in strict custom, they could be disinherited for ever, as they had been born after their father's felony had been committed. But the Capetians rarely took so rigid a stand on their rights, and Louis may possibly have had doubts about the justice of such a disinheritance. At all events, he preferred to reach an agreement with the children's mother — a policy which had other reasons to recommend it also. Countess Mary of Clermont had possible claims of her own on the county of Alençon, which had been disregarded when Philip Augustus annexed the county on the death of Count Robert III in 1219. Louis VIII therefore came to terms with her in July 1225 at Chinon. Mary renounced the county of Alençon, and ceded Doullens, Saint-Riquier and

Avesnes-le-Comte to the crown. The *communes* of Ponthieu took
an oath of loyalty to the king, and it was stipulated that the castles
of the county should be delivered up to him on demand. In return,
Simon of Dammartin's children recovered their rights of inheritance, and Mary received back the remainder of Ponthieu. She
was pardoned her *rachat*, and was given a cash payment of 2000
livres parisis.

Other instances can be given. In June 1224 Louis VIII bought
the castle of Montreuil from Guillaume de Masnières for 200 *livres
parisis*, and in December he agreed to pay an annual rent of 100
livres tournois to Galeran d'Ivri, Viscount of Meulan, for his
property at Beaufort in Anjou. St. Louis acquired the county of
Mâcon in 1239 for 10,000 *livres tournois* and a life-rent of 1000
livres; the previous lord, Jean de Braine, who held the county by
right of his marriage, was childless. Philip III used much the same
methods in 1281, when he paid Count Arnoux III 3000 *livres
tournois* and a life-rent of 1000 *livres* for his county of Guines; he
was also generous enough to pay off the count's debts. Two other
cases occurred in the same year: Count Renaud of Guelders
surrendered his lands in Normandy, including the port of Harfleur,
in return for a life pension equal to their revenues; and Gui de
Mauléon, knight, exchanged the castle and barony of Montmorillon for a cash payment of 1200 *livres tournois* and an annual rent
of 130 *livres.*

Philip the Fair made many purchases. He bought Edward I of
England's rights in Quercy in 1289, giving in exchange an annual
rent of 3000 *livres*. In 1286 he bought the county of Chartres; in
1291, Beaugenci; in 1293, the fief of Montpellieret (the first step
towards the Valois acquisition of Montpellier in the fourteenth
century); in 1302, the viscounties of Lomagne and Auvillars; in
1306, the viscounty of La Soule. In 1301, he advanced a considerable sum of money to Hugh XIII of Lusignan, Count of La
Marche and Angoulême, on the security of the latter's counties.
Hugh died before he had repaid the debt; the succession was
disputed, and complicated by the destruction of his will. Philip
the Fair saw his chance to intervene, and in 1308 Hugh's heirs
ceded the two counties to the crown in return for a financial

settlement. An even more important acquisition, that of the county of Burgundy, was virtually a purchase also. The consent of Count Otho IV to the marriage of Joan of Burgundy and the king's second son Philip (which gave the latter immediate possession of the county) was only secured by a payment of 100,000 *livres tournois* and a life-rent of 10,000 *livres*.

These examples are sufficient to demonstrate that royal encroachment on the great fiefs was parallelled by a remarkably widespread policy of small-scale acquisition. It would be difficult to exaggerate the importance of this policy, which did as much as the annexation of the great fiefs to create the enormous domain shown by the *État des paroisses et des feux* of 1328. Equally, a study of the policy confirms the conclusions suggested by the history of the great fiefs. It was a peaceful policy, based on legal rights, carried through by lawyers who knew the importance of a good title and were anxious to avoid the hatreds and tensions which would have accompanied the use of force. Even when, in the last resort, force had to be used, the crown and its advisers were always careful to work for a final settlement. It was always considered important that the dispossessed proprietor or his heirs should eventually acknowledge the validity of the legal right used to justify a royal seizure.

*   *   *   *

Successful as they were in annexation and expansion, the Capetians never had any intention of extending their domain over all France. The idea of a kingdom comprising only lands administered directly by the crown was not one which ever suggested itself to them or to their servants. Their ideal, rather, was that the king should have a domain large enough to sustain him in all necessary state; round this domain there should cluster fiefs great and small, held directly or mediately from the crown by vassals prepared to respect their feudal obligations.

A study of royal alienations will make the point more clearly. At no time did the Capetians ever abstain from making gifts of lands or rights. They made such gifts when they were still weak and struggling, and they continued to make them after their fortunes had changed. To them, as to their nobles, *largesse* was the distinguishing mark of the feudal baron, and being good barons they accordingly practised *largesse*. On more than one occasion in the thirteenth and early fourteenth centuries they distributed their hard-earned gains with a liberality bordering on the excessive.

This attitude of mind was dangerous enough when it led to no more than small concessions. When it operated in favour of members of the royal house, it was liable to produce alienations so large as to be a serious threat to the territorial strength of the monarchy. But the dangers involved in the creation of *apanages* for the princes of the blood royal never seem to have become obvious to the dynasty. Royal servants might on occasion warn their masters against excessive generosity towards subjects, but they never showed any opposition to the endowment of the royal house itself. The ordinance of Moulins of 1566, which belatedly proclaimed the inalienability of the royal domain, still allowed of two exceptions, one of which was 'in the case of *apanages* for the younger sons of the house of France'.

Apanages for younger sons went back to the earliest days of the Capetian dynasty. Their purpose, no doubt, was to make the members of the royal family more ready to accept the notion of the indivisibility of the crown — a doctrine which was never formally proclaimed, but which was implicit in all royal policy. Thus Henry I, after his accession, surrendered to his younger brother the duchy of Burgundy, which Robert the Pious had taken so much trouble to conquer. The subsequent absence of similar creations for a whole century can hardly be attributed to policy; though the continuity of the dynasty was maintained, there were few younger sons to be provided for. But it may be noticed that Louis VI did not endow his younger sons in this way. He may have had in mind the behaviour of his own half-brother, Philip, the son of Philip I and Bertrada de Montfort; in 1130 Louis had been compelled to reclaim the county of Mantes, given to Philip in 1104. This reluctance to disperse the domain may also have been due to a very natural wish to retain the conquests which had cost him so much effort and warfare.

The first Capetian to create *apanages* on a large scale was Louis VIII. He began by providing for his half-brother, Philip Hurepel, the son of Philip Augustus and Agnes of Méran. When still an infant, Philip had been betrothed in 1201 to Matilda, daughter of Renaud of Dammartin, one of the most powerful lords in northern France, who held the counties of Dammartin, Boulogne and Mortain. Renaud joined the coalition of 1214, and was captured at Bouvines. His possessions were seized, and the marriage of his daughter to Philip Hurepel carried through; Philip received the county of Boulogne. In 1224 Louis VIII, obeying the last wishes of his father, endowed his half-brother with an *apanage* comprising the counties of Boulogne, Domfront, Mortain and Clermont, one quarter of the county of Dammartin, the greater part of the county of Aumale, and the lands of Alisai and Lillebonne. Thus the lands confiscated from Renaud of Dammartin did not fall in to the crown. Ironically, even King Louis' generosity did not ensure Philip Hurepel's loyalty, for he was one of the leaders of the feudal coalition against the regent Blanche of Castile. It was fortunate for the monarchy that the *apanage* reverted to the crown on Philip's childless death. Even so, the county of Boulogne passed to a collateral line, and did not return to the domain until several centuries later.

Out of the twelve children of King Louis' marriage, five sons were still alive when he made his will in June 1225. Louis, the eldest, was the heir to the kingdom and required no special provision. Robert, the second son, was promised Artois, which had been the dowry of his grandmother, Isabella of Hainault, with the exception of the portions set aside as the dower of Blanche of Castile. John, the third son, was to receive the counties of Anjou and Maine, and Alphonse, the fourth son, the county of Poitou and the Auvergne. The king's fifth son, and any who might be born in the future, were to enter holy orders, and therefore to receive nothing. In fact, the fifth and sixth sons died young, as did Prince John; the seventh and last son, Charles, eventually received the *apanage* designed for John.

This comprehensive settlement involved the dispersal of one-third of the entire royal domain. Of all the confiscated Angevin lands, only Normandy was retained. One clause of the will certainly anticipated that if Philip Hurepel left no heir his *apanage* would revert to the crown, and the same may have been intended in the case of the other *apanages* also. The risk was nonetheless great, but the dynasty was exceedingly fortunate in the outcome. Philip Hurepel and Alphonse of Poitiers left no heirs, and their lands returned to the domain. Anjou followed in 1328, when Charles of Anjou's great-grandson, Philip VI of Valois, became King of France. But Robert of Artois' *apanage* was not recovered until the Treaty of the Pyrenees in 1659, after a complicated history which had involved its passage by marriage into the hands of first the house of Burgundy and then the house of Habsburg.

Whatever his opinion of their wisdom, St. Louis scrupulously respected his father's instructions, but he was conspicuously less generous to his own sons. John Tristan received only the county of Valois, Peter those of Alençon and Perche, and Robert that of Clermont-en-Beauvaisis. Both John and Peter died without heirs (the former at Tunis in 1270, the latter in 1284), and their fiefs reverted to the crown. Robert of Clermont was the ancestor of a long line which culminated in the house of Bourbon, later to be kings of France. His county was re-annexed in 1327, but only through an exchange which cost the crown the county of La Marche, and the castellanies of Issoudun, Saint-Pierre-le-Moutier, and Montferrand.

Philip III had three sons to provide for. The elder of his surviving sons by Isabella of Aragon, Philip, came to the throne. To the younger, Charles, his father gave, by royal letters of 26 February 1284, the county of Valois, which had been the *apanage* of the dead John Tristan. The letters added the castellanies of Béthisy and Verberie to those of Crépy, La Ferté-Milon and Pierrefonds, which had constituted the original county. They also contained a clause, by now obligatory, stipulating the return of the *apanage* to the crown should the recipient have no heirs. The endowment, in expectation of success in Aragon, was a modest one. The new king, Philip the Fair, was, however, generous in compensating his brother for the loss of his expected crown. Charles' *apanage* had already been augmented as a result of his marriage to Margaret of Anjou, who brought him the counties of Anjou and Maine, which in 1290 contained 145,534 hearths in 1514 parishes. In 1291 King Philip added the county of Alençon, which had reverted to the crown on the death in 1284 of Peter of Alençon. He also gave Charles the castellanies of Châteauneuf-en-Thimerais and Senonches, which the crown had secured by an exchange in 1283; in 1293 he added the county of Chartres (acquired by the crown in 1286), besides a number of gifts of lesser importance.

Philip III's youngest son, Louis (the child of Mary of Brabant), was not forgotten. After his father's death he was styled Count of Évreux. He was later given possession of the county, to which Philip the Fair added the lordship of Beaumont-le-Roger, Meulan, and the castellanies of Étampes, Dourdan, La Ferté-Alais and Gien.

Philip the Fair was less generous to his own sons — not from any premonition that all three would become kings, but more probably because he simply assumed that they would behave as well to each other as he had done to his own brothers. Prince Louis succeeded in 1305 to his mother's large inheritance of Navarre, Champagne and Brie. Philip, the second son of the king, received the county of Poitiers (comprising not the whole of Poitou, but only the town of Poitiers and its *banlieu*). His father also bought for him, at a high price, the hand of the daughter of Count Otho of Burgundy, and with her the rich imperial county of Burgundy and the lordship of Salins. The youngest prince, Charles, was given the county of La Marche to supplement that of Bigorre, his share of his mother's inheritance.

The last three Capetian rulers had no sons to receive *apanages*. Louis X, however, considerably increased the revenues of his brother Philip at his own accession. Philip's annual income of 20,000 *livres*, of which the county of Poitiers provided only 7000 *livres*, was increased by gifts to 50,000 *livres*. When Philip in his turn became king, he gave his brother Charles of La Marche the castellanies of Niort, Montmorillon and Fontenay. He also increased the *apanage* of his uncle Louis of Évreux by giving him the county of Longueville, which Louis X had confiscated from

Enguerrand de Marigny. It should be noted, however, that the *apanages* of the three sons of Philip IV all returned more or less completely to the royal domain, for all three inherited the crown.

For three centuries, therefore, Capetian policy was ambivalent. On the one hand, it aimed at acquiring lands, at placing other lands under royal suzerainty, at restoring the *Regnum Francorum*. On the other, it simultaneously involved the alienation of these same acquisitions in favour of the cadet members of the dynasty, and thereby the real danger of a return to that very fragmentation of the *Regnum* which the kings wished to prevent. The rule that *apanages* should return to the crown in default of heirs did not remove the contradiction. This rule was common to all fiefs, and the Capetians in fact owed some of their own acquisitions to it. Nor can royal policy be defended by protesting that the excessive generosity of Louis VIII was never repeated, for such generosity would have been increasingly difficult after the time of St. Louis, as the royal financial position deteriorated. The later Capetians found it more convenient to make gifts of annual revenues — in effect, temporary alienations — to members of the royal house, and to royal friends and servants. By doing so they retained the ability to default on payment, or even to revoke the grants. They also used their increasing international power to establish, or to try to establish, their cadets outside France. Junior members of the family were quite ready to suggest such a policy on their own account. Charles of Anjou owed his Sicilian kingdom to his brother's help. Philip III met disaster in an attempt to set his younger son, Charles of Valois, on the throne of Aragon. Philip the Fair gave financial support to the Italian, Byzantine and imperial ambitions of the same Charles of Valois, and in addition established his own younger son, Philip, in the imperial county of Burgundy. No Capetian ruler appears to have seen any future danger to France from these foreign ambitions, any more than from the creation of the *apanages*.

Something of the real intentions and desires of the Capetians may perhaps emerge from this study of their territorial consolidation of their kingdom. No modern ideas of territorial unification lay behind their enrichment of the crown of France. They never sought to become the direct owners of all France, to remove all the great fiefs, to dismantle the feudal structure of the kingdom. As long as their vassals, direct or mesne, performed their feudal duties and services, the kings were well content. They were no different from other barons of the age, anxious to muster as many knights as possible under their banners and to see their *curia* attended by as many vassals as possible. They did not assess the importance of their domain in economic, not even in political terms, but predominantly in military terms. Possession or suzerainty meant warriors, not revenues; lances were more important than crops. Indeed, the only land as such which attracted their attention was the forest, not so much for its revenue as for the great noble pastime of the hunt. Ready to give other lands, the Capetians were tight-fisted when it came to grants of woods or of timber; they were readier to grant fields than warrens or chases.

The dynasty had nothing of the peasant's attitude to land. The kings never looked upon it as something to be collected, to be hoarded, to be exploited with prudence. Nor did they have the outlook of far-seeing statesmen. They never saw the value of a secure territorial base, on which a centralised state might with patience be built. Nor were they even anxious to create an un-challenged despotism. Rather, they looked on their kingdom as a great domain, in which God had enfeoffed them, and which it was in no way wrong for them to entrust to their blood-relations or to their loyal servants. In itself the domain was not vital to them; what mattered was that vassals great and small should acknowledge the king's sovereign right, and do their proper services. From this viewpoint, it is easier to see why they so seldom used force, but preferred to work towards agreements which left no hatreds behind them. In so doing they were making themselves masters of their kingdom. They were also creating the territorial basis of the French nation — but that achievement was neither deliberate nor conscious.

10

The Machinery of Government

The task of the Capetians did not stop short at establishing their sovereignty and subjecting the fiefs and lordships of France to their authority. To make their work permanent they had to enlist the services of reliable administrators, capable of holding all their territories together, for without a strong and efficient administration their political achievement would have been ephemeral. To produce their administrative system they employed the methods which had stood them in good stead in other fields of activity, neither working to a preconceived plan nor creating new institutions, but instead adapting and developing what already existed. Institutions which appeared to endanger the monarchy were shorn of their power and significance; and any new institution, springing from novel exigencies, had to prove its value before the monarchy would confer any kind of definitive status on it.

The attitude of the Capetians towards change, though sensible, was probably unconscious. They resembled their contemporaries in their respect for tradition, and refrained from violent suppression and bold innovation alike. Their original ideal was to govern like Charlemagne, and, later, like St. Louis: not that they preserved any clear memory of how their forerunners had governed. The great rulers of the past stood for a vague ideal of good government which embodied the personal conceptions of kingship entertained by each succeeding king and his entourage. When the Capetians brought about developments in existing institutions of government, they did so on the pretext of restoring them to their original state. The administrative machinery they had inherited from their predecessors was retained, though it acquired new characteristics. Officials kept their old titles; but their characters changed.

When Hugh Capet came to the throne the remnants of Carolingian administration were preserved as a matter of course. To all outward appearances there was no change. Government by the Palace went on, and the great officers of state retained their functions. But Carolingian administration no longer served any practical purpose, for the effect of the king's actions was more or less limited to the royal domain and he was confined to the role of a feudal magnate. Public administration was almost the direct antithesis of feudalism, and there was little place for it in a society held together by feudal ties. A genuine administrative system did not grow up until feudalism began to decay.

The *cadres* of Carolingian administration which the Capetians preserved had small significance — scarcely any in relation to the kingdom as a whole, for the great Carolingian officers of state had become powerful feudal barons and their example had been followed by the less important functionaries. The regalian rights had been usurped by these men, or allowed to fall into their clutches. The regular administration of royal justice was a thing of the past, there were no royal revenues, and the king could hardly muster his own army without baronial consent. He still surrounded himself with great office-bearers, but their functions were now in practice almost exclusively confined to the royal household and royal domain, outside which their authority was all but nominal.

During the first two centuries of Capetian rule the king could only secure the means of royal action by summoning to court his great barons, the men with whom true power lay, and appealing for their support. Without it he was, as sovereign, powerless; but it was by no means always withheld, and even when not unanimous it could be useful. Baronial support gave Robert the Pious the means necessary to bring to a successful conclusion his stubborn and protracted campaigns to win control of Burgundy.[1] But the goodwill of the barons was only forthcoming for royal policy when the latter did not clash with their particularist interests.

The only administrative machinery apparently in existence

[1] See pp. 101–2.

during the first period of Capetian rule was that necessary for the organisation and control of the royal domain; and not much is known about it. Historians are probably right to suppose (though they have little concrete evidence to go on) that its main features from 987 onwards were those which emerge fairly clearly in the reign of Louis VI, when the documents at last become something more than a mere collection of fragments. This early royal administration was a rudimentary affair, comprising a few great palatine officers in the king's household, and a handful of royal representatives, called *prévôts*, stationed in different parts of the domain. Its development was naturally influenced by contemporary social trends. For the great royal offices of constable, butler, chamberlain, seneschal (or *dapifer*), and chancellor, though not hereditary, were granted for life — a long step on the road to hereditary tenure; and they seem to have remained the preserve of the small group of families which held the most important feudal lordships within the royal domain. The constable was usually a Chaumont, a Montmorency, or a Clermont; the chamberlain a Galeran, a Dammartin, or a Beaumont; the seneschal a Rochefort; the butler a La Tour. In Louis VI's time the Garlande family tried, with momentary success, to engross the offices of seneschal chancellor, and butler. Étienne de Garlande held the offices and carried out the functions of both seneschal and chancellor; but he grew too powerful for the peace of mind of Louis VI, who was egged on by Queen Adelaide and St. Bernard to strip him of his offices and exclude him from the royal household. After five years of rebellion the fallen favourite gave in and abandoned all claim to be seneschal by hereditary right. The manner in which those who followed him at the chancery — Algrin d'Étampes, Cadurc, Simon, and Hugues de Champfleury — went out of office suggests that the king's relationship with successive chancellors was also beset with difficulty.

The only great royal offices which entailed serious administrative functions were those of seneschal and chancellor. The seneschal was the head of the king's household, and the *prévôts* seem also to have been under his authority. He controlled the royal finances, commanded the army, and shared with the other great officers extensive judicial powers. The chancellor was the head of the secretariat of the central administration, such as it was. He kept the seal which was employed to authenticate royal acts and deputised for the king in his high capacity as supreme judge over all his kingdom. Had these two offices become hereditary, the king would have risked declining swiftly to a purely honorary role in which he would have wielded only the semblance of power.

By the later twelfth century the Capetians had come to see this danger clearly. But it was unthinkable that they should suppress the great offices of state, which had been handed down from the Carolingian emperors, and were in their own eyes indispensable to the royal prestige and dignity. They solved the difficulty not by extinguishing the great offices but by appointing nonentities to some of them and leaving those of seneschal and chancellor vacant. After the fall of Étienne de Garlande in 1127 Louis VI appointed no seneschal until 1131, when he gave the office to his cousin Raoul of Vermandois. After Raoul died there was a short vacancy, followed in 1154 by the appointment of Thibaud V, Count of Blois and Chartres, who held office thenceforth until his death in 1191. Not only were Raoul and Thibaud related to the royal family and so regarded as likely to be steadfastly loyal to the crown; they were also great barons, Thibaud especially, who were often kept away from court by the administrative cares of their own domains. With them the office of seneschal became what the king wanted it to be, increasingly honorary and decreasingly dangerous. Nevertheless, the seneschal still retained the right to exercise all his old powers. Philip Augustus saw a danger in this, and thought it better not to appoint a successor to Thibaud V. Thus the office of seneschal was not suppressed, but simply left vacant.[1] Up to 1191, royal diplomas had been witnessed by the chancellor's four great colleagues — the constable, butler, chamberlain, and seneschal. Thereafter, until the extinction of the Capetian dynasty in 1328, they used the words *dapifero nullo* to

---

[1] Further proof that the office of seneschal survived can be found in the accounts of the *prévôts*, most of whom were obliged under the terms of their leases to pay the seneschal an agreed sum on All Saints' Day (1 November), to meet the expenses of the assize he held annually. When the office of seneschal fell vacant, the seneschal's due was collected on behalf of the king, and the *prévôt* had to show it among his receipts, but it was kept separate from the farm of his *prévôté*.

emphasise the fact that the office of seneschal continued to exist but remained unfilled.

After the disgrace of Étienne de Garlande in 1127 the chancellorship stayed vacant. But Étienne had learned his lesson and he was reappointed in 1132. When Hugues de Champfleury fell in 1172 the office was again left vacant, this time for seven years, and yet again for thirty-eight years (1185–1223) after the death of Hugues du Puiset. When the chancellor Guérin, who was also Bishop of Senlis and a Knight Hospitaller, died in 1227, no one was appointed to succeed him until 1314, by which time the king was too strong to have any fear of his chancellor. But while the office of seneschal could be dispensed with altogether, the chancery was a vital organ of administration, and had to have a head. Consequently a keeper of the seal was appointed, a much less exalted dignitary who held office solely at the royal pleasure, which could be withdrawn.

To carry out the work which they hesitated to leave in the hands of the great officers of state the Capetian kings appointed household functionaries — in particular, the *palatini*. Most of these officers were recruited from the minor nobility of the royal domain, now that it had been reduced to obedience; but some of them were of different origin, like Henri le Lorrain, whose enemies alleged that he came of servile stock until King Louis VI cleared him of the imputation. These members of the royal entourage had no precise official status. They were rather those of the king's friends and *familiares* whom he selected to perform the multifarious short-lived governmental tasks on which his authority rested. For apart from the chancery and its subordinate offices the royal court seems to have had no fixed organisation.

This way of doing things hardly deserves to be called 'administration'. The king was a great landed proprietor living on his domain, the local administration of which was in the hands of his farmers, the *prévôts*. Each of them bought his *prévôté* by auction, and in return for an agreed farm administered the royal lands and pocketed the royal aues within the *prévôté* and the neighbouring lordships. Outside the domain the king could act only on the political, not on the administrative plane, and depended on establishing harmony with his prelates and barons through the medium of the assemblies which he regularly convoked. And if some exceptional administrative measure chanced to be applicable outside the domain, the king would prefer to request a baron or bishop to execute it and to act in his own part of France as a temporary representative of the 'royal administration'.

But it must be confessed that the administrative machine may have been more complex than its extremely meagre documentation suggests. A well-established governmental and administrative system appears in the reign of Philip Augustus, and conceivably it was in existence before his accession. On the other hand, it was Philip Augustus who added to the royal domain the great province of Normandy, which had the most efficient administration in Europe, evolved from the time of the earliest dukes onward. Norman administration owed much to the fact that William the Conqueror had acquired the throne of England in 1066 and, determined to be master in his own house, had exploited his conquest to organise feudal society in both England and Normandy on the basis of respect for the rights of the ruler, in contrast to its basis in France, which was the enfeeblement of royal power and the usurpation of regalian rights.

Philip Augustus acquired not only Normandy but also a considerable part of the territories where the heavy-handed Angevins had established firm control by introducing an administration akin to that of Normandy. Angevin administration had been too thoroughgoing not to have called forth protests from the populace of these territories, but they had soon fallen into the habit of obedience. Thus Philip's territorial gains not only enlarged the area of the royal domain; they also made it impossible for the rudimentary administration of the earlier Capetians to be regarded any longer as adequate. Profound changes would clearly be needed if the monarchy was to retain its new acquisitions.

In Philip Augustus' time the Capetian monarchy was taking on a range of new burdens and commitments bearing no relation to those of the past, and was assuming a great political role which the old patriarchal administration was quite incapable of supporting and financing. It was no longer possible for local administration in the royal domain to be left to the *prévôts*, simple farmers who had habitually referred straight to the king every single political issue which confronted them. The crown needed increasingly specialised administrators in ever greater numbers. It needed responsible intermediaries to keep it in touch with its local agents, and permanent representatives to supervise the districts into which the enlarged royal domain and the expanding area of royal activity had now to be divided. The royal court could no longer be a mere gathering of the king's friends and his personal clerks, with no precise functions but looked upon (with no heed paid to their qualifications) as suitable to be entrusted with every variety of royal task.

Change was rarely swift and often fumbling, the more so as the king and his counsellors were not always sufficiently aware of the novelty of the difficulties facing them and looked to the past to provide them with solutions. The people they ruled had an equally defective sense of the transformation taking place, and failed to understand that particularism and a purely local approach to problems of government were now obsolescent. There was no planning of the changes that occurred; they followed no pre-ordained sequence; and they were hampered by resistance to innovation as such and by respect, touching in itself, for established institutions, though many of the latter now had to function in highly anomalous conditions.

A full picture of Capetian administration in the thirteenth century cannot be presented here.[1] But the most important of the changes and innovations which the monarchy brought about will be considered, and an attempt will be made to discover the principles underlying these changes — though they were principles which were probably not formulated, even unconsciously, by the Capetians.

The first great change of the thirteenth century was the appointment of officials nominated and paid by the king and holding office entirely at his pleasure. Until the accession of Philip Augustus in 1180, the Capetian monarchy, as far as can be

---

[1] Such a picture will be found in F. Lot and R. Fawtier, *Histoire des institutions françaises au moyen âge*, vol. ii: *Institutions royales: les droits du Roi exercés par le Roi* (Paris, 1958).

deduced from the surviving documents, seems to have employed two kinds of official. Those in the first category were the officials of the central administration — the great officers of state and the chancery clerks. They were appointed by the king, but held office for life, though they were liable to summary dismissal, and took in one form or another a share of the profits of their offices. The second category consisted of the *prévôts*, whose appointment was not entirely under royal control, since the king auctioned it to the highest bidder. In the beginning the *prévôtés* may have been held of the king as fiefs. Some of them were hereditary, and it is likely that in the earliest years of Capetian rule they did not come under any kind of uniform system. But in due course there was a fairly rapid and complete change to the system of farming the *prévôtés*. The purchaser compounded for the revenues of the office by paying the sum fixed at the auction, and recouped himself by exploiting the lands and rights committed to his charge. He might have to hand over his *prévôté* at any time to a bidder offering a higher farm unless he were prepared to match the higher figure himself; and this process might be repeated several times.

The inconveniences of this method of appointing and rewarding royal officials are obvious. The man who had purchased office was by virtue of his cash outlay free of all or very nearly all royal surveillance and control. Having a personal interest in the exploitation of his office, he easily succumbed to the temptation to widen its powers, squeeze every conceivable revenue out of it, strive to arrange that his heir should succeed him in it, and generally treat it as private property.

Under Philip Augustus there appeared an official of entirely different type, the *bailli*, not invented by the Capetians but borrowed by them from the Anglo-Norman monarchy. The kings of England had been compelled to find a solution to the difficulties of making rapid progresses throughout their extensive territories on both sides of the Channel. To control England, Normandy, Anjou, Poitou, and Aquitaine simultaneously they had to create large numbers of local officials and invest them with full powers to act on their behalf. Some were mobile commissioners of enquiry and itinerant justices. Others were *baillis* and seneschals rooted in their own particular localities. The *baillis* of Normandy and the seneschals of the other Angevin continental fiefs were officials of a new kind. They could not farm their offices, since the duration of their tenure was never fixed; nor could any particular section of the revenues committed to their charge be pocketed by them as wages, for every farthing they handled had to be accounted for under rigorous royal supervision. Consequently they had to be paid fixed stipends augmented by various perquisites in kind. The Angevins had produced a type of official new in feudal society, the direct representative of royal authority, appointed and salaried by the king and revocable at his pleasure. Philip Augustus copied this prototype, and when he conquered most of the Angevin lands and found administration everywhere in the hands of officials of this kind, he introduced them throughout his royal domain, though not without modifications.

The first royal *baillis* of whom there is precise record are those mentioned in the so-called testament which Philip Augustus drew up in 1190, on the eve of his departure on Crusade,[1] and by which he established *baillis* in certain territories 'distinguished by their own names' — that is, by the names of the *baillis* to whom their administration was committed. Each *bailli* was to hold in his district a monthly assize, at which plaintiffs might obtain speedy justice, the royal rights should be safeguarded, and the fines due to the king should be recorded in writing. Thrice yearly the *bailli* was to come to Paris and account for the administration of his *bailliage* to the regents — the Queen Mother Adela of Champagne and the Archbishop of Rheims. He was not to be removed from office without royal authorisation, unless guilty of murder, homicide, rape, or treason; and he was also to control the royal *prévôts* and to appoint four *prudhommes* to stay with each *prévôt*, who was to govern on their advice. At Paris the number of *prudhommes* was established at six, whom the king himself nominated. No *bailli* was to remove a *prévôt* from office without royal permission, except on the same grounds as those on which the regents might dismiss a *bailli*.

[1] H. F. Delaborde, *Recueil des actes de Philippe Auguste*, vol. i (Paris, 1916), pp. 416–20, no. 345.

The districts allotted to the earliest *baillis* were not given geographical designations. That this was so even as late as 1202–3 appears from the document sometimes wrongly called the first budget of the French monarchy,[1] in which we read, for instance, of the receipts and expenses of Guillaume de La Chapelle, Hugues de Gravelle, and Renaud de Béthisy, not those of the *bailli* of Orléans, the *bailli* of Étampes, and the *bailli* of Sens. Only with the accounts of 1248 do the *baillis* acquire geographical designations.[2] Probably their growing financial responsibilities produced a closer geographical definition of the districts they administered. If financial administration is to be effective it requires stable and well-defined territorial units, especially at a period of history when the rapid collection of taxes is still exceedingly difficult and payments tend to be dragged out over long years. The royal *baillis* and seneschals, who to begin with were commissioners of inquiry, quickly developed considerable judicial and financial functions, but the latter were of greater importance because the more the monarchy's power increased the greater grew its need for money. Michelet's famous observations on the importance of gold in fourteenth-century history are equally applicable to the thirteenth century. From Philip Augustus to Charles IV all the later Capetian kings were preoccupied by acute financial problems.

The *baillis* and seneschals were the king's representatives. His powers were delegated and his problems were passed on to them. Like him they came to direct most of their energies to the quest for increased revenues, and their judicial functions gradually became of secondary importance. At the end of the thirteenth century they lost their seats in the *Parlement*, and ended by becoming directly subordinate to the *Commission des Comptes*, the financial section of the *Curia Regis*, which was definitively organised as the *Chambre des Comptes* in the course of the fourteenth century. The new developments did not mean the immediate disappearance of older arrangements. The *prévôts* continued for a considerable period to acquire their *prévôtés* by

---

[1] Published by Brussel, *Nouvel examen de l'usage général des fiefs en France*, vol. ii (Paris, 1750), pp. cxxxix–ccx; and photographically reproduced in the appendix to F. Lot and R. Fawtier, *Le premier budget de la monarchie* (Paris, 1932).
[2] *R.H.F.*, xxi, pp. 270–84.

auction, and the sale of various other offices also persisted. In 1314–15 there were complaints from the south about the sale of the offices of *viguier*, *bayle*, and notary. The *baillis* and seneschals never succeeded in defining in absolutely clear terms the geographical boundaries of their districts, and no reliable map of the *bailliages* and *sénéchaussées* can be drawn. For the limits of some districts were altered when new officials were appointed; other districts were carved out, then suppressed, then re-established;[1] the royal lands in the charge of the local administrators fluctuated in extent because of alienations and new acquisitions; the lordships in which the *baillis* and seneschals were commissioned to guard the royal rights were never the same for very long; and the administrative district to which a particular lordship was attached was not always known for certain. The royal government never possessed an administrative map of France or a year-book containing a list of the royal officials and their districts and powers. In the *bailliages* and *sénéchaussées* the archives seem to have been the personal property of the officials, who took them away with them when they were transferred elsewhere.[2] In consequence the historian must refrain from making Capetian administration appear too schematised when there was still much internal anomaly and confusion. Several centuries were to pass before modern principles of organisation were imposed on it.

The trend towards the specialisation of officials was another new feature of the reign of Philip Augustus. Conceivably it originated about the middle of the twelfth century, though this is far from certain; but in the thirteenth it indubitably became pronounced in several branches of the administration as a logical consequence of the increase in royal powers and the expansion of the royal domain. As long as the king was no more than a great landed proprietor, he had required only one type of local official, to exploit his domainial lands and rights, and his rare opportunities

---

[1] The known examples are catalogued by L. L. Borrelli de Serres, *Recherches sur divers services publics du XIII⁶ au XVII⁶ siècle*, vol. iii (Paris, 1904), Appendix B.

[2] For an amusing letter from Simon de Montigny, *bailli* of Troyes and Meaux, to Simon de Billy, his successor in the *bailliage* of Orléans, see Ch.-V. Langlois, 'Registres perdus de la Chambre des Comptes', in *Notices et Extraits*, vol. xl (Paris, 1916), pp. 82–3. Notwithstanding its title this work contains a vivid study of central administration in action under the later Capetians.

of taking action in the parts of his kingdom lying outside the domain did not call for a numerous administrative staff. The political tasks they produced could be left to the members of the royal entourage. Nevertheless, the royal court sitting as a judicial tribunal seems to have included as early as the reign of Louis VII, and perhaps earlier, a number of *familiares* relatively expert in the law. As the king exercised his royal powers ever more extensively he found the personnel of his administration increasingly inadequate. Every branch of the royal activities came to need its own group of competent officials.

The resultant trend towards specialisation was slow, and its character varied from place to place. For instance, it is certain that Norman administration as it existed when Philip Augustus seized Normandy in 1204 included a number of specialised officials. The same was true of Anjou and to some extent the other lands the Angevins had ruled. When Champagne was acquired by the crown, its administration was well developed, and the Capetians needed to add little. The monarchy was profiting from the work of the great feudal dynasties, which in many respects was superior to its own. By contrast many of the smaller lordships of France seem to have had only a rudimentary administrative organisation, resembling that of the old royal domain of the earlier Capetians. The situation was probably similar in the South, although Simon de Montfort seems to have striven to improve it.

Specialisation at the king's court started a general movement which gradually affected every part of the royal domain. This process has been frequently described by historians, though never with sufficient emphasis on the slow pace at which the judicial and financial commissions at the court developed into permanent and independently organised structures. In 1203, accounts were being rendered at the Temple, as the general account for that year shows. Hence there already existed a little commission of specialists to investigate the accounts of the *baillis* and the accounts of the *marches*.[1] Yet the *Chambre des Comptes* always considered as its

[1] The *marches* were frontier districts under the control of the *baillis*. Their expenses, strictly military, were met with funds from the royal treasury, not from local revenues, and formed a special account. The *marches* seem to have disappeared after the reign of Philip Augustus.

foundation charter the ordinance of Vivier-en-Brie, issued in
1320. Again, in the reign of Philip Augustus and thereafter regular
sessions of the king's court were specialising in judicial business;
but it was Philip III's ordinance of 1278 and Philip V's two
ordinances of 1319 and 1320 which organised the *Parlement* as the
judicial section of the *Curia Regis*.

Nor did the forms of the past disappear completely. The *Curia
Regis* continued to exist in its organic form (if the expression may
be permitted); and on one occasion it forgathered as such. Until
the middle of the fourteenth century the members of the specialised
sections of the *Curia* received not only special wages for sessions
of the latter but also ordinary wages when they were 'at court'
(*in curia*). Although the *Parlement* and the *Chambre des Comptes*
had permanent staffs which prepared their work for them, neither
section officially operated or really existed except during its
periodic sessions, which varied in duration. The king's *conseil*, to
which the sovereign summoned whom he pleased and which was
attended by the princes of the blood royal, the great prelates and
lords, the king's *familiares*, and the members of the *Parlement*
and the *Chambre des Comptes*, was a faithful copy of the assembly
of the *palatini* who helped the earliest Capetians to govern.

There was also a strong development of specialisation in the
lower ranges of royal administration. Gradually there appeared
beside the *bailli* or seneschal new officials charged with helping
him with his various responsibilities: receivers, local justices,
procureurs, forest officials, *capitaines*, and others.

All these officials, whether employed in central government or
in local administration, held office exclusively at the royal pleasure.
Except for judicial officials they were not protected in their
appointments by any kind of professional safeguard. Their tenure
of office derived in no way from rights based either on past
services to the king or on any kind of unwritten contract made
with him.

The outlook which developed among the royal officials was
another novel feature of administrative history in the thirteenth
century. In earlier centuries the royal administration had been
looked on simply as a source of profit. Even a royal official as

devoted as the Abbot Suger was more concerned with the welfare of his abbey of Saint-Denis than with the good of the kingdom; and most royal administrators entered the king's service for personal gain. Once a *prévôt* had paid the farm of his *prévôté* his main concern was to recoup himself for his outlay, and then to pile up the biggest profit he could wring out of his allotted portion of the royal domain, even at the cost of ruining it. The great officers of state likewise strove to make their offices profitable and hereditary and to get permanently into their own hands the royal authority delegated to them.

Royal officials were only human, and this kind of acquisitiveness never disappeared, but it grew rarer, and in the thirteenth and fourteenth centuries most of them were approaching their duties in a different spirit, and displayed a striking zeal for royal interests and rights in which they had no apparent personal interest. They took to claiming not only what was the king's due but also anything which they thought would be to his advantage, even when his right to it was by no means obvious. They often exceeded the king's own instructions and sometimes flouted his personal wishes — for example, with regard to projected alienations of royal lands — if they judged that these ran counter to the monarchy's true interests.

That the royal servants had become more royalist than the king was a change of far-reaching importance. Historians have frequently drawn attention to it, but without seriously asking themselves what caused it or why men should be eager to give the king such devoted service and regard themselves as honoured to be allowed to do so. It is not as though the Capetians lavished generous salaries on their officials. In modern terms their pay was modest. The *bailli* of Vermandois received 739 *livres* in 1269, a little more than 500 *livres* in 1285, 292 *livres* in 1305, 500 *livres* in 1323 (though this was just after he had added the post of receiver to that of *bailli*), and 292 *livres* at the beginning of the reign of the first Valois king, Philip VI, in 1328. It is true that a *bailli* might receive gifts, or *courtoisies*, as they were called; but the ordinance of 1256 limited their value to 10 *sous* a week (25 or 26 *livres* a year), and laid down that they must never consist of gold or silver, but only of meat, fruit, or wine. Philippe de Beaumanoir, *bailli* to Philip III and Philip IV, commented that 'only an exceedingly unfair official would override anybody's rights in return for gifts of that order'.[1]

The stipends of the more important local officials offer some clue to what their subordinates must have received. The high dignitaries of central government were not much better treated. In 1299 Pierre Flote received 500 *livres* as keeper of the seal, and one of the king's treasurers received 600 *livres*. Their salaries were augmented by certain payments in kind, such as robes, food, and fuel; but perquisites of this sort were small beer. The tradition of the underpaid French official goes back to the very dawn of administrative history. And the question inevitably arises whether wages in cash and kind represent only a fraction of the benefits a royal administrator extracted from his office. Lord Sandwich once gave it as his opinion to Samuel Pepys that a man grew rich not by the stipend of his place but by the opportunities of making money which place afforded. But the evidence submitted to the royal commissioners of inquiry sent into the provinces to hear the complaints of the king's subjects hardly suggests that this pronouncement was applicable to later Capetian France. The surviving records of these inquiries give an impression that what was complained of was not so much venality as oppression and extortion; but the proceeds of extortion were destined for the king's coffers, not the pockets of his officers. When corruption was alleged, the accusation was usually couched in such vague phrases that it is likely to have been little more than the expression of the ancient and childish belief that every man has his price. The historian must also make allowances for the spite of those who had sought to buy an official's favour and failed. It must have suited such people to think and say that they would have had more success in corrupting him if they had offered a bigger bribe. The last thing they wanted to believe in was his integrity. Some of the charges brought were no doubt justified, but isolated instances of corruption are no grounds for a sweeping generalisation.

Thus the attractiveness of service in the royal administration

[1] *Coutumes de Beauvaisis*, ed. A. Salmon (Paris, 1899), vol. i, p. 21, § 29.

G

can hardly be put down merely to the hope of material gain. One of the most notable of the royal officials, Philippe de Beaumanoir, produced a famous catalogue of the virtues of the good *bailli*.[1] It is fair to say that Beaumanoir did not always practise the virtues he preached. Nevertheless, he had a high and disinterested conception of his office of *bailli*, even though he himself was not always capable of living up to it.

The outlook of the royal officials may well be explicable by the social milieu from which they were chiefly recruited. Only the more important of them are known to the historian, and they were as a rule members of the lesser nobility, knights, burgesses, or clerks holding minor dignities. Men of some substance, not penniless fortune-hunters, they were not attracted into the royal service merely by opportunities for making money. On the other hand, before taking the king's livery they had never tasted the pleasures of power. The social groups they came from were not accustomed to command except as the subordinates of a higher authority, and on their own they could now do little to alter this situation. A knight had small chance of becoming a great lord; and without the royal favour it was impossible for a burgess to become a knight and exceedingly difficult for a clerk to attain to one of the more exalted ecclesiastical dignities, let alone a bishop's mitre or cardinal's hat. But the king could raise a man above his original station, grant him a pension, or invest him with a fief.

Such royal rewards certainly came the way of successful officials. Even when they were distributed with a sparing hand, members of these social groups were induced into the royal service by the irresistible lure of power. Every royal official, from the *conseiller* of the *Parlement* or the *Chambre des Comptes*, the *bailli* and the seneschal, down to the simple serjeant who carried the fleur-de-lys baton, was a representative of the greatest power in the kingdom and wielded in his own sphere an authority superior to all others. The Capetians were bent on seeing to it that the dignity of their officials was maintained. They rarely refused to uphold their actions, and even when they did the career of the disavowed official was not prejudiced. By contrast, the slightest offence

[1] *Coutumes de Beauvaisis*, i, pp. 16–17, § 12–22.

against one of the king's servants was regarded as a crime worthy of the heaviest punishment. A monk of Saint-Valéry once, without malicious intent, grasped the *bailli* of Amiens by the shoulder when the latter was visiting his monastery. The upshot was that the abbey was fined 800 *livres*. The step was perhaps excessive; but it is a vivid, if exceptional, instance of the French king's determination to ensure respect for the persons of his officials.

In short, the royal administration was a service which attracted Frenchmen of the middle classes because it offered them a path to wealth, position, and rank, delegated sovereign power to them, and afforded them almost complete protection against misfortune. It is not surprising that they became fiercely devoted to the dynasty which had put them in such a favoured situation, and that they were the foremost zealots of the new cult of monarchy which played so vital a part in the future shaping of the state.

One last innovation of the Capetians remains to be considered: their choice of Paris as the capital, the king's permanent residence, and the seat of his government. This choice was a starting-point for important developments to which the devotion of the royal officials made a great contribution.

In the ancient world Rome had been the unique example of a political capital of the modern type, its special position deriving from the part it played in the creation of the Roman Empire. In the middle ages western Europeans were strangers to the idea that there should be a single royal residence sited in the principal city of the kingdom and that a town without long-established ties with the reigning dynasty should be chosen as capital. The very conception of a capital clashed with the feudal notion of monarchy. A feudal king was expected to be itinerant, constantly touring his widely dispersed domain lands, living on their produce, and visiting his vassals, high and low, to make sure of their loyalty and enjoy his prerogative of hospitality (*gîte*), which gave him the right to live at the subject's expense for periods varying in different cases from eight days to a single mealtime. This was how the earliest Capetians lived, travelling wherever they had *gîte* to exploit, staying in one after another of the rather primitive town houses and country mansions which were known as the royal 'palaces'.

From Louis VII's reign onwards they resided more frequently in Paris. From the earliest times the king had had a palace there without enjoying the lordship of the city. Now he apparently came to dominate Paris. But vestiges of the old tradition of royal wandering lingered on as long as the dynasty lasted, as is clear from the itineraries of the Capetian kings compiled from their *acta* by the editors of the *Historiens de la France*.[1] On the other hand, the different departments of the central government, as they emerged, came to be fixed at Paris. By 1300 the process was complete. Paris had become both the political and the administrative capital of the kingdom.

It is not clear why Paris was chosen. Arguments from geography and economic history tend to neglect the fact that the great expansion of Paris as a city came after the Capetians had selected it as their capital, and that their choice itself was the turning-point in the city's history. It may well have been decided by factors which would look unimportant to a modern eye. As the chief town of the Île-de-France, Paris was the centre of a great belt of forest land, unmatched as hunting country by any other stretch of territory which the Capetians, with their passion for the chase, were likely to acquire. And a royal administration based on Paris could always be put in rapid touch with the king, except on the rare occasions when he took an outstandingly long journey.

The Capetian monarchy was the first, and for a long time the only régime in western Europe with a fixed capital of this kind. What is even more important, Paris showed from the start a determination not to relinquish one jot of this position. There was one court of appeal in Capetian France, the *Parlement* of Paris. When the crown acquired the inheritance of Alphonse of Poitiers there was an effort at decentralisation, but the court of appeal set up at Toulouse had only a brief existence. The Exchequer of Normandy continued to hold two sessions a year for

[1] For the period 1226–1328 see *R.H.F.*, xxi, pp. 408–99. For the earlier reigns the itineraries appear in the prefaces to the catalogues of royal *acta* mentioned *supra*, pp. 8–9.

political purposes at Rouen, and the great law-days of Champagne continued to be held at Troyes; but it was the *conseillers* of the *Parlement* of Paris who came to do justice there in the king's name, turning these solemn assizes into mere temporary delegated sessions of the *Parlement*. The situation was similar in the field of finance. The *Chambre des Comptes* was the sole financial court, and it too seconded necessary personnel to the sessions of the Exchequer of Normandy. From Philip II's reign onwards the royal archives were deposited at Paris, and the royal treasure was kept at the Paris Temple under the guard of the Knights Templars. The chancery itself, which might have been expected to accompany the king on his travels, rapidly acquired the habit of sitting close to the major departments of the *Curia* and serving them as a general secretariat, thereby preventing them from evolving departmental chanceries of their own.

The centralisation of the directing organs of royal government and their permanent establishment in what was swiftly becoming the greatest city in France strengthened the administration and gave it cohesion, so that its different sections were able to agree on joint policy and then move to common action, pool their resources, and undertake mutual aid, and draw all the important business of state into their hands. In these circumstances the ordinary routine of administration, centred on Paris, was bound to work towards the unification of France under the monarchy. But the king's idea of political unity was not that of his officials. He wished to bind his realm together with feudal ties alone, and saw only good in the existence of the great fiefs, provided that their lords scrupulously performed their feudal services and honoured their feudal obligations. His officials wanted a single authority to rule in the land unchallenged, the authority which the king had delegated to them. Their devotion to the royal power was almost mystical in its intensity, and they regarded any limitation placed on it as an anomaly which it was their duty to extirpate. This attitude became much more pronounced when their ranks were swollen by new colleagues recruited from the dynasty's newly acquired southern territories, where the Roman Law idea of the prince whose will alone is law reigned supreme.

They believed that the king should be absolute master in his kingdom, the sole fountainhead of legislation and justice, untrammelled in his control of the crown's financial and military resources. The means they used to these ends were far from characteristic of their royal masters. Although they were capable of dying heroically on the field of battle, like Pierre Flote at Courtrai, they were fundamentally bureaucratic, and seized on law as their indispensable weapon. They developed an insatiable curiosity to discover the origins of any rights which conflicted with those of the king and placed checks on his power. This curiosity had important consequences in a society the basis of which was the usurpation of regalian rights. The royal officials were hostile to every method of invoking force to settle a dispute in law, and sought to abolish private war and the judicial duel. Nor would they admit any right to be established until its origin had been explained and its history reconstructed for them. In the course of this kind of historical research, they plunged into endless discussions of the titles submitted to them, and frequently revealed that their good faith was only relative, subjecting documents put in evidence against them to pitiless scrutiny, but resting content with dubious proofs of the validity of the rights they claimed for the crown.

It is not surprising that the royal officials incurred unpopularity in their own day and have not escaped the censure of modern historians. Their challenge to the *status quo* led them to be taken for revolutionaries, though they imagined their goal to be the restoration of the conditions of a remote past. Their aversion to the use of force and preference for the processes of law won them the reputation of being unscrupulous and tortuous. But it is pointless for the historian to subject them to moral judgments. What matters is their achievement, and that was considerable.

It was owing to them that the king became the source of all justice in France. His judicial supremacy had never been seriously contested in principle, but the practice fell marvellously short of the theory. Not until the king's power had grown to formidable stature and royal justice had become easily accessible was his jurisdictional supremacy remembered and recourse had to it. As long as the Capetians had been confined to their ancestral domain and had ruled by means of a rudimentary administration, scarcely anyone but the vassals of the domain had sought justice at their court. A few exceptional pleas not originating in the domain came there to be judged, usually because a plaintiff wished to spite his suzerain or because one of the suitors was a bishop or a monastery more hopeful of justice at the royal court than at that of the magnate within whose fief the plea had arisen. But the territorial expansion of the monarchy changed the situation. The number of the crown's immediate vassals increased. The king replaced the great vassals whose lands he had annexed with himself as direct suzerain, and cases previously reserved for local feudal jurisdiction came before his court. In addition, the annexation to the royal domain of the former domain lands (in the strict sense) of great vassals called for the appointment of increasing numbers of royal officials and led to their gradual dissemination in every part of the kingdom, so that there were few districts without a resident royal official in more or less close proximity.

The king's essential function was that of judge, and consequently his representatives were all judges in varying degrees and all watched jealously for every opportunity to exercise royal jurisdiction. The *baillis* and seneschals were judges of first instance at the assizes they held, and judges of appeal in cases involving the crown's immediate vassals. But there persisted in France for long centuries numerous peculiar jurisdictions, which were independent of royal justice and derived from grants or usurpations of the sovereign's judicial power. The royal officials, using a variety of methods, conducted an age-long struggle against these liberties. Sometimes, though less often than has been supposed, they claimed from them the cognisance of certain pleas on the grounds that they were *cas royaux* belonging to the king. In 1315 the crown was requested to define such pleas. Louis X's government replied that 'the king's majesty has cognisance of pleas which by right or ancient custom may belong and ought to belong to the sovereign prince and to no other person'.[1] This manifestly opened the door wide to arbitrary action on the king's

[1] *Ordonnances*, i, 606.

part in the future. On many occasions the royal officials departed from the principle of the full competence of royal justice, and produced the theory that it survived in a latent form in instances where the king had granted it away. This was how they justified their use of the *prévention* to draw pleas before the royal courts. The royal judge claimed cognisance of the plea before the judge of the peculiar could claim it, and alleged that the latter had been negligent. The claim was also made that the king's courts should have cognisance of all contracts sealed with the royal seal; and every plea involving persons, establishments, or institutions under the royal protection was claimed for the crown. Thus the jurisdictional peculiars, both lay and ecclesiastical, suffered from a series of encroachments and resumptions steadily kept up by the royal courts; and the work of undermining their foundations was completed by the exercise of the royal right of appeal.

It had always been possible to appeal to the king's court from a judgment pronounced in a lower court, but until the twelfth century the appeal could only be heard by the king himself. Long journeys, heavy expenses, and serious delays inevitably resulted. Once the king had *baillis* and seneschals nearly everywhere, representing him in the fullness of his powers, they could hear appeals on his behalf. The appeal no longer needed to be taken directly to the king's court; it was more readily available to the subject; and if necessary a supplementary appeal could be made from the court of the *bailli* or seneschal to the supreme tribunal, the *Parlement* of Paris.

In the development of royal power, royal justice played a part which it is difficult to exaggerate, although final judgment on it is not easy to pronounce, and not all royal judges were miniature Solomons. But the appeal offered a serious guarantee against the denial of justice and unjust judgments in lower courts, both royal and franchisal; and the *Parlement* seems to have had a creditable conception of its judicial duties. Peculiar jurisdictions did not by any means all disappear, but an appeal lay to the king's court from every one of them. And the function of supreme judge, constantly exercised through the medium of the *Parlement* or the courts of *bailliage* and *sénéchaussée*, transformed the king into a personage everywhere present in his realm in the role of Lion of Justice. With the mass of his subjects it was his most popular role.

The royal officials played the leading part in this development. Here again they were not following the king's instructions. The king saw nothing unsuitable in the existence of baronial jurisdiction, though he had more sympathy with the attitude of his officials towards ecclesiastical jurisdiction. When questions of jurisdiction arose, he often repudiated the actions of his officials and renewed the franchisal privileges they were striving to liquidate; but he was powerless to restrain the excessive zeal of those who served him. In consequence, men accused him of bad faith and saddled him with the responsibility for the fruitless protests that were raised. This may well have been unfair; for the Capetian monarchy could only issue orders, which were obeyed in proportion as they pleased the officials charged with carrying them out. And as the officials did not see eye to eye with the king on this matter, the royal circulars enjoining respect for peculiar jurisdictions went to swell the endless bundles of similar dead letters in the crown archives.

The royal officials also wanted the king to be the source of all legislation, and on this issue they were apparently in complete accord with him. Royal legislation was in its application at first limited to the royal domain; and it required the general consent of the barons and bishops. But gradually it became applicable to every part of the kingdom and was increasingly promulgated by the king acting only on the advice of his great officers of state. Capetian legislation, however, affected only the *droit public*. *Droit privé* remained fixed by custom, which the monarchy for a long time made no move to alter.

In respect of *droit public* feudal custom attributed to the king the power of making, according to Beaumanoir, 'such laws for the common profit as shall please him'.[1] Before the reign of Philip Augustus the king made scarcely any use of this power. But the strengthening of his sovereignty and its extension to the entire kingdom led him to increase and multiply his *établissements* and *ordonnances* and to strive to make them accepted as applicable

---

[1] *Coutumes de Beauvaisis*, ii, p. 24, § 1043.

everywhere. This policy created its own difficulties; for those who admitted the principle of royal legislation also averred that 'each baron is sovereign in his barony'; and such baronial 'sovereignty' was opposed to the royal sovereignty in legislative matters.

The difficulty was resolved by leaving the king with his power to legislate, but only with the assistance of his sovereign barons. In this way *établissements* made in common could be safeguarded against meeting with resistance when they were put into practice. The king was behaving in accordance with the convention of the time, like a baron who was unable to act without the 'counsel' of his vassals. But it quickly became impossible for the king to have the great vassals of the crown — let alone the whole body of vassals — at hand for consultation. He was driven to take counsel only with men who could come to court immediately on summons. And so it was no longer possible for the king to command that *établissements* should be applied in the baronies; he had instead to pray the barons to give their permission. Once more he is seen to be appealing to the goodwill of his vassals rather than insisting on their obedience.

The king very soon let it be known that he thought his request should be favourably received, and that any refusal would be taken amiss. In 1223, in an *ordonnance* dealing with the Jews, he declared that this new law would be binding both on those men who had 'sworn' to it, that is, accepted it, and on those who had not.[1] In 1230 another *ordonnance* dealing with the Jews contained the clause: 'And if any of our barons shall refuse to accept this *établissement*, we shall constrain them to do so, and our other barons shall be bound to help us constrain them with all their power and in good faith.'[2]

The practice of mentioning the consent of the magnates continued for a long time, but this consent was a mere formality, since the king's *Conseil* was deemed to be representative of the magnates. In reality, from the reign of St. Louis onwards, and especially after Louis had returned from the first of his Crusades, the King of France was determined to legislate as he pleased,

[1] *Ordonnances*, i, 48.   [2] *L.T.C.*, ii, p. 16, no. 1615.

though with the advice of his *Conseil*. His ability to do so increased as his domain expanded and his power in the kingdom grew. With the accession of Philip the Fair and the virtual annexation of Champagne to the royal domain, the only great fiefs left in France were Brittany, Burgundy, Flanders (which, however, was in Philip's hands for part of his reign), and Aquitaine (which was seized by both Philip IV and Charles IV in turn and considerably subdued under Charles); and the king went a step farther and began to refer, when legislating, to the plenitude of his royal power, to his right to make laws by virtue of his office, and to his intention to make *établissements* for as long as he should be pleased to do so.

Yet appearances were respected. The great feudatories were requested to apply the royal legislation in their lands. Still, no refusal was likely, and the greatest of the vassals, Brittany and Burgundy, were ready to obey the king.

The royal officials put the new laws into execution with zeal. Every infringement was treated by them as an attack on the royal rights, which called for the machinery of justice to be set in motion. Taken as a whole, royal legislation was usually progressive, and there was no difficulty in securing recognition of this fact. During the constitutional movement of 1314–15 the baronial charters contained many protests about the administration of royal justice, but no challenge to the king's right to legislate for the whole kingdom.

Did the power of legislation extend to the field of finance? The king's servants were logical men who argued that it did; but they either dared not or could not press home the view that the king was the sole judge of the monarchy's needs and so could impose the necessary taxes on all his subjects. The ancient Roman idea of a direct arbitrary tax was unknown in Capetian France. Even the king doubted his right in financial matters. The expressions of regret for the subsidies they had exacted from their people, which their biographers put into the mouths of the dying Capetians, were certainly not mere common form.

But the growing monarchy had new needs, to meet which new sources of revenue would have to be found; for the revenues of the domain in its strict sense were soon found to be inadequate, allowing the king to 'live of his own', as the saying went, but not allowing him to reign. Capitalism was only in its early stages of growth, and loans could not give the king everything he needed, quite apart from the awkward fact that they had to be repaid. Manipulation of the coinage began by yielding the royal mint a profit but always ended in a loss for the treasury when the depreciated coin began to flow back to it. All the dynasty's other financial expedients in the period c. 1250–1328 were no more than palliatives. The last Capetians were always short of money. Their administration failed them in this vital field, for direct royal taxation had not been established in France when the dynasty died out in 1328. On the other hand the Capetians had prepared much of the ground for its introduction by their successors.

The needs of the kingdom's defence provided them with the justification for raising substantial sums of money from their subjects from time to time. Their exploitation of the ancient military service with the feudal host paved the way for the advent of direct taxation in France. The first step was to extend host-service throughout the kingdom, and here the crown's territorial expansion was of great importance. The dukes of Normandy, the counts of Toulouse, and the counts of Champagne and Brie had been wont to send the royal host no more than a meagre percentage of their knights. But after the king had stepped into the shoes of these particular magnates, the entire armed force of their territories was mustered to the royal host, as it had rallied in former times to the banner of duke or count when his fief was threatened. The raising of armed forces on this scale, however, while possible for a region of limited extent, could not conceivably be undertaken for the whole French kingdom at the height of Capetian power; nor was it to be desired, for the problems of mobilisation, victualling, and the chain of command would have been too great, quite apart from the countless differences which would have arisen in an army composed of men with such manifold and conflicting privileges, customs, and obligations. But the old Carolingian system of mobilising only the men of regions threatened by the enemy could hardly be resuscitated. It had failed to cope with the Viking invasions, and would also have deprived the crown of substantial forces and put the onus of military responsibility on the same parts of the kingdom every time. On the other hand the mustering of all the armed forces in France would have produced a rabble, poor in quality and beyond the reach of discipline. It was in the monarchy's interests to raise a much smaller force, of serious military value, and to pay for it by taxing those exempt from military service.

The Capetians were not slow to grasp this idea, as is evidenced by a celebrated document of 1194, the *prisée des sergents*,[1] which lists the communes and abbeys of the royal domain and the quotas of serjeants and numbers of carts they were under the obligation to send to the royal host; but each of the most important communes, even at this early date, is shown as having commuted this service into a cash payment, based on the wages of the serjeants and the value of the carts due from it. In the account of 1202–3 this document is repeated almost in its entirety, but all the services due have now been commuted to cash payments to the impressive total of 26,435 *livres parisis*.[2]

This practice of converting the military service of commoners into money was established by Louis IX throughout the domain he had inherited from his father. Later, when the heritage of Alphonse of Poitiers had been acquired by the crown, the royal government took the size of the population and its resources as a basis for assessing the quotas of serjeants and the cart-service due from the plebeian communities, since there was no reliable evidence already available. Similarly there appeared in 1272 the first of the royal *acta* which led to the establishment of arbitrary taxation to supply the king with troops in place of the military service men owed to their feudal lords under conditions dictated by convention and tradition. It only remained to apply the principle of commutation to the military service of the nobility, and to extend it throughout the kingdom, not merely to the royal domain. Philip IV must have the credit for effecting this change, though he was not its originator.

[1] *R.H.F.*, xxiii, 722–3. See also the valuable appendix to the study of 'Les prisées du service roturier au xiii⁰ siècle' in L. L. Borrelli de Serres, *Recherches sur divers services publics*, i, 465–527.
[2] Lot and Fawtier, *Le premier budget de la monarchie française*, p. 19.

By the early thirteenth century the principle had been accepted that the vassal of noble status summoned to the feudal host could compound for his service with a money payment if he wished. But this was a personal arrangement between him and the crown; there was no general tax, regularly applicable in such cases. A step forward was taken in 1272, when Philip III summoned the feudal host to punish the rebellious Count of Foix, and a number of nobles refused to serve. As a result an ordinance was issued in 1274, fixing a scale of values for the commutation of military service. The vassal was to pay a fine for absence, and also the estimated total of what his service with the host would have cost him had he performed it.[1] But he was still free to choose between service and commutation. Philip IV went further, though not without taking precautions. During his war with Edward I of England he levied four general taxes: a hundredth in 1294, and fiftieths in 1295, 1299, and 1301. The novelty of these war taxes was that they were imposed on all the king's non-noble subjects. The nobles were exempt; but the exigencies of the war in Flanders drove the monarchy to make some, and in due course all of the nobles in France liable to taxes of this kind.

In 1302 the *arrière-ban* was proclaimed, calling on all the able-bodied men in the kingdom to muster in arms on a stated day. But a nobleman of military age with an annual income of 50 *livres* or more was allowed to buy exemption by paying the crown half of his annual revenues. Women, children, and disabled men holding noble fiefs paid one-quarter of their incomes. The crown, however, instructed its collectors not to levy these imposts on any baron's lands without his consent.

An ordinance of 17 October 1303, issued 'with the counsel and deliberation' of a number of barons 'because we could not have at this counsel and deliberation our other prelates and barons of our kingdom of France', laid down that every nobleman and ecclesiastic without exception was to furnish the king, for every 500 *livres* of revenues from land, with 'a warrior of gentle birth well armed and mounted on a horse worth 50 *livres tournois*, the said horse to be covered with a coat of mail and a coat of arms'. Commoners

[1] *Ordonnances*, xi, 351.

were to send six serjeants for every hundred hearths. All personnel mustered were to serve four months.[1]

Income from land, not the fief, was the basis for this new arrangement as it applied to the nobility, although it allowed personal military service. But it roused such a storm of protest that the crown transformed it into a straightforward cash levy. For each man-at-arms due (that is, for every 500 *livres* of income from land) the nobles and clergy were to pay 50 *livres*; and a money composition was also to be accepted in lieu of the serjeants owed by groups of commoners. The levy was not repeated in the lifetime of Philip IV. A general subsidy of this nature was determined on in 1313, to finance the war in Flanders, but was abandoned, according to Geoffrey des Nès, when the Flemings once again promised to carry out the Treaty of Athis-sur-Orge. A new subsidy, similar in character but only sketchily defined, was given up in the face of general discontent in 1314.

The basis of the subsidies levied in 1315, 1318, 1319, and 1324 is still obscure, but conjecturally they were less stringent versions of those taken by Philip IV. The details are of small importance; the significant facts are that the king was levying money throughout his kingdom and that the nobility, as well as the clergy and commoners, paid its share. The Church's contributions to the royal treasury included both the proceeds of the crusading tenths ordained by the Papacy and the subsidies granted to the king by the provincial assemblies of the clergy. It should be remembered that the Bull *Etsi de Statu* (31 July 1297) recognised that the king had the right in cases of 'dangerous necessity' — which he himself was to define — to request the clergy that without first asking for papal permission they should contribute to the defence of the realm.

All this was done without any public statement of principle or any reference to the idea of regular taxation. Admittedly the royal officials, who received anxious instructions to do nothing that would disgruntle the taxpayer, went about their work with tact and caution. The result was that the king, by claiming only the feudal military service customarily due to him, put himself in a

[1] *Ibid.*, i, 383–5.

position to secure at need financial support from his entire kingdom.

The royal officials had achieved much. They had brought the power of the crown to bear in every part of the kingdom, progressively extended the scope of royal jurisdiction and legislation, and secured increasing respect for both. They had insisted relentlessly on the performance of every service owed to the king, and had gone ahead with the task of converting personal obligations into fiscal obligations. In consequence, the king had become the sole fountainhead of justice and legislation and the supreme head of all the military forces in France; and it had been made possible for him to call successfully on all his subjects to give him military aid.

When the Capetian dynasty died out in 1328, none of these developments had been more than outlined, and their underlying principles remained unformulated. If the sovereign rights of the king were to be successfully exercised whenever the need to invoke them arose, there would still have to be much patient negotiation. The administrative machine still had many imperfections, and could not operate efficiently unless account was taken of numerous survivals from the era when royal power was feeble and royal rights were more nominal than real. Nevertheless, great advances had been made during the three centuries of Capetian rule, although not all the credit for them is due to kings and their servants, and they can only be fully understood in the light of contemporary developments in French society.

22

The Impact of Social Change

The French nation grew up within the bounds of space, authority and government created by the Capetian kings. These bounds were on the whole well and clearly defined; they had in the main been reached without the use of force. But of themselves they did not create a nation. Before that could come to pass, it was necessary that the inhabitants of the realm should accept the Capetian achievement. That in the end they did so was at least in part due to the patience of the kings and their servants, but the main reason was a quite different one. The anchoring of the various elements of French society within the Capetian state was the result of fundamental social changes, which destroyed once and for all the barriers inevitable in a feudal age. Changes and results were alike unconscious; but the results in no way did violence to the pattern of French history.

Feudal institutions and ways of thought reached their zenith in France during the first century of Capetian rule. Then France was nothing more than a mosaic of virtually independent fiefs, out of which a few adventurers on the grand scale — descendants of the servants and ministers of the Carolingian kings — were beginning to carve territories for themselves. The trend was towards the development of feudal principalities, and not towards the restoration of a kingdom united under a strong crown. Socially as well as politically, the noble possessors of fiefs were unchallenged. The greater clergy, well endowed with lands and deeply involved in lay feudal society, was virtually indistinguishable from the lay nobility. The great mass of the population, in town and country alike, had no political importance. The routine of cultivation dominated their lives, for there was no industry and only local commerce, and agriculture was the only activity known to the great majority. It was, moreover, an agriculture with narrow horizons, and men moved little from their native villages.

For all that, France was on the eve of a demographic crisis. Our information is far from adequate, but it is certain that the population of the kingdom increased considerably during the eleventh century. If the reasons for this are obscure, it is at least clear that its results included a difficult problem for the nobility — how to set their children up in life.

Neither before nor after the eleventh century did the nobles work with their own hands. They were warriors, who lived on the produce of their estates, and whose sole business was war. But their warfare was no more highly developed than the agriculture of their serfs. As a result, a military society with a relatively low mortality rate found itself forced to live off a limited number of fiefs, of which the productive capacity was static. Many of these fiefs were barely adequate to maintain their holders, and sub-division only drove the noble class as a whole down to the starvation level. The rise in population, therefore, created an urgent need for some outlet for the younger sons of the nobility, who could neither be fed nor endowed on the family estates.

Not surprisingly, there was an increasing tendency, as the century advanced, for the nobility to adventure beyond the frontiers of France in search of new lands. The Norman conquest of Sicily and southern Italy was the starting-point. William of Normandy's expedition to England in 1066 drew feudal adventurers from outside Normandy, whilst from 1064 onwards expeditions to Spain attracted knights from all parts of France. In particular, the nobles of southern France, close neighbours of Christian Spain, accompanied by those of Burgundy (who were influenced by the views of Cluny), made war on the Moslems of Spain in campaigns which were the precursors of the Western Crusades in Syria and Palestine.

In the late eleventh century, during the whole of the twelfth, and for a good part of the thirteenth, Crusades to the Holy Land drained off the surplus nobility of France. No adequate study of the effect of this enormously significant event upon the evolution of the kingdom has ever been made. There are excellent assess-

ments of the expeditions themselves, and of their
consequences outside France, but as yet there is no eva
their relationship to the social and political growth of the
state.

The first step in such a study would be an informed estimate or
the numbers of those who went on Crusade, of those who
remained in the East, and of those who died on the various
enterprises. Even so exaggerated a figure as the contemporary
estimate of 600,000 deaths on the First Crusade between Nicaea
and Jerusalem has a certain negative value. But even more important would be a detailed study of individual cases, to give precision
to generalisations as to the effect of the Crusades on the fortunes
of the nobility. Such a study would throw light on the process by
which the resident-proprietor changed into the landlord. A study
of noble dynasties would be equally valuable; it would show how
far residence in the East, with its climatic as well as military
dangers, led to the extinction of individual houses. There are
reasons to suspect that the noble class of the thirteenth century
was very different in composition from that of the eleventh. It
would be helpful to have this suspicion confirmed or disproved;
if it should in fact be correct, then the origins of the new nobility
require investigation.

Professional scholars have tended to neglect genealogical
history of this kind, leaving it to the untrained amateur. In
consequence, works on the subject are much more rare than
linguistic, onomastic and economic studies, and are all too often
mediocre into the bargain. Yet a large-scale enquiry into the
history of families, their marriage connections, and the changes
in their landed property, would be as valuable as a feudal geography. Both are amongst the most urgent needs of the present
generation of French scholars, and there is a very real danger that
they will not be provided whilst the original documents survive.

It is an established fact that significant numbers of the nobility
went on Crusade. It is also certain that they paid their own way,
although as a class they could not lay their hands on large sums of
ready money. Our knowledge of the supply arrangements of the
Crusades is scanty. Once arrived in Moslem countries the

expeditions no doubt lived off the land, but that could account for only a comparatively short part of the whole journey. Whether they took the land routes or travelled in Italian or Provençal fleets, there was always a long journey of several months' duration before the Crusaders reached a land where plunder was legitimate. And all the time transport charges had to be met, dead or spent horses had to be replaced, equipment had to be collected or renewed. Such expenses were bound to be considerable, and many of the Crusaders were unable to meet them out of their revenues, even when augmented by the customary feudal aid levied from vassals on the occasion of a Crusade.

The necessary funds could be found only by borrowing or by the sale of lands. Such sales were frequent, and townsmen and peasants were not alone in benefiting. Princes who did not go to the East bought up whole fiefs from those who did; thus King Philip I purchased the town and *banlieu* of Bourges from Eudes Arpin. But petty sales to commoners were certainly the most frequent.

The emigration of members of the nobility also helped to reduce the disorder of the kingdom. It removed the most turbulent element in society, at a time when the great feudal principalities were emerging and the Capetians were beginning to tame their domain. The most troublesome of all royal vassals, Hugh du Puiset, in fact ended his life across the Mediterranean. Although the economic results of the Crusades — the opening of the Mediterranean, the growth in scale and complexity of Italian commerce, the reappearance of towns and a *bourgeois* class — have long been appreciated, it has not always been sufficiently emphasised that for two centuries the French nobility was the chief source of men, money and materials for the conquest and maintenance of the Latin lands in the East — a fact with social and economic as well as political implications.

The Crusading movement brought advantages to others besides those who actually went to the Holy Land. Stay-at-homes, the Capetians amongst them, profited also. Only three French kings actually went on Crusade: Louis VII, Philip Augustus and St. Louis. Philip Augustus stayed only briefly. The kings, although good enough Christians to be ready to fight the infidel, were not prepared to abandon their royal duties in order to do so. Whilst the nobility ruined itself and was decimated in the East, the Capetians inaugurated the policy, eventually so successful, of pressure on their feudal vassals. Its coincidence in time with the Crusading era is striking. Jerusalem was taken on 15 July 1099, and in the next year the crown prince, who was to reign as Louis VI, made his first attack on the vassals of the royal domain. The last Crusade ground to a halt outside the walls of Tunis in 1270; a year later, on 22 August 1271, Alphonse of Poitiers and his wife died at Savona, without heirs, and Languedoc fell in to the crown.

There were other, less obvious, advantages for the crown also. In the long run the Crusades led the aristocracy to look upon the king as its natural employer. Life in the East and the development of commerce between East and West brought about a change in the values of the nobility. The uncouth baron of the eleventh century, and his often equally unpolished wife, gave way to the gentleman and his lady, with their greater refinement and a taste for luxury even in daily life. The change can be exaggerated, and too much can be deduced from it. But the noble circles for which Chrétien de Troyes wrote, and which listened to the amorous adventures of Lancelot, were very different from those which had taken pleasure in the simpler heroics of the *Chanson de Roland*.

Jealousy of the increasingly wealthy and luxurious town merchants also affected the nobility. This jealousy found an echo in the vexation of Philip the Fair's queen, Joan of Navarre, on seeing the rich clothing of the townswomen of Flanders. An attempt to match the *bourgeois* style of life started many of the nobility on the path of financial ruin. Stationary incomes — to the fixing of which the practice of giving long-term land leases, automatically renewed, contributed considerably — could not sustain the expenses involved, and the result was all too often the pawning of lands and a further reduction in income.

This downward road has yet to be mapped with precision, but its end can be clearly seen. As early as the middle of the thirteenth century the family lands of a large proportion of the aristocracy had disappeared. Division amongst co-heirs had assisted the process. There remained only rents or *cens*, whose value tended to diminish with variations in the value of money, over and above the reduction already caused by the increase in the amount of coin in circulation and the rise in the cost of living.

With their economic superiority lost, the impoverished nobles took refuge in the privileges of blood. They refused to accept into their ranks anyone who was not the son of a knight, and became in fact a closed caste. The change was unwise, and its consequences serious: a long process of intermarriage led to physical deterioration, whilst isolation from the mass of the population was in the long run even more debilitating.

Poor, no longer landholders on a large scale, cut off from the other classes of society, and leaderless into the bargain, the new nobility could turn to one refuge only — the king's service. By the middle of the thirteenth century they were entering that service with increasing frequency. There they found the means of subsistence, and sometimes even financial fortune. There too they were able to continue to exercise power and authority — if no longer on their own account, at least by delegation from the crown.

The Capetians were generous masters to their new servants. Even more significantly, the kings never made their mastery obvious. They always behaved as the first amongst a class of equals, as rulers of the gentlefolk of their kingdom. The ideal of feudal kingship, with the right which it gave to the king to intervene in the family arrangements of his vassals, was not yet dead. It helped to create the feeling that the nobility of France, knit closely together by marriage alliances, formed a single great family, whose head and natural protector was the king. The Capetians never attempted to set barriers between themselves and their subjects. Etiquette did not play a large part in the day-to-day life of the royal court. The king's nobles shared the routine of his private life as well as the government of his kingdom. There was never any question of the Capetians being the opponents or enemies of their aristocracy; on the contrary, they were always careful to preserve the closed character of noble status. The *Parlement* reflected the views of the nobles when it took steps to restrict the right of entry into the class, by forbidding anyone but the king to knight a commoner. The kings themselves took the same standpoint; they made it more difficult for non-nobles to acquire noble fiefs, and they carefully avoided any decision on the delicate question as to whether the tenure of noble land conferred noble status.

Further, by making the royal court the centre of the social life of the nobility, the kings grouped their nobles closely around themselves. The origins of this court life are obscure; it may have begun as early as the reign of Philip Augustus, but it equally possibly developed only after the marriage of Philip III to the young Mary of Brabant. In the latter king's reign there certainly existed a circle of lords and ladies in permanent attendance on the king and queen, and leading a leisured and largely frivolous life. Superficially of little importance, this had in fact some significance. The king's court was beginning to provide a permanent centre for the life of the nobility; in so doing, it was bringing under firm royal guidance the descendants of an older generation of feudalists, who had become strong by refusing to be thus bound to the disintegrating monarchy of their own time.

*   *   *   *

The court of the last Capetians was not composed entirely of these rootless nobles. To it there came also the members of the richer *bourgeoisie* of Paris — a group who had become almost indistinguishable from the aristocracy, if we are to judge by Pierre Gentien's curious poem, the *Tournoiement as dames de Paris*.[1] The *bourgeoisie* of the whole kingdom, indeed, had followed the nobility in one respect: they too had come to look upon the king as the focus of the loyalties of their class.

The emergence of a class of rich townsmen owed something at least to the Crusades, which re-opened the Mediterranean trade-routes and sparked off the revival of commerce on a grand scale. The relative peace which followed the departure of the more turbulent nobles to the East allowed the townspeople to carry

[1] Ed. Mario Pelaez, in *Studj Romanzi*, vol. xiv (1917), pp. 5–67; *v*. Ch.-V. Langlois, in *Histoire littéraire de la France*, vol. xxxv, pp. 284–301.

on their work and trade in greater freedom and security. As a result, they were able to build up fortunes of a new kind, in which landed wealth no longer played the originating or even the most important part. Although in some ways unstable, these new fortunes were more flexible, easier to control, and capable of much more rapid expansion.

In changing circumstances, it was impossible for the town merchants and craftsmen to remain within the framework of strict dependence which had restricted them in the feudal age. Too weak to break out individually, they found the necessary means in the *conjuratio*. By means of such sworn associations they were able to form *communes* (to use their own term), and to force their way into the feudal hierarchy; as collective units they were there able to secure defined and respected rights and duties, through the use of force or, as was more frequently the case, of money.

Although the crown benefited from the appearance of the *communes*, the royal attitude to them has been distorted by legend. It has long been an article of belief that the Capetians were very well disposed to the *communes*, and Louis VI has even been styled 'the father of the communes'. But such views are not now accepted, and it is held rather that the royal attitude was not based on principles, but sprang from circumstances. As in so many other matters, the kings had no set plan and no long-term aims; the local and immediate needs of royal policy were the decisive factors. On the other hand, the crown was adroit enough to draw its profit from a movement which was directed against the local authority of the aristocracy and the Church. The communal movement created a whole series of often rich and powerful lordships inside the great fiefs, and grew up through a series of conflicts with lords who had come to regret their consent to the first vital steps in the process. It was inevitable that the appearance of the *communes* should weaken the capacity of these lords, lay and religious alike, to resist the advance of royal authority throughout the kingdom.

The crown reaped two further advantages. The establishment of a *commune* provided more opportunities for the exercise of royal suzerainty or sovereignty. Royal confirmation of town charters originally granted by the immediate lords could be doubly profitable for the king. Confirmation brought ready cash; it also supplied the legal basis for a future intervention to protect the *commune* and guarantee its rights. Also, the *communes* were a source of valuable military assistance for a not over-powerful crown. The towns possessed their own militias, and although these were perhaps of no great value in a pitched battle (the legend of their deeds at Bouvines is a legend only), they could give useful service behind walls. The defence of Mantes saved Paris in 1188, and the fact that Philip Augustus tended to confine his foundation or confirmation charters to *communes* on the frontiers of the domain — in the Vexin, Picardy, Soissonnais, and Laonnais — is significant.

The kings were well aware of the importance to the townspeople of *communes* and town privileges. Although they were not prodigal of communal charters in the ancient domain, they respected and confirmed existing ones when they annexed new lands. This respect for communal institutions brought them the gratitude of the *bourgeoisie*, and was the origin of the idea that the king was, in general terms, the protector and lord of all the towns of France.

The French *communes* never came to occupy the position or exercise the influence of their equivalents in Italy and Flanders. For all that, their development, even under a certain degree of royal patronage, was in some ways a potential danger to the royal unification of the kingdom. It involved the creation of new lordships which were none the less real for being collective, and there was always the danger that leagues of *communes* might appear, or that a single *commune* might come to dominate the others. Further, the institution was not by definition anti-feudal; it could without difficulty be fitted into the political framework of a feudal society, and even strengthen it — as happened in some other parts of western Europe. In France, where towns never reached an excessive size, this danger hardly arose; the emergence of a strong monarchy in the thirteenth century helped to prevent the possibility. On the other hand, the French *communes* did develop a strongly local and particularist spirit. The member of a *commune* was closely attached both to his institution and to the town which it governed. He was bound to possess a house in the town, in which he must live for at least part of the year. It was not beyond the bounds of probability that he might come to think and act in much the same way as the petty feudalists of the eleventh century, isolated from the main currents of contemporary life. Here again, however, Capetian policy, whether deliberately or otherwise, succeeded in weakening municipal solidarity and in detaching the townsmen from their town communities.

It is certain that not all townsmen were members of their local *communes*, although the exact proportions cannot be established. Within the *communes* themselves there were divisions between the richer members and the remainder. The former were wealthy in their own right, or belonged to families of rich antecedents. They tended to keep the offices of municipal government in their own hands, and the *communes* thus became collective lordships under the control of small groups of select families. They were in no sense democratic bodies. It was natural for those excluded from these municipal oligarchies to become resentful, and to accuse — often with reason — their members of keeping all profits to themselves, of allowing all burdens to fall on the other inhabitants, and of ruining the town's finances to their own advantage. By the thirteenth century two parties had developed, which were in violent opposition to each other. Beaumanoir noticed this, and commented that he had seen 'many disputes in the *bonnes villes*, with the poor fighting the rich, and sometimes even the rich fighting each other'.[1]

These disputes were resolved only by the intervention of the crown, usually on the side of the *bourgeois* oligarchy. Royal intervention tended to put the towns and townspeople in the king's power. It was difficult for them to refuse financial aid to the crown when it had come to their help in a difficult situation — a fact of which the Capetians were well aware. The last kings of the dynasty multiplied the aids and tallages which they demanded from the *bourgeois* ruling groups in the towns, until in the end the oligarchs were ruined and had to beg the government to take over

[1] *Coutumes de Beauvaisis*, ii, p.267, § 1520.

their finances, and sometimes even the whole municipal administration.

By the end of the thirteenth century the organised municipal community was well on the way to disappearance. The *bourgeoisie* could no longer look to it for an outlet for their ambitions. Instead, the king's service promised wealth and honour. It was becoming easier for a *bourgeois* to turn to that service, for his own status was beginning to change. Its basis was altering; from being territorial, it was becoming personal. Although there were still *bourgeois* of individual towns, there were now far more *bourgeois du roi*.

Originally, the *bourgeois* was an inhabitant of a town, with a certain degree of freedom inside it, but remaining the man of the lord of the town. Once outside his town, or the lands of his lord, he became no more than a foreigner, an *aubain*; he no longer had a protector, and his safety depended on the possibly expensive benevolence of the lord on whose lands he happened to be. The twelfth-century *bourgeois* were not thereby completely deterred from travel, but their journeys were hazardous and costly, and they tended to remain closely attached to their towns and lords.

In the thirteenth century, documents begin to show *bourgeois* from outside the royal domain declaring themselves *bourgeois du roi* in royal towns or before royal *prévôts*; the practice is probably older than the first surviving documents which mention it. A *bourgeois* who made such a declaration, and was inscribed on the lists, was not required to reside in the royal town or *bourg* in which he was listed. Wherever he went he was protected by royal authority, for he had become a king's man, and could call on the aid of royal agents who were always ready to enforce their master's rights. Thereafter the king, their new protector, was more important for these *bourgeois du roi* than the towns from which they had derived their original status. They were, in fact, the first element in feudal society to lose their local ties and to become, properly speaking, 'nation-wide'. Further, the expansion of the royal domain and the increase in 'new declarations' (shown by the ordinances which attempted to limit them) led to an increase in the numbers of the *bourgeois du roi*, and eventually to the grouping of the entire *bourgeois* class around the king.

The Capetians did not repulse these new followers. The king was as much their king as he was the king of the gentlefolk, and so he took their counsel, allowed them easy access to his person, and opened the royal administration to them. Before much time had passed he began to grant them knighthood and nobility. It would be no exaggeration to maintain that in return the *bourgeois du roi* — apparently the creation and certainly the favoured dependents of the crown — were the first in the kingdom to develop the idea of loyalty to the monarchy — an idea which was the forerunner of patriotism proper.

The events of 1314–15 support such a claim. In the face of a belated attempt by the aristocracy to limit the dangerous advance of royal authority, by extorting a solemn recognition of its privileges from the king, the *bourgeoisie* stood by the crown through a crisis as serious as that in contemporary England. They were at best indifferent, at worst openly hostile to a reaction which threatened to force them back into an old and unfavourable position. Only in Burgundy did the towns join the feudal coalitions, and elsewhere royal officials were able to give the insurgents to understand that in case of need the crown could rely on the support of the great mass of its subjects. The *bourgeoisie* might not have shaken themselves finally clear of local preoccupations, but they had certainly reached a point at which they understood that the interests of their class were bound up with those of the kingdom.

In this, and in escaping from feudal localism, the townsmen were not alone. Craftsmen and peasants alike had also been slowly escaping from the bonds which tied them to the soil. The communal movement was wider than the limits of the towns proper, for there were many rural *communes*. Even beyond the communities which received charters of privileges of the type of those of Lorris or Beaumont, the condition of the villein slowly improved, and his attachment to the land weakened. For reasons of immediate profit both kings and lords enfranchised many serfs. In addition, the pattern of land-exploitation was changing. Leases (either for a money-rent or for a fixed share of the produce) were replacing direct occupation, and gave greater freedom to the peasant. The policing of the royal domain, and the re-establishment of a state of relative order, which reached its highest point in the thirteenth century, also helped towards greater rural prosperity. Evidence for this prosperity can be seen in the systematic policy of enfranchisement carried out by the dynasty at the turn of the thirteenth and fourteenth centuries; rural serfs were then able to offer quite considerable sums as the purchase-price of their freedom.

The rise in general prosperity brought advantages to the crown. Peasants and artisans had an increasingly positive interest in the maintenance of peace and good order — conditions which they ascribed to the action of their kings. To them the king was the protector of their weakness. His justice was easily accessible, and his agents, whilst by no means beyond reproach, were far superior to those of the local lords, and indeed to those lords themselves. Royal authority was the effective curb on local tyranny, and the peasant and artisan knew it. They might lie outside the realm of effective political action, with no likelihood of being able seriously to hinder the growth of the king's power, but they had a real interest in the success of royal policy, and their attitude cut the ground from under any possible noble opposition to the crown. Also, it made the work of royal agents easier; a less well-disposed population could have put considerable difficulties in the way of royal policies.

* * * *

The close links which joined the Capetians and the clergy of their kingdom have been noticed already. They dated from the earliest days of the dynasty, and they were in no way weakened by the economic and social changes of the eleventh and twelfth centuries.

The rise and emancipation of the *bourgeoisie* often took place at the expense of the Church. It was not that the townsmen lacked devoutness, as the age understood it. But they were not, as a class, particularly well disposed towards the clergy. Their hostility may have owed something to the existence of a large number of nominal 'clerks', who sheltered under 'benefit of clergy' whilst entering into commercial and industrial life. The nobles, also, had reasons to be hostile. The Church remained wealthy, drawing much of its prosperity from past noble liberality towards God and His saints. As their own resources dwindled, the nobles came to regret this generosity of their ancestors, and to cast about for every chance to regain control of pious gifts. It was an additional inducement that often enough the clergy had not respected the purposes laid down by the original donors. Further, the intricate intermingling of lay and religious lands produced many lawsuits; church courts, faced by such cases, tended to favour churchmen. Both the *bourgeoisie* and the nobility, therefore, were on the whole hostile to the Church, and a gulf began to widen between churchmen and the rest of society. The static nature of religious society in an age of accelerating social change did nothing to narrow the gulf.

Some new elements did appear inside the Church, such as the orders of mendicant friars. Of these, the Franciscans and Dominicans were the most important in France. They possessed a 'rule' of their own, but they differed profoundly from the monastic orders proper — Benedictines, Cluniacs, and the offshoots of the latter — with their great abbeys and large estates. The friars had no loyalty except to their orders; they professed their obedience in particular provinces, but were not thereafter tied to them. With their international character, their lack of local ties, and their absolute obedience to the Papacy, these orders were a possible centre of resistance to the growth of royal authority. But the possibility never became a reality. The Capetians were well disposed to both the Franciscans and the Dominicans, and the kings from St. Louis onwards endowed them with a stream of gifts — more often in the shape of annual rents or *cens* than of actual lands. The orders, in their turn, became willing servants of their protectors and benefactors. They remained faithful to the crown in the great quarrel between Philip the Fair and Pope Boniface VIII. The Franciscans had the greater reason to take up this attitude; the 'spiritual' element in the order was unlikely to look kindly upon a Pope who had interfered forcefully in its internal politics. But the Dominicans were not behindhand. In a letter of 22 July 1303 the Provincial of the French Dominicans invited the brethren of his province to adhere to the royal appeal to a Council of the Church.[1]

The advent of the mendicant friars helped to deepen the divisions inside the Church, to the ultimate benefit of the monarchy. The secular clergy were aggrieved by papal support of the friars' claim to hear confessions; older churches and monasteries were jealous of the diversion of lay generosity to their new rivals. In consequence, both monks and secular clergy turned to the crown for support; the Papacy, the supporter and protector of the new orders, was too suspect.

The international organisation of the friars was only one example of the increasing exploitation of the French Church by alien, and particularly by Italian, clergy. The policy of the Curia on collation to benefices was an even more obvious instance. The tendency was probably exaggerated by uninformed public opinion, and never reached the intensity it attained in England. But there was some basis of fact behind the numerous complaints of Italian intrusion. It is not too difficult to detect in this situation one of the motive forces behind the emergence of a strongly nationalistic frame of mind amongst the French clergy, the precursor of the so-called 'Gallicanism' of the late fourteenth century.

The growth of monarchic authority was not confined to France alone. Inside the Church, papal control was transforming a Christian republic into a monarchy with markedly absolutist tendencies. The theories of the Gregorian Reformation came increasingly close to reality under Innocent III and his successors, in the shape of a movement which aimed at uniting the Western Church under unchallenged papal headship. The intention was nothing less than that the Pope should have the initiating control in all matters spiritual, and a free hand with the temporalities of the Church. This entailed the suppression or modification of many extremely old local habits and traditions, and above all the disappearance of all the particular characteristics which the Western Church had derived from the society in which it had

[1] E. Picot, *Documents relatifs aux États Généraux et Assemblées réunies sous Philippe le Bel* (Paris, 1901), p. 383, no. 407.

grown up. Similar to that of the Capetians, this programme was far more difficult to carry through, for it involved conflict with a vastly greater number of local interests, whose resistance was much more obstinate than any encountered by the French monarchy.

In France at least, the new policy was on the surface a reversal of an old-established papal programme. The Popes had long acted as the champions of the liberties of the Church against lay encroachment. They had upheld free election to bishoprics and abbacies; they had attacked lay patronage; they had maintained the judicial and financial privileges of the clergy. Now they had come to stand for the reduction, even for the suppression, of free election; for an unqualified papal right to the disposition of benefices; for a reservation of the most lucrative law-suits to judgment in Roman courts; for a savage policy of taxation of the local churches and the possessions of the clergy; and for an unchallengeable exercise of power by legates over the local churches — involving a stream of papal orders, correction of alleged abuses, and distribution of praise and blame, all in a manner that was not always tactful.

Even if the Popes had been French such conduct would have caused discontent. But the Papacy was fast becoming an Italian institution. Thirty-four Popes reigned between the beginning of the twelfth century and the accession of the house of Valois: twenty-six of these were Italians, one was English, one Portugese, and six French (in the modern sense of the term). These Popes lived at Rome, or in the Patrimony, surrounded by a predominantly Italian Curia. It was this Curia which took decisions on the filling of vacant benefices — not always without the suspicion of simony. Inevitably, papal policy was an Italian policy. The Popes were Italians, served by Italians, possessing extensive Italian lands, and often members of Italian families whose quarrels were a serious complicating factor in the affairs of the Curia. And the Italian policies of the Popes were expensive. They involved wars and alliances, and they compelled the Curia to levy money from reluctant non-Italian churches. With a crowning lack of tact, this money was paid into the coffers of the Italian bankers who served the Papacy. It was hardly surprising that there were protests.

Slowly but surely the French clergy, under the impact of this new Papacy, developed a feeling of detachment. They never openly became hostile towards the Holy See, but they came to mistrust it. The Popes were accused, with some exaggeration, of ruining the Church in France for the benefit of the Italian Curia and the family ambitions of Italian Popes. Once this outlook became widespread, the French Church was impelled to turn to the crown for support. It was unpopular with lay society, and even subject to attack by it; now it had come to distrust its own head. The king seemed a possible — indeed the only possible — protector of local liberties against an aggressive Papacy, as well as a defender against enemies at home. The crown, for its part, was prepared to give the Church what it wanted. The king protested, often energetically, against the excesses of papal agents and tax-collectors; he multiplied the royal charters recognising and confirming the liberties and privileges of the churches of his kingdom; he was open-handed and accessible to the clergy, giving them places in his administration, and encouraging them by a piety as real as it was edifying. It was hardly surprising that in return the Church became a firm supporter of the crown.

The intention of Philip Augustus, St. Louis and Philip the Fair was to attain a position of uncontested sovereignty. They were fortunate in that circumstances and their own policies made it possible for them to appear as the fathers and equals of their nobles, the protectors of their most humble subjects, and the defenders of the Church of their kingdom and its liberties. They were fortunate because as a result they secured a willing obedience that might have proved hard to command, and because in consequence all the diverse parts of the society of their kingdom came to take their places inside the framework which the dynasty had worked to create.

H

1 2

The Intellectual and Moral Climate

The Capetian achievements, territorial, political, administrative, and their acceptance by the French people, were the vital advances along the road towards the creation of France. But by themselves these products of three centuries of patient state-building were not enough, and if they were to endure they had somehow to be induced to come together in a single organic whole. Breath must enter into the dry bones.

Probably the Capetians did not look at the problem in this light. It must be re-emphasised that they were not deliberately working for posterity. They were men of action, living in the present. Their immediate difficulties bulked too large to allow them the leisure, even if they had had the inclination, to take the long view. The nation in its modern sense was an idea they did not grasp, any more than their contemporaries grasped it. Nevertheless, their efforts undoubtedly made a vital contribution to bringing the French nation to its eventual birth.

A nation is made up, first and foremost, of people who speak the same language: not, that is to say, a group of different tongues all going back to a single remote linguistic root, but a language in which the differences between one local dialect and another are not too great to prevent the various regional groups from easily understanding each other. This was emphatically not the situation when the Valois dynasty succeeded the Capetians in 1328. There was a deep cleavage between the speech of the north, *langue d'oïl*, and the speech of the south, *langue d'oc*. In addition, a Celtic language was spoken in Brittany and a Germanic language in Flanders; and the clergy used Latin as a spoken language. Thus five widely differentiated languages were current in the kingdom of France at the time when the House of Capet died out.

One of these five languages, however — *langue d'oïl*, spoken in the royal domain, the region of which Paris was the hub — was gaining ascendancy over the rest by becoming the principal language of literature. *Langue d'oïl* was also the language in which the royal commands were issued. The proceedings of the *Parlement* of Paris were conducted in *langue d'oïl*. And the royal administration used it frequently, though concurrently with Latin and *langue d'oc*.

The monarchy was responsible for the central government's use of French — as we may now call *langue d'oïl*. But the Capetians made only an indirect and tardy contribution towards the choice of it as the language of literature. Excepting only Robert the Pious, Hugh Capet's descendants down to and including St. Louis seem to have had little interest in the things of the mind. It is remarkable how slight a role the King of France plays in the literature which has survived from the twelfth and thirteenth centuries. Lacking the evidence of other works which have now disappeared, we should be unwise to draw sweeping conclusions from this fact. All the same, our present knowledge strongly suggests that the great feudal courts of Champagne and Flanders and Burgundy performed a far more important part in the development of French literature than did the court of the Capetian kings.

This situation changed when Philip III came to the throne in 1285 and married the young Mary of Brabant. With Philip — whose confessor, the Dominican Laurent d'Orléans, though born a Florentine, wrote a French work, the *Somme le Roi*, the very considerable success of which is not at all easy to understand — the French king and his entourage began to take an interest in literature and the royal court to be a wellspring of literary patronage. At the court of Philip IV the great ladies — foreshadowing the Cartesian beauties of the seventeenth century — took up enthusiastically the teachings of that prodigiously encyclopaedic and highly original writer, Master Ramón Llull of Majorca: or so at least Llull tells us.

As the Capetian dynasty neared its end, the King of France was beginning to take in the world of letters the place he occupied in the world of affairs. The Valois were to inherit and develop this tradition. Under royal influence *langue d'oïl* became decisively the language of French literature. But the Capetians had not initiated this process, for it was in full swing by the time they came to give it added momentum.

In the present state of research it is still by no means clear exactly how far *langue d'oïl* owed its growing predominance to its status as the language of the royal court. A convincing answer has still to be given to the question of exactly what company the Capetians kept at their court in the twelfth and thirteenth centuries. And without further evidence on the point it seems implausible that the court's cultural life suddenly leapt up to full vigour in the reign of Philip III. Since *langue d'oïl* was current in the entourages of Philip Augustus, Blanche of Castile, and St. Louis it was conceivably already the language of fashion for the French nobility and *bourgeoisie* in general. But these are problems to which there are no satisfactory solutions yet available.

Though for centuries the Capetians looked with indifference upon French intellectual life, they nevertheless made, perhaps unwittingly, a contribution of crucial importance to its centralisation in Paris. Mediaeval universities were not necessarily royal foundations. More often they were the product of papal initiative, for education came under the aegis of the Church. But obviously a papal move to found a university could bear little fruit without the goodwill of secular authority. Boniface VIII, for instance, founded by letters apostolic a *studium generale* at Pamiers in 1295, but this new university never existed except on paper. The hostility of Count Raymond VII created inordinate difficulties for the infant University of Toulouse. And in 1312 King Philip IV suppressed the University of Orléans, which Pope Clement V had founded only six years previously.

Universities in Capetian France, then, were not exclusively in the province of the ecclesiastical authorities. In their future the king also had a voice. Apart from various *studia* which usually specialised in the study of Roman Law, there were in France only two fully constituted universities, or *studia generalia*: Toulouse, founded in 1229, and Paris. The antiquity of the University of

Paris and its high prestige, especially in the thirteenth century, help to explain the early struggles of the newer foundations. Their prospects were almost hopelessly blighted by Parisian competition. Angers and particularly Orléans only flourished because they taught Roman Law, which in Paris was forbidden by the crown.

In the thirteenth century the University of Paris was not always on the best of terms with the monarchy. There was an especially bitter and prolonged conflict between them when Blanche of Castile was regent. But their struggles were never so exacerbated that reconciliation was out of the question. When a dispute between them was touched off by some act of violence committed by the royal officers against masters or students, the king, contrary to his usual practice, would come down heavily upon his offending servants. Both Philip Augustus and Philip the Fair summarily punished that high and mighty dignitary the *prévôt* of Paris for his oppressions of the university. The monarchy's generally benevolent attitude towards the university may well have sprung from consideration of Parisian business interests. The presence of such an important body of consumers in the capital was good for trade and was therefore to be encouraged. On the other hand the king may have kept on such good terms with the university because he grasped that its support might one day be exceedingly valuable to him. Whatever his motive, it is of great interest that the university, an ecclesiastical and papal creation, deliberately sought his alliance. In return, the Capetians in the thirteenth century neither founded nor permitted to be founded any new universities capable in the long run of weakening the supremacy of Paris. Nor did they at all encourage those other universities, such as Toulouse, Angers, and Orléans, which had already come into being, either in the old royal domain, or in lands subsequently annexed.

It is a reasonable conclusion that the Capetians wanted only one university, one *studium generale*, in their kingdom — the University of Paris. This policy had far-reaching consequences. Paris, already the seat of monarchy, the royal city *par excellence*, came more and more to be France's intellectual capital.

There is a danger of exaggerating the importance of the universities in the middle ages, especially before the fourteenth century; of looking at them in too modern a light. But even though the number of men in France who received a university education was only a tiny proportion of the population, the existence of the University of Paris, unique of its kind in the kingdom, undoubtedly contributed much to the spiritual and intellectual unification of the French people. It frustrated the development of provincial centres of university life, which could have been awkward, even dangerous for the monarchy. Conversely, if there had been any parallel in the provinces to the loyalism of the University of Paris it could only have prejudiced the work of unifying France. This trend declared itself strongly in the fourteenth century. But it was in the thirteenth that Paris had established her intellectual supremacy and that her university's authority grew powerful under royal protection.

Since many of the royal servants were graduates of the University of Paris, it became a sort of annexe to the great corporations in the service of the state which the Capetians were organising. The last kings of the dynasty consulted the university on a number of weighty issues. It gave the crown its opinion as to the validity of the abdication of Pope Celestine V. It rallied to the support of Philip the Fair in his quarrel with Boniface VIII. In 1317 it was consulted on the question of the succession to the French throne. Each time its opinion was sought, the university produced the answer the king wanted. These consultations enhanced the prestige of both parties. For men observed that the university commanded the sovereign's utmost respect and that he freely took counsel, especially on the difficult terrain where the secular marched with the spiritual, at a fountainhead of incomparable wisdom, flowing entirely for his benefit.

The prestige of the University of Paris, its loyalty to the crown, and the royal favours it received combined to make the city in which it stood the intellectual capital of France. The attention of every Frenchman with an interest in the things of the mind was focussed on Paris. The great city provided, for a wide diversity of social groups, the intellectual unification and centralisation which

— whatever may be said for and against them — had so profound an influence on the development of French unity.

This development was the more important because France had no ecclesiastical capital. The Primate of the Church in France had his see not at Paris but at Sens. His primacy was far from being universally acknowledged, and was challenged, often successfully, by rival primates in the provinces. The lack of an ecclesiastical capital and of a generally accepted head of the Church in France was to some extent compensated for by the University of Paris. Christian thought in France was under the university's direction. Many of the thirteenth-century and fourteenth-century French bishops and archbishops had been educated in the Paris Faculties of Theology and Canon Law. The university gave spiritual unity to the French Church and not surprisingly captured it intellectually. The future leaders of French ecclesiastical life learned devotion to the monarchy in the Schools of Paris. A royalist university, honoured and protected by the king, took the lead in countering the 'Catholic' influence of the Holy See and laying the spiritual foundations and training the *cadres* of the Gallican Church. But whether the kings who fostered and encouraged and sought the counsel of their capital's growing university foresaw that their policy would have such consequences is far from certain.

The extent of Capetian influence on the development of France's language and literature is difficult to assess; on intellectual life it can be measured rather more exactly. But no satisfactory solution can be offered to the important problem of the dynasty's place in the history of the visual arts. What the Capetians contributed to the establishment of a specifically French school of artists remains an open question.

It was in the French royal domain that Gothic art made its earliest appearance in the twelfth century. It seems clear that Norman and Burgundian and other influences from outside the royal domain helped to shape the Gothic style, but the fact remains that the first wholly Gothic buildings were put up in the Île-de-France.

Churches built in the Gothic style now began to appear rapidly on all sides. Local schools of architecture in the full flowering of their development were suddenly supplanted by Gothic, and only rarely can a transitional phase be shown to have occurred to make the change less abrupt. Churches begun in the Romanesque style were finished off in the Gothic of the royal domain.

The adoption of the architectural style of the Île-de-France sometimes coincided, as in Languedoc, with the establishment of Capetian political domination. But Gothic appeared in too many places where Capetian power did not penetrate to justify the theory that the two developments were indissolubly linked with each other. And it is known that the Capetian kings built few churches except their palace chapels at Paris and Saint-Germain-en-Laye. The movement which was beginning to cover France with Gothic churches was in fact created by the spontaneous efforts of innumerable individuals. The product of purely local forces, it had no discernible central organisation or control.

Various explanations have been offered for the widespread popularity of Gothic. In particular it has been stressed that Gothic was a method of building which offered new solutions to the problems architects had long encountered in the construction of large and well-lit edifices. But even if Gothic originated as a series of new devices in architectural engineering, it was far more than a mere way of building. The revolution was aesthetic as well as technical, inaugurating an age of discovery in the resources of the plastic arts. Its birth and success are not to be explained away by the simple statement that the potentialities of the pointed arch had been realised.

The beauties of the Gothic style were not its only attraction. For it was the style of the royal domain and in consequence fashionable everywhere. Fashion is a matter of taste, not of reason, and there have been periods in the history of art when bad taste has triumphed. It is a fair assumption that the prestige of the Capetian monarchy helped to create a preference for the artistic styles favoured in the royal domain and the great royal city of Paris. When a clerk who had studied at the University of Paris acquired a benefice or an ecclesiastical dignity it was natural that he should want to rebuild his church in the 'Parisian' manner. Very little is known of the artists of this period, but some of them seem to have been remarkably cultivated men. The architect Villard de Honnecourt certainly was. In those days apprentices in the arts may well have mixed freely with university students as they do today. The student who got preferment and rose in the world would eventually want to employ artists himself and would give his old artist friends the benefit of his patronage. The aesthetic fashions of the *bourgeoisie* were learned from the great lords; those of the great lords from the royal domain.

It is conceivable that to copy royal fashions in the arts was a method of paying court to the powerful kings of the thirteenth century. The artists themselves are almost completely anonymous. But systematic research on their patrons, though very difficult to carry out, might clarify the motives which led them to adopt the new styles and to employ the artists of the royal domain. This may well have been a way of demonstrating loyalty, paying one's addresses to the royal officers, or pleasing a bishop noted for his devotion to the crown. The question is worth investigating.

To sum up: at the very time when the Capetian kings were bringing together under their authority the various territorial lordships of the kingdom, the vernacular spoken in the royal domain was beginning to be accepted and spoken throughout France and to become the predominant language of literature. A new art-form, created by the eclectic artists of the royal domain, was spreading to every corner of the kingdom, and was ultimately to establish itself all over Europe. At Paris, the seat of government and the king's own city, the university had won an undisputed ascendancy over the minds of the French clergy. Rival universities — those already in existence and those which were to be founded in the fourteenth century — were doomed to obscurity or the pursuit of a few specialised studies.

The political achievement of the Capetians had included the bringing together of the great fiefs of the kingdom and their subjection to closer control; in the realm of thought and culture the dynasty had accomplished, consciously or not, a similar *rassemblement* of the leading minds of France. And there is a last process of this kind to be considered. It might fittingly be called the *rassemblement* of the mass of the crown's subjects.

H 2

At the beginning of the fourteenth century Philip IV twice appealed, on religious issues, to the public opinion of his entire kingdom (not merely that of the populace of the royal domain) and gathered together its representatives. In 1303, at the most critical stage of his conflict with Boniface VIII, Philip decided to appeal to the Church Universal, sitting in a general council, against a pope whose legitimacy and orthodoxy he now denied. He resolved to appeal to a general council not only in his own name but also in the name of his whole realm. Consequently the people had to be consulted first. An assembly of delegates from the different estates of society was decided on, and a great campaign was launched to secure the support of the French people for the request for a general council which Philip had put forward in their name. The people of each town and village assembled in church or market-place, cloister or cemetery, heard the royal commissioners give an account of the situation, and with virtual unanimity declared themselves in favour of the royal policy, though it is true that some of those present saw in the projected general council a forum in which the pope would be able to justify his own cause.

Some historians have regarded Philip's campaign to recruit support for his demand for a council as no more than a dishonest farce. They deny that the Frenchmen who were consulted were allowed to voice their true opinions. There were, however, groups which openly refused to support the king.[1] Whether these historians are right or wrong is of no consequence. For even if consultation was a sham, the fact that even a pretence of it took place was of great importance. For the first time a question affecting the whole realm had been placed before all the king's subjects, without distinction of class or sex. (The official reports from various urban and rural communities mention the names of women who took part in their local assemblies.) Frenchmen had their first opportunity ever to realise that they all belonged to one community and that there was indeed a kingdom of France.

[1] At the end of the seventeenth century the Trésor des Chartes still preserved 596 declarations of unconditional support for Philip IV, 93 of limited and conditional support, and 18 refusals of support.

The opportunity arose again in 1308, once more in connection with the affairs of the Church. The king proposed to appeal to Pope Clement V to suppress the 'heresy' of the Templars, and summoned to Tours delegates from every part of the kingdom: nobles, townsmen, clerks. 'Townsmen' were defined so broadly that there was hardly a community in France which was not called on to be represented. Once again the Frenchmen the king consulted gave him the answer he wanted.

The consultations of 1303 and 1308 suggest that there already existed unanimity on certain issues among the different communities of Philip IV's kingdom. And it is probable that these consultations, by giving unanimity a chance to make itself known, helped to confirm and strengthen it. Its main source was the subject's loyalty to his king and his veneration for the French crown and the House of Capet. The influence of Louis IX can be detected here, for he had stood before his people as an ideal sovereign, whose personal virtues enhanced the kingly office both in his lifetime and after. The effect of Louis IX's services to the monarchy was magnified when his grandson's skilful diplomacy procured his canonisation from Boniface VIII.

But the King of France was not France; or rather, if he represented France, his people, though they venerated him, failed to grasp exactly what it was he represented. Their loyalty to monarchy was not yet patriotism, in the noblest sense of that word, but it had set their feet on the path towards genuine national sentiment.

For patriotism to come to birth in France, Frenchmen would have to go through a crisis in which those who were loyal to the monarchy would be baffled as to which royal claimant to support. With the king in temporary eclipse, the kingdom, the *patrie*, France, would become visible. Then and only then would there be a French nation.

The great crisis of the fifteenth century was to bring this about. But the Capetians had pointed the way unmistakably. They had united France territorially, endowed monarchy with new vigour and renown, invested the crown with the halo of sanctity, created an administration which was to bind the kingdom together for centuries, and begun to accustom their subjects to feel alike and think alike and express themselves alike. The House of Capet had drafted the broad outlines of the French nation. It was for the future to complete the work.

EPILOGUE

With the completion of our survey, the question arises: had the Capetians a policy from the outset, and, if so, what was its nature? A dynasty's policy may be defined as a comprehensive and durable plan of government devised by the founder or one of his successors at a precise period of time, and thereafter carried out in detail by those who come after. But none of the Capetians formulated a policy of this kind; and the *Enseignements* of St. Louis to his son were exclusively moral precepts. On the other hand we may arguably speak of policy when all the reigning kings of a dynasty approach their task in the same way, and work with reasonable consistency towards the same goal as their predecessors. That the Capetians did this is a fair deduction from the present study, not a deceptive product of the analytical layout of the work; other accounts of Capetian history, strictly chronological in their arrangement, would yield the same conclusion.

None of the Capetians was a man of genius or even an intellectual. But all of them were intelligent hard-working men, living in the world of their present and finding the daily round of governmental duties occupation enough without speculating on the likely historical effect of their actions. They had no need to shape their policy: hard necessity did that for them.

To survive as a dynasty they had to keep firm control of the succession to the throne. Hence their practice for two centuries of associating the king's eldest son with his father on the throne. Thus the heir was trained in the business of kingship during his father's lifetime, and was in the best possible position to carry on the latter's work after his death. As king-designate he came to know and co-operate with his father's counsellors and naturally retained their services when he became sole king. In due course his own eldest son went through a similar apprenticeship. Nearly all the Capetians were respectful and obedient sons who modelled themselves on their fathers, and in consequence the government of France acquired a peculiarly continuous quality.

By the thirteenth century the Capetians no longer felt serious anxiety on the score of their survival as the ruling dynasty, and gave up the practice of associating the heir with his father on the throne. But nothing was lost, for by then the dynasty had gained considerable territorial power and was also capable of effective action beyond the limits of the royal domain. Moreover, the Capetian kings of the time were the ablest, or perhaps the luckiest of their line, and each in turn was spurred on by his father's successes to follow the same road in pursuit of the same objects. Thus from 987 to 1328 Capetian rule had a continuity and a homogeneity which originated not in long-term planning but in each king's readiness to take his predecessor as his pattern.

Capetian policy as we have defined it grew out of the conditions of Hugh Capet's time, which endured for nearly two hundred years. The king was weak, and his domain, though not negligible in size, was a prey to the feudal disorder characteristic of the period. The Capetians could not think of making conquests abroad. On the contrary, they had their work cut out to re-establish order in the royal domain and to protect the crown's interests against the encroachments of over-mighty subjects. They were not strong enough to be able to rely very much on force, but, as we have shown, they made skilful use of their suzerain rights. This was only possible because they were prudent enough to refrain from attempting revolutionary changes, and because as feudal kings they claimed from feudal society only what was their due. Their claims were not excessive so long as the feudal system retained its vigour, for the king could do nothing without the consent and goodwill of his vassals. But for various reasons the feudal system, though theoretically intact, began to crumble in the thirteenth century, and the monarchy benefited from both aspects of this state of affairs.

The Capetians made their appeal to sovereign right only slowly to begin with, for they seem to have grasped that time was on their side, and they were always clever enough to show at least formal respect for the rights of others. They readily proclaimed and confirmed the rights of their vassals almost as if they knew that when the day came to absorb great fiefs into their domain they would be able to claim those rights for themselves.

They were not an excessively ambitious dynasty, and refrained from pursuing will-o'-the-wisp schemes or involving themselves in any of the fanatical religious movements of their time. In St. Louis they produced the ideal crusader, but it was as well that he did not appear on the scene until the monarchy was sufficiently strongly entrenched to be able to afford this luxury and at a time when the general enthusiasm for crusading was waning. And Louis' death on crusade was even more opportune for his dynasty, which was able to shine in — and profit from — the reflected glory of a martyr for the Faith.

The Capetians made good use of their numerous opportunities to increase their power and possessions; but they were never in a hurry and always had the good sense to employ force sparingly, even when they had an utterly free hand. Its use was at times necessary but always repugnant to them. It was as if they understood that force wins only transient victories and that whatever is to last must be founded firmly on right. Their early difficulties had imposed on them a policy which they carried out with moderation and wisdom; and they kept their heads and adhered faithfully to the same line of conduct throughout the years when their power was steadily mounting. It was their good fortune to disappear before their prodigious successes had had time to persuade them into forgetting the lessons of their earlier days.

We must finally ask what, if anything, their policy had contributed to the creation of France. It has already been observed that in 1328 France was still in the making, not yet made. Her territorial framework was more or less complete, she had a settled political régime and the main elements of an efficient administrative system, and her inhabitants were united in their loyalty to the crown. But these things had not made a nation of her. Like the little ship in Kipling's story, making her first voyage across the Atlantic, the France of 1328 had yet to find herself. But most of the essentials needed to bring the French nation to birth were in existence; and the Capetians had contributed decisively to their development, and endowed them with a number of their permanent characteristics. France inherited from the dynasty her territorial cohesion (produced with a minimum of force), her tendency to be absorbed in her own affairs and neglect events in the world outside, her unresisting acceptance of the leadership of Paris, her submission to a powerful and devoted administration, and her cult of kingship, in which all her people shared, and which was eventually to merge into the cult of *la patrie*. She had been organised by able kings, who put right before might and so helped to engender her horror of constraint and her mediaeval passion for liberties which became her modern passion for Liberty. Such were the services — performed without realisation of the magnitude of the task undertaken — rendered by the kings of the House of Capet to the French nation which was still unborn when they were succeeded in 1328 by their kinsmen of the cadet House of Valois. Their achievement had been founded, albeit unconsciously, on the practice of a principle formulated centuries after by Montesquieu: 'He who would govern men must not drive them but lead them.'[1]

[1] Montesquieu, *Mes pensées*, vol. ii, fo. 204ᵛ.

A SELECT READING LIST

THIS list is not intended to provide an exhaustive bibliography of Capetian history. It contains secondary works only, and does not include the studies of individual reigns noted in Chapter I.

AUDOIN, E., *Essai sur l'armée royale au temps de Philippe Auguste* (Paris, 1913).

BLOCH, M., *Les rois thaumaturges* (Strasbourg, 1924).

BLOCH, M., *La société féodale*, 2 vols. (Paris, 1939).

BORRELLI DE SERRES, L. L., *Recherches sur divers services publics du XIIIᵉ au XVIIᵉ siècles*, 3 vols. (Paris, 1895–1904).

BORRELLI DE SERRES, L. L., *La réunion des provinces septentrionales à la couronne par Philippe Auguste* (Paris, 1899).

BOUSSARD, J., *Le gouvernement d'Henri II Plantagenêt* (Paris, 1955).

BOUTARIC, E., *Saint Louis et Alphonse de Poitiers* (Paris, 1870).

BRACHET, A., *Pathologie mentale des rois de France* (Paris, 1903).

COVILLE, A., *Les états de Normandie, leurs origines et leur développement au XIVᵉ siècle* (Paris, 1894).

CROZET, R., *Histoire de Champagne* (Paris, 1933).

DHONDT, J., *Études sur la naissance des principautés territoriales en France (IX–Xᵉ siècles)* (Bruges, 1948).

DOGNON, P., *Les institutions politiques et administratives du pays de Languedoc du XIIIᵉ siècle aux guerres de réligion* (Toulouse, 1892).

DUCOUDRAY, G., *Les origines du Parlement de Paris et de la justice aux XIIIᵉ et XIVᵉ siècles* (Paris, 1902).

ESMEIN, A., *Cours élémentaire d'histoire du droit français*, 14th edition (Paris, 1921).

FLACH, J., *Les origines de l'ancienne France*, 4 vols. (Paris, 1886–1917).

GANSHOF, F. L., *La Flandre sous les premiers comtes*, 3rd edition (Brussels, 1949).

GAVRILOVITCH, M., *Étude sur le traité de Paris de 1259 entre Louis IX, roi de France, et Henri III, roi d'Angleterre* (Paris, Bibl. de l'École des Hautes-Études, 1899).

GLOTZ, G., editor, *Histoire Générale: Histoire du Moyen Âge*, vol. IV, part 2, by C. Petit-Dutaillis (Paris, 1937); vol. VI, part 1, by R. Fawtier (Paris, 1938).

GUILHIERMOZ, P., *Essai sur l'origine de la noblesse en France au moyen âge* (Paris, 1902).

HALPHEN, L., *Le comté d'Anjou au XIe siècle* (Paris, 1906).

HALPHEN, L., 'La place de la royauté dans le système féodal', in *Anuario de historia de derecho espanol*, 1932, pp. 313–21; reprinted in *Revue Historique*, vol. 172, 1933, pp. 249–56, and in L. Halphen, *A travers l'histoire du moyen âge* (Paris, 1950), pp. 266–74.

HASKINS, C. H., *Norman Institutions* (Cambridge, Mass., 1918).

LAVISSE, E., *Histoire de France*, vols. II and III (Paris, 1901, 1903).

LONGNON, A., *Atlas historique de la France depuis César jusqu'à nos jours*, 6 parts (Paris, 1885–9).

LONGNON, A., and DELABORDE, H. F., *La formation de l'unité française* (Paris, 1922).

LOT, F., and FAWTIER, R., *Histoire des institutions françaises au moyen âge*, vol. I, Institutions seigneuriales: les droits du Roi exercés par les grands vassaux (Paris, 1957); vol. II, Institutions royales: les droits du Roi exercés par le Roi (Paris, 1958).

LOT, F., and FAWTIER, R., *Le premier budget de la monarchie française* (Paris, Bibl. de l'École des Hautes-Études, 1932).

LUCHAIRE, A., *Les communes françaises* (Paris, 1890).

LUCHAIRE, A., *Histoire des institutions monarchiques de la France sous les premiers Capétiens directs*, 2 vols., 2nd edition (Paris, 1891).

LUCHAIRE, A., *Manuel des institutions françaises, période des Capétiens directs* (Paris, 1892).

LUCHAIRE, A., *La société française au temps de Philippe Auguste* (Paris, 1909; English translation, London, 1912).

MARTIN, O., *Histoire de la coutume de la prévôté et vicomté de Paris*, 2 vols. (Paris, 1922 and 1926).

MICHEL, R., *L'administration royale dans la sénéchaussée de Beaucaire au temps de Saint Louis* (Paris, 1910).

NEWMAN, W. M., *Le domaine royal sous les premiers Capétiens* (Paris, 1937).

PERRICHET, L., *La grande chancellerie de France des origines à 1328* (Paris, 1912).

PETIT-DUTAILLIS, C., *La monarchie féodale en France et en Angleterre* (Paris, 1933; English translation, London, 1936).

PETIT-DUTAILLIS, C., *Les communes françaises* (Paris, 1947).

PIRENNE, H., *Histoire de Belgique*, vol. I, to 1300, 5th edition (Brussels, 1929); vol. II, 1300–1477, 4th edition (Brussels, 1947).

POWICKE, F. M., *The Loss of Normandy, 1189–1204* (Manchester, 1913).

RICHARD, J., *Les ducs de Bourgogne et la formation du duché* (Dijon, 1954).

STRAYER, J. R., *The administration of Normandy under St. Louis* (Cambridge, Mass., Monographs of the Medieval Academy of America, No. 6, 1932).

STRAYER, J. R., 'Philip the Fair — a "constitutional" king?', in *American Historical Review*, vol. LXII, 1956–7, pp. 18–32.

VIOLLET, P., *Histoire des institutions politiques et administratives de la France*, 3 vols. (Paris, 1890–1903).

WAQUET, H., *Le bailliage de Vermandois aux XIIIe et XIVe siècles* (Paris, Bibl. de l'École des Hautes-Études, 1919).

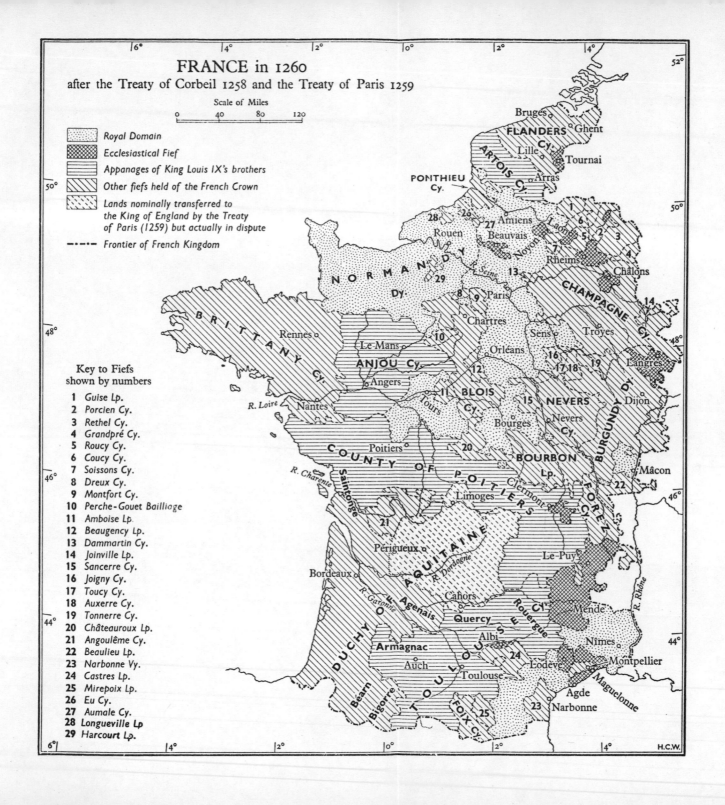

FRANCE in 1260
after the Treaty of Corbeil 1258 and the Treaty of Paris 1259

Scale of Miles
0   40   80   120

Royal Domain

Ecclesiastical Fief

Appanages of King Louis IX's brothers

Other fiefs held of the French Crown

Lands nominally transferred to the King of England by the Treaty of Paris (1259) but actually in dispute

—·—·— Frontier of French Kingdom

Key to Fiefs shown by numbers

1 Guise Lp.
2 Porcien Cy.
3 Rethel Cy.
4 Grandpré Cy.
5 Roucy Cy.
6 Coucy Cy.
7 Soissons Cy.
8 Dreux Cy.
9 Montfort Cy.
10 Perche-Gouet Bailliage
11 Amboise Lp.
12 Beaugency Lp.
13 Dammartin Cy.
14 Joinville Lp.
15 Sancerre Cy.
16 Joigny Cy.
17 Toucy Cy.
18 Auxerre Cy.
19 Tonnerre Cy.
20 Châteauroux Lp.
21 Angoulême Cy.
22 Beaulieu Lp.
23 Narbonne Vy.
24 Castres Lp.
25 Mirepoix Lp.
26 Eu Cy.
27 Aumale Cy.
28 Longueville Lp
29 Harcourt Lp.

FLANDERS Cy.
Bruges
Ghent
ARTOIS Cy.
Lille
Tournai
PONTHIEU Cy.
Arras
28
26
27 Amiens
Rouen
Beauvais
Noyon
Rheims
Châlons
NORMANDY Dy.
29
R. Seine
13
Laon
CHAMPAGNE Cy.
1
6
5 2 3
4
7
14
8
9 Paris
Chartres
Sens
Troyes
Langres
BRITTANY Cy.
Rennes
Le-Mans
10
ANJOU Cy.
Angers
12
Orléans
16
17 18
19
Dijon
BLOIS Cy.
NEVERS
Nevers Cy.
BURGUNDY Dy.
R. Loire
Nantes
Tours
11
15
Poitiers
Bourges
20
BOURBON Lp.
Mâcon
22
COUNTY OF POITIERS
Clermont
FOREZ
R. Charente
Saintonge
Limoges
Le-Puy
21
Périgueux
AQUITAINE
R. Dordogne
R. Rhône
Bordeaux
Cahors
Nîmes
DUCHY OF Agenais
R. Garonne
Quercy
Mende
Montpellier
Armagnac
Albi
24
Lodève
Agde
Maguelonne
Auch
Toulouse
Béarn
Bigorre
FOIX Cy.
TOULOUSE
25
23
Narbonne
Rouergue Cy.

Le-Puy

H.C.W.

THE CHURCH IN FRANCE
at the death of St. Louis (1270)

Scale of Miles

0   40   80   120

—·—·— Frontier of French Kingdom
— — — Boundaries of Ecclesiastical Provinces
⚑ Archbishoprics   ⚑ Bishoprics   ++ Royal Abbeys

Thérouanne   Tournai
Arras
Amiens
R H E I M S
Rouen   Beauvais Noyon   Laon
                          Soissons
Bayeux   Lisieux   Rheims
Coutances   Senlis   Châlons
R O U E N   Évreux
St. Pol de Léon   Paris   Meaux
Tréguier   St. Malo   Chartres
St. Brieuc   Dol   Avranches Sées
Quimper   Rennes   Le Mans   Sens   Troyes
T O U R S   Orléans Auxerre   Langres
Vannes   48°
Angers   Tours
Nantes
                    Nevers   Autun
                    Bourges   Châlon
Poitiers   L
B O R D E A U X   Mâcon
                    Limoges   Y
Saintes   Angoulême   Clermont   O
            Périgueux   N
Bordeaux   B O U R G E S
            Bazas   Le Puy
A C   Agen   Cahors Rodez   Mende
Dax   Aire Lectoure   Albi   Uzès
Bayonne Auch   Lodève Nîmes
A U C H   Toulouse N A R B O N N E Maguelonne
Lescar   Carcassonne   Béziers
Oloron Tarbes Couserans   Narbonne
Comminges   Pamiers
            (founded 1295)

An enlargement of the Paris area

Senlis
Meaux
Paris
Chartres
Sens
Orléans
Auxerre

H.C.W.

INDEX

Adalbero, Abp. of Rheims, 10, 48
Adela of Champagne, Q. of K. Louis VII, 27–8, 51, 56, 77, 85, 113, 126, 177
Adelaide of Anjou, Q. of K. Louis V, 55
Adelaide of Maurienne, Q. of K. Louis VI, 19, 27
Administrative system, royal, 169–98, 229, 230
Agenais, 119, 123, 124 n., 125, 152
Agnes of Méran, Q. of K. Philip II, 52, 164
Albigensian heretics (Catharists), 26, 27, 119
Albigeois, 119, 120, 123, 124 n.
Alençon, Ct. of — v. Alençon, Peter, Ct. of; Robert III
cty. of, 160, 165, 166
Peter, Ct. of, son of K. Louis IX, 54, 165, 166
Alexander III, Pope, 23, 85, 119
Algrin d'Étampes, royal chancellor, 171
Alphonse of Poitiers — v. Poitiers, Alphonse of
Alsace, Philip of, Ct. of Flanders, 111, 112, 113, 114
Amiénois, 66, 108, 112, 114
Amiens, 113
award of, 33, 116
bpric. of, 71, 80, 112
cty. of, 80, 108, 112, 113, 114
treaty of (1186), 113, 114
treaty of (1279), 125
Anagni, 38, 42, 43, 95
Angers, university of, 219
Angevin and Anglo-Norman administration, 174, 176–7
Anglo-Norman and Angevin administration, 174, 176–7
Anglo-Norman royal house, 20–1, 23–4, 26, 137–55
Angoulême, Ct. of — v. Lusignan, Hugh XIII of cty. of, 138, 146
Anjou, Charles of, son of K. Louis VIII, 31, 35, 54, 125, 164, 165, 167
Ct. of — v. Fulk Nerra; Fulk Réchin; Fulk the Young; Geoffrey the Bearded; Geoffrey the Fair; Geoffrey Martel; Henry II, K. of England
cty. of, 18, 23, 24, 28, 110, 137, 141, 143, 144, 145, 147, 149, 150, 152, 164, 165, 176, 180
house of, 20–1, 23–4, 136–58
Anna of Kiev, Q. of K. Henry I, 27, 103

Apanages, 125, 163–7
Aquitaine, dy. of, 23, 24, 36, 37, 51, 106–7, 110, 141, 143, 148–55 passim, 176, 193
dukes of, 36, 153, 155 — v. also William VIII; William IX; William X; Edward I, K. of England
nobility of, 36, 153, 155
Aragon, K. of — v. James I; James II
Archives, private, 7, 10–11
royal, 6–11, 187
Arnoul, Abp. of Rheims, 73
Arnoul II, Ct. of Flanders, 50
Arnoul III, Ct. of Flanders, 105
Arras, 42, 62, 111
Arthur I, Ct of Brittany, 26, 134, 145–9 passim
Arthur II, D. of Brittany, 135
Artois, 66, 111, 112, 113, 114, 164
Ct. of — v. Artois, Robert, Ct. of
Robert, Ct. of, son of K. Louis VIII, 46 n., 54, 56, 164, 165
Athis-sur-Orge, treaty of (1305), 118, 197
Autun, cty. of, 101
Auvergne, cty. of, 66, 118, 119, 125, 138, 144, 150, 158, 164
Auxerre, cty. of, 101, 103

Baillis, royal, 33, 176–84 passim, 190
Baldwin IV, the Bearded, Ct. of Flanders, 50
Baldwin V, Ct. of Flanders, 103, 104–5
Baldwin VI, Ct. of Flanders, 105
Baldwin IX, Ct. of Flanders and Hainault, 62
Baldwin X, Ct. of Flanders and Emperor of Constantinople, 114, 115
Baldwin II, Ct. of Hainault, 105
Baldwin III, Ct. of Hainault, 27
Baldwin V, Ct. of Hainault, 111, 113, 114
Beaucaire-Nîmes, seneschalcy of, 86, 122
Beaumanoir, Philippe de, 46 n., 183, 184, 191, 208
Beaumont, Ct. of — v. Matthew house of, 160
Beaumont-sur-Oise, cty. of, 108, 160
Benedict XI, Pope, 38
Berry, 66, 144, 146
Bertha of Frisia, Q. of K. Philip I, 105
Bertha of Burgundy, Q. of K. Robert II, 50–1